THE SOUL OF CREATIVITY

THE SOUL OF CREATIVITY

FORGING A MORAL RIGHTS LAW FOR THE UNITED STATES

Roberta Rosenthal Kwall

STANFORD LAW BOOKS
An Imprint of Stanford University Press
Stanford, California

Stanford University Press
Stanford, California

Printed in the United States of America on acid-free,
archival-quality paper.

Library of Congress Cataloging-in-Publication Data

Kwall, Roberta Rosenthal, 1955–
The soul of creativity : forging a moral rights law for the United States / Roberta
Rosenthal Kwall.
p.   cm.
Includes bibliographical references and index.
ISBN 978-0-8047-5643-3 (cloth : alk. paper)—ISBN 978-0-8047-6367-7
(pbk. : alk. paper)   1. Copyright—Moral rights—United States.   2. Authors—Legal
status, laws, etc.—United States.   3. Creation (Literary, artistic, etc.)   I. Title.
KF3012.K85 2010
346.7304'82—dc22   2009029227

Typeset by Westchester Book Group in 10/15 sabon.

For my first teachers, Abe & Millie Rosenthal
and my beshert, *Jeffrey L. Kwall*

Contents

Acknowledgments   ix

Introduction   xiii

1   Authorship and Textual Integrity   1

2   The Intrinsic Dimension of Human Creativity   11

3   The Current Legal Framework   23

4   International Norms   37

5   Ownership of the Author's Message
and the Public Domain   53

6   Marginally Original and Functional Works of Authorship   69

7   Authors in Disguise and Collaborative Works   87

8   Personas   111

9   Human Rights Laws and Authorship Norms   133

10   Looking Forward to Legal Reform   147

Notes   167

Index   237

Acknowledgments

THE SEEDS OF THIS BOOK have been germinating for many years. I wrote my first law review article on moral rights back in 1985, and I have been contemplating themes relating to moral rights ever since that time. Over this period, my thinking has been illuminated by the many conversations I have had with colleagues and the comments I have received on prior articles addressing various aspects of moral rights.

This book delineates both my vision of the theoretical basis for moral rights, and my view of how moral rights can best be legislated in the United States. I am grateful to the following individuals in particular for their helpful comments and suggestions at various points throughout the drafting process and for taking the time to provide me with important feedback: Elizabeth Adeney, Kenneth Crews, Adolf Dietz, Graeme Dinwoodie, Wendy Gordon, Sheldon Halpern, Justin Hughes, Lewis Hyde, Craig Joyce, J. Thomas McCarthy, Neil Netanel, David Nimmer, Martin Redish, Mark Rose, Rebecca Tushnet, Russ VerSteeg, Keith Werhan, Peter Yu, and Diane Zimmerman. I also express my appreciation to the two editors at Stanford University Press with whom I worked during the course of this project: Amanda Moran and Kate Wahl. In addition, I am grateful to Lawrence Arendt for his repository of grammatical knowledge and for his preparation of the index.

I have also benefited from the feedback I received during the many presentations of parts of this work over the past few years. These venues include workshops and conferences sponsored by the following law schools: Albany, Boston University, Louis D. Brandeis (Kentucky), Brooklyn, Cardozo, Case Western, Columbia, George Washington, Houston, Illinois, Indiana (Bloomington), John Marshall, University of Kentucky, Marquette, Michigan State, New York University, Notre Dame, University of Pittsburgh, Radzyner (Israel), University of Washington, and Yale. I also wish to acknowledge the helpful comments from participants at the Intellectual Property Scholars Conference Series sponsored by Berkeley, Cardozo, DePaul, and Stanford law schools. In addition, I am grateful to all of my colleagues at DePaul for their attendance and feedback at several brown-bag workshops at which I presented portions of this work, and especially to Susan Bandes, Jeffrey Shaman, Stephen Siegel, and Katherine Strandburg for helpful suggestions along the way. I also wish to thank my dear friend Leslie Silbermann for her support and encouragement at every stage of the process.

Many students also have assisted with aspects of this book and I feel truly blessed to have had the good fortune to work with such talented people at an early stage of their legal careers. From DePaul University College of Law, I wish to thank Maryam Fakouri, Simon Gurda, Kari Kammel, Craig Mandell, Michelle Marek, Emilie Potenet-Stec, Jeremy Roe, Kimber Russell, Valerie Sherman, Charles Silverman, Michael Silverman, Nikhil Sriraman, and Aaron White. From Tulane Law School, where I taught during the Spring 2008 semester, I thank Adeolu Bakare, Susan Jaffer, and Johanna Roth.

Of course, the generosity of one's dean also deserves special mention, and in this regard I wish to say a special thank you to Glen Weissenberger, former Dean of DePaul University College of Law, for the generous summer research grants that facilitated the completion of this project. I also thank Lawrence Ponoroff, former Dean of Tulane Law School, for providing student research assistance support during my visit.

Given that I have been writing about moral rights for over twenty years, it is inevitable that some material from several of my previously published law review articles would appear in this work in a revised format. These prior articles include: *Originality in Context*, 44 HOUS. L. REV. 871 (2007); *Authors in Disguise: Why the Visual Artists Rights Act Got it Wrong*, 2007 UTAH L. REV. 741; *Inspiration and Innovation: The Intrinsic Dimension of the Artistic Soul*, 81 NOTRE DAME L. REV. 1945 (2006); *The Attribution Right in the United States: Caught in the Crossfire Between Copyright and § 43(a)*, 77 WASH. L. REV. 985 (2002); *Author-Stories: Narrative's Implications for Moral Rights and Copyright's Joint Authorship Doctrine*, 75 S. CAL. L. REV. 1 (2001); *Preserving Personality and Reputational Interests of Constructed Personas Through Moral*

Rights: A Blueprint for the 21st Century, 2001 U. ILL. L. REV. 151; *Fame*, 73 IND. L.J. 1 (1997); *How Fine Art Fares Post-VARA*, 1 MARQ. INTELL. PROP. L. REV. 1 (1997); *The Right of Publicity vs. The First Amendment: A Property and Liability Rule Analysis*, 70 IND. L.J. 47 (1994); and *Copyright and the Moral Right—Is An American Marriage Possible?* 38 VAND. L. REV. 1 (1985). In addition, the works of numerous authors and scholars from a variety of disciplines provided the raw material for the contemplation and analysis reflected in this book.

Finally, I dedicate this book to the three people who have played the most influential roles in my life: my parents (Millie and Abe Rosenthal) and my husband, Jeffrey Kwall. I am grateful for their love, support, encouragement, and for providing me with the inspiration to achieve my goals.

Introduction

THE ACT OF CREATIVE AUTHORSHIP implicates the honor, dignity, and artistic spirit of the author in a fundamentally personal way, embodying the author's intrinsic dimension of creativity. In many countries, copyright laws, which are concerned generally with authors' rights, emphasize author autonomy, personal connectedness to one's original work, and the integrity of the author's message through a doctrine known as moral rights. In contrast, American copyright law rewards economic incentives almost exclusively and lacks adequate moral rights protections. As a whole, our copyright law fails to take into account that human creativity embodies an intrinsic dimension, a process characterized by inspirational motivations. Steeped in a utilitarian tradition, copyright law in the United States is concerned with calibrating the optimal level of economic incentive to promote creativity. Such a perspective emphasizes the merchandising and dissemination of intellectual works. Absent from the discussion, however, is a focus on the intrinsic workings of creative enterprise. This intrinsic dimension of creativity explores the creative impulse as emanating from inner drives that exist in the human soul. These drives do not depend upon external reward or recognition but instead are motivated by powerful desires for challenge, personal satisfaction, or the creation of works with a particular meaning or significance for the author. When a work of authorship is understood as an embodiment of the author's personal meaning and message, the author's desire to maintain the original form and content of her work becomes manifest.

By way of definition, I use the terms *inspirational* or *spiritual* as shorthand designations for the type of relationship authors maintain with their creations. This relationship does not emphasize artistic creation for the sake of reaping economic reward. Instead, I believe this relationship is one characterized by a dual sense of self-connectedness to the work, and self-imposed distance with respect to the work. In other words, this relationship requires the author to infuse herself into her work, while simultaneously maintaining the appropriate distance and perspective so that the work can emerge. Perhaps the best analogy to the type of relationship I am proposing is that of a parent and child. The parenting experience, perhaps one of the most humbling of all, requires the same delicate balance as that needed to produce highly creative works of authorship. Parents must learn when to become invested and when to take a step back and allow their offspring to grapple with life's challenges on their own. Moreover, both parents and authors know that their relationship with their "offspring" (both human and intangible) requires a strong degree of faith—not necessarily in God or a higher power, but faith in oneself as a creator, and in the vision of one's emerging work.[1] Ultimately, this perspective places an equal degree of importance on the process of nurturing one's creation as it does on the ultimate product. Significantly, this perspective, though it is shared by many authors, psychologists, scholars of creative theory, and even theologians, is very different from the economically driven approach that has shaped the law governing authors' rights in the United States.

As the twenty-first century progresses, the world will likely continue toward an orientation that is based on information processing rather than pure knowledge. Creative thinking is particularly essential in this environment,[2] and our legal structure must reflect a fuller comprehension of the creative being so that it can respond more effectively to all aspects of authors' needs. The theoretical premise of this book is that the law can, and should, be shaped in response to all relevant forces motivating creativity, not just those concerned with economic reward. It seeks to augment the law's understanding of human artistic enterprise in the United States by illuminating the intrinsic dimension of creativity. By emphasizing the importance of inspirational motivations as an integral part of the creation process, this book calls for the incorporation of a variety of viewpoints into the dialogue on authors' rights. By no means does this discussion intend to disregard the traditional economically based model for authors' rights in the United States. It does, however, argue that the economic model alone is not a sufficient basis for formulating the direction of the law and thus calls for consideration of the intrinsic dimension of innovation as a supplement to the conventionally understood economic incentive paradigm.[3]

The United States' resistance to exploring more fully the implications of the intrinsic dimension of the creative process has resulted in a legal system lacking sufficient moral rights protections so that authors by and large do not have the ability to safeguard their works from textual integrity violations such as lack of attribution, misattribution, and mutilation. The failure of American law to embrace a multidimensional perspective of human creativity is problematic on several fronts, which is explored throughout this book. On the most global level, my argument is that once the intrinsic dimension of the creative process is more fully understood, it will be possible to think more expansively about legal protections that will facilitate safeguarding the messages conveyed by works of authorship. But how do we begin to unbundle the intrinsic dimension of creativity? I suggest this can be done through an examination of a variety of narratives that seek to explain human creativity as inspirationally motivated. I rely on a diverse group of narratives, including firsthand testimonials from authors, literary and psychological works, and even the Creation narratives in Genesis and other theologically based sources. Interestingly, all of these narratives contain consistent insights about the intrinsic dimension of human creativity. Collectively they suggest that the philosophies supporting authors' personal rights embody long-standing and widely held norms of authorship.

The ultimate challenge, however, is to craft legal measures that will facilitate authors' ability to safeguard the textual integrity of their works without sacrificing too much of the current legal structure in place. I leave to others the enormously complex task of evaluating the balance the current copyright system strikes as a general matter and instead, I concentrate on the issue of textual integrity. Most recently, Congressional action and heated litigation involving copyright law have been focused on other avenues such as access circumvention,[4] term extension,[5] file sharing,[6] and other technology-driven agendas. Given the uncertainties created by these controversial topics, enhanced protection for the textual integrity of works of authorship is an unlikely topic for center stage, absent a greater degree of public awareness of the issues involved in the discourse. This book attempts to open the dialogue on moral rights in the United States by highlighting the problem of safeguarding textual integrity. As such, it treats issues of vital importance to those who use the creative process to reveal themselves to the outside world.

Chapter 1 explores the relationship between authorship and textual integrity. An author's ability to safeguard the integrity of her texts is explained as a fundamental component of authorship morality. A complete view of the creative process embraces widely held foundational norms of authorship. Once the relationship between authorship and textual integrity is fully mined, it is easier to understand more fully not only the importance of authors being able to safeguard the integrity of their texts but also how legal doctrines can facilitate this objective.

Chapter 2 develops the theory of the intrinsic dimension of creativity relied upon throughout the remainder of this book. Drawing from psychological and theological sources, as well as personal narratives of authors, this chapter illustrates that authorship largely is the product of "inner labor"–an intrinsic process motivated by inspirational forces. This chapter examines the inspirational motivations that comprise the intrinsic dimension of creativity and addresses their relevance to authors' rights.

Chapter 3 discusses the legal structure governing authors' rights in the United States. Initially, this chapter traces the philosophical foundations of American copyright law and their relationship to the relevant copyright doctrines. Specifically, it analyzes the traditional economic incentive paradigm and its impact on copyright law. It then provides an overview of moral rights, trademark and unfair competition, right of publicity, and other relevant common law doctrines. This chapter demonstrates the overall inadequacy of the current intellectual property legal framework with respect to safeguarding textual integrity.

Chapter 4 explores in general terms the treatment accorded authors in foreign jurisdictions. In contrast to the United States, many countries maintain authors' rights protections that enable authors to safeguard the integrity of their texts far more readily than authors in this country. Thus, the United States is out of step with global norms by not recognizing more substantial authors' rights. Moreover, the Internet environment makes the United States' deficiency particularly problematic because violations of textual integrity can occur with unprecedented ease, and the results can be disseminated to countless recipients with the mere press of a key. Yet, these differences cannot be so easily remedied because certain cultural and legal differences preclude the wholesale adoption of another country's approach absent careful consideration of its fit into our existing legal framework.

Chapter 5 explores the United States' historical concern for the preservation of the public domain and its impact on our laws regarding textual integrity. Initially, this chapter addresses why enhanced moral rights protection fosters the objectives of the Copyright Clause. It also discusses the problem confronting authors in safeguarding the integrity of their messages in the face of the United States' strong public domain tradition emphasizing public access and use of information. This chapter further illustrates the consistency between the type of moral rights protection I advocate and several current free speech and public domain theories proposed by legal scholars.

Chapters 6 through 8 discuss three distinct types of challenges for authors in maintaining textual integrity. Chapter 6 addresses works whose level of originality, while perhaps sufficient to obtain copyright protection, is nonetheless arguably too low to qualify for the stronger protections for textual integrity addressed in this book. Chapter 7 discusses works of authorship that are not written by a single known author such as anonymous works, works written under a pseudonym, and works for hire under copyright law. If the purpose of providing enhanced textual integrity protection is to safeguard the author's message, it would seem as though the author's identity should be preserved and publicly known. Yet, it is not possible to access authorship identity for all types of works. This chapter also explores the complexities of maintaining textual integrity in the context of collaborative works, which are becoming increasingly prevalent. Chapter 8 is devoted to a somewhat different type of text. This chapter addresses the issues implicated when the text in question is a public persona constructed by an individual rather than a more conventionally understood work of authorship.

Chapter 9 examines a relatively uncharted area within the study of American intellectual property law—the role of human rights and authorship norms. The history of the International Bill of Human Rights demonstrates that although there may not have been a universal consensus as to whether moral rights are human rights, there was a significant recognition that these interests are deemed worthy of protection in a human rights framework. Thus, rather than focusing on whether moral rights are within the scope of human rights, the better question is whether the widespread recognition of moral rights means they should be considered as "authorship norms." This chapter ultimately calls for a broader spectrum of theoretical justifications for copyright law than the utilitarian framework typically invoked to justify copyright protections. A more fluid view of copyright generally allows for the incorporation of enhanced moral rights into our legal system.

The final chapter of this book offers a proposal for how, in light of the theoretical position I develop, the law in the United States can be reformulated to incorporate measures manifesting a greater sensitivity to authors' needs in maintaining the integrity of their texts. As stated earlier, the challenge is to formulate a set of reforms that will incorporate authorship morality through new measures designed to supplement, but not displace completely, the current legal system. This challenge is substantial but it can be accomplished. The key to crafting such reforms lies in paying greater attention to the intrinsic dimension of creativity and all of the forces motivating authorship rather than just those that are based on economic incentives.

THE SOUL OF CREATIVITY

CHAPTER I

Authorship and Textual Integrity

A SKEPTIC MIGHT ASSERT that it is wrong for people to identify with the intellectual products of their capacities and therefore, would question whether individuals should have any particular entitlements to such products. Justin Hughes fittingly captured this view with the following observation: "To transpose Robert Nozick's classic query, why should we think putting our personality out into the world gives us rights to the things we create? Why should we not assume that when we mix our personality with the world, we lose part of our personality instead of gaining part of the world?"[1] Postmodernist skeptics advance the related argument that no single work manifests creativity and innovation deriving from a unitary source. Drawing on this view, legal scholars have criticized copyright law as a whole for its implicit reliance on the Romantic view of authorship.[2] If true artistic creativity is, in essence, a fiction, then no reason exists for privileging authors above other producers when it comes to issues of textual integrity.[3]

Moreover, literary theorists document that the concept of "authorship," as we understand that term today, is a relatively recent phenomenon that began to take shape in the eighteenth century.[4] English professor Martha Woodmansee reminds us that how we see the concept of "authorship" today was not inevitable given that the heritage of the Renaissance was to view authors as either "craftsmen" who mastered what was put before them for the enjoyment of the "cultivated audience of the court," or alternatively as "inspired" by external forces.[5] The idea that an author is personally responsible for her work may be inconsistent with the first, and perhaps even to some degree with the second, of these conceptions. According to Woodmansee, the notion of personal responsibility emerged later, in part as a result of the influence by a class of professional writers in the eighteenth century who sought to justify legal protection for their efforts.[6]

To some there is appeal in the view that once we create we should lose that which we have infused in our work. I suggest, however, that the rationale underlying this position contradicts the norms of artistic protection. Although authors freely borrow from the landscape of existing cultural production, a work of creative authorship nonetheless manifests the author's individual process of creativity and artistic autonomy. The postmodern critique ignores the reality that when an author borrows from the cultural fabric in crafting her work, it is still the unique combination of past efforts and the author's original contributions that invests the author's work with its autonomous unique and inviolate stamp. As Fred Yen has observed: "Authorship is therefore not the creation of works which spring like Athena from the head of Zeus, but the conscious and unconscious intake, digestion, and transformation of input gained from the author's experience within a broader society."[7] Perhaps the authorship construct in which we indulge today was "neither natural nor inevitable,"[8] but it is without doubt the one that has prevailed and thus, cannot be completely eliminated from the discourse. Further, by questioning the ability of authors to draw upon personal originality as their creative inspiration, notwithstanding liberal borrowing from the existing artistic landscape, the postmodern scholars arguably do not sufficiently account for the inspirational dimension of authorship. Indeed, the very act of authorship entails an infusion of the creator's mind, heart, and soul into her work. Many authors of creative works maintain a certain type of relationship with their artistic "children." This relationship is unique among other types of human production given the highly personalized and intrinsic nature of creative authorship.

Although a creator's audience may indeed find meaning in a creator's work that is distinct from the author's, the focus here is on a "meaning" and "message" personal to the creator. Courts use the words *meaning* and *message* together, but typically they do not define or distinguish these terms.[9] The concepts of a work's "meaning" and "message" as used in this book are related in that they are dependent upon the creator's subjective vision rather than the vision of the creator's audience, but these terms nonetheless embrace somewhat distinct ideas. The creator's meaning personifies what the work stands for on a level personal to the author, whereas the creator's message represents what the author is intending to communicate externally on a more universal level. A work's "meaning" therefore exemplifies the idea of "why I as the creator got involved in doing this work and what I see in it." In contrast, a work's "message" embodies the notion of "what I as creator expect others to see in it, and what I hope they'll take from it."[10]

Let's unbundle these concepts with an example. In my office hangs an exquisite colorful print called *Bereshit Micrography* by Leon Azoulay. The print contains the complete book of Genesis executed in Hebrew microcalligraphy and depicts the Creation, Noah's ark and a rainbow, and other images from the book of Genesis. Although I cannot say with certainty what the meaning of this work is for the author, one could posit that he created this edition of 350 prints as a testament to the mysteries of Divine creation. Azoulay was raised in the ancient town of Tsfat, Israel, the birthplace of Jewish mysticism known as Kabbalah. His biography indicates that this environment inspired him to search for a means of expressing his passion for both painting and the Bible.[11] Azoulay's personal meaning essentially can be viewed as including whatever qualities he believes the work intrinsically embodies. The message of the print, on the other hand, is the narrative the author seeks to communicate to his audience. The author's message likely will include his own personal meaning but it might also extend beyond it. For example, hypothetically speaking, Azoulay's microcalligraphy of Genesis may be intended to communicate that unless man controls his evil tendencies, suffering will occur as it did in the Garden of Eden.

When a work of authorship manifests a meaning and message specific to the author, attribution and integrity protections together safeguard the author's original conceptions. Charles Beitz, a professor of politics at Princeton University, has observed that even if a particular creator's work lacks a clear "propositional content" in that the creator is simply attempting to "produce an interesting object for interpretation," the argument for moral rights protection remains strong because "the creator might reasonably believe that preservation of the work in its original form is necessary for the success of the aim."[12] Moreover, preservation of the author's meaning and message during the lifetime of the author facilitates the development of authorship dignity. It is human nature to care about how one's product is packaged for external consumption. And when the packaging violates the original author's vision of the work's meaning and message, there is an assault to the author's dignity. This assault, though arguably justifiable in light of other people's enjoyment of free speech and artistic freedom, nonetheless violates a well-established code of authorship morality. There is, quite simply, something wrong with damaging a work's textual integrity. Authorship morality depends upon the observance of certain foundational norms regarding authorship. The difficulty facing the United States, however, is how to craft legal protection for these authorship norms that are compatible with our current understanding of both copyright and free speech.

A legal system committed to authorship morality should be concerned with recognizing authors' dignity interests. Edward Bloustein emphasized the importance of dignity recognition in his classic explanation of the inviolate personality as "the individual's independence, dignity and integrity," which "defines man's essence as a unique and self-determining being."[13] Linking this description of the inviolate personality to the subject of authors' rights, he continued: "It is because our Western ethico-religious tradition posits such dignity and independence of will in the individual that the common law secures to man 'literary and artistic property'—the right to determine 'to what extent his thoughts, sentiments, emotions shall be communicated to others.'"[14] Bloustein's observations underscore the link between dignity as a construct and its embodiment in externalities that command respect and attention. Thus, as a behavioral category, dignity can find realization only in its external embodiments that allow the inner personality to commodify itself. Commodification of the products of authorship allows an author's inner personality to explain and interpret itself to the outside world. If a person succeeds in communicating her message, she can claim dignity. In the words of theologian Rabbi Joseph Soloveitchik, "the silent person, whose message remains hidden and suppressed in the in-depth personality, cannot be considered dignified."[15] As these philosophical observations suggest, authorship dignity cannot be assessed absent the author's externalized message, and this message, in turn, reflects the inner dimensions of the author's creative process. Thus, appropriate regard for a work's meaning and for the external embodiment of an author's work as the means through which her message is communicated to the public facilitates the acquisition of authorship dignity.[16] Moreover, a legal system concerned with safeguarding authorship dignity is designed to ensure that the author's choice of signature and presentation will be respected to the fullest extent possible. These are the vital elements of the work's meaning and the author's intended message to the world.[17]

In addition, there are practical benefits to designing a legal system of authors' rights that promote authorship morality. Laws governing authors' rights can be ignored if they fail to embrace widely shared norms regarding authorship. Psychology professor Tom Tyler has demonstrated that the most important factor in shaping compliance with the law is public perception of right and wrong.[18] Tyler observes that "the law can have an important symbolic function if it accords with public views about what is fair, but it loses that power as the formal law diverges from public morality."[19] In other words, people are more likely to obey laws that reflect public morality.

Tyler also proposes legitimacy as a factor fostering voluntary compliance. In the context of legislative mandates, legitimacy derives from public perception regarding the fairness of the decision-making process. Simply put, "[p]eople are more likely to regard as fair, and to accept, decisions in which they participated."[20] Broad-based participation is the key to ensuring that the decision-making process is perceived as fair, which in turn promotes compliance. In the context of intellectual property laws specifically, Tyler urges broader citizen participation so that people come to "believe that the rules established serve reasonable social purposes and are not simply efforts to create profits for special interest groups, such as large corporations."[21]

In other countries, the intrinsic dimension of the creative process is recognized independently of the external commodity through moral rights laws that protect the personal, as opposed to the economic, rights of authors. The most prominent components of moral rights laws are the right of attribution and the right of integrity. The right of attribution safeguards the author's right to be recognized as the creator of her work. The right of integrity guarantees that the author's work truly represents her creative personality, and is free of distortions that misrepresent her creative expression. Central to moral rights is the idea of respect for the author's meaning and message as embodied in a tangible commodity because these elements reflect the intrinsic creative process. On a theoretical level, moral rights focus on inspirational motivations and the intrinsic dimension of creativity; attribution and integrity rights are protected because they are regarded as integral components of a work's meaning and message as conceived by the original author. In other words, both the right of attribution and the right of integrity function to safeguard the author's meaning and message, and thus are designed to increase an author's ability to safeguard the integrity of her texts.

Attribution is a vital, and perhaps the most widely endorsed, component of authorship dignity. A focus on the intrinsic dimension of human creativity sees the author's choice of attribution as very much part of her meaning and message and as such, it plays a central role in communicating the essence of an author's work to her audience. As Chapter 7 explores more fully, even anonymous or pseudonymous works can be seen as reflecting a branding choice that is a fundamental part of the author's meaning and message. When the author's attribution of choice is omitted without permission of the author, the original work is somehow incomplete. Consider, for example, Stanford Law School's Creative Commons Project, which offers participating authors easy, predefined terms for licensing free use and even modifications of their work.[22] In electing the terms in which to participate, virtually all authors require attribution of their work.[23] In fact, because of this overwhelming preference on the part of authors, Creative Commons changed its default license option to include attribution.[24] Attribution thus functions as a significant, and widely acknowledged, means of safeguarding the overall integrity of an author's text. In discussing the right of attribution, Susan Liemer has observed that the "goal is to protect the personal association between the artist and her art" because even if two works look similar, they arise out of distinct minds, bodies, creative efforts, and processes.[25]

The moral right of integrity also represents a foundational authorship value. Objectionable distortions, modifications, presentations, and even destruction of an author's work damage authorship dignity because the author's external embodiment of her meaning and message no longer represents her intrinsic creative process. The resulting damage is particularly acute when the modified work is linked to the author through specific attribution or widespread public recognition.

The following examples illustrate some of the difficulties authors face in safeguarding the integrity of their texts. A clear attribution violation was the impetus for the lawsuit in *Batiste v. Island Records, Inc.*[26] According to the facts of this case, a song written, performed, and recorded by the plaintiffs, the Batiste brothers, was digitally sampled by the defendant Cordes, and included in one of Cordes's musical compositions released by the defendant record company. Before the release of Cordes's composition, the record company secured the permission to use the plaintiffs' song from Bolden, a local music publisher and record producer to whom one of the plaintiffs had assigned the copyright in the plaintiffs' song. The record company also paid Bolden a $15,000 advance against the record royalties.[27] The liner notes accompanying the defendant's album credited only one of the plaintiff brothers as a cowriter of the defendant's song, and stated that the song sampled by Cordes was performed by the plaintiffs' band and used under a license by Bolden.[28] The court ultimately found in favor of the defendant because limitations of both copyright law and the law of unfair competition precluded the availability of mandated attribution for the brother whose name was omitted as an author.

With respect to the right of integrity, consider the plight of deceased sculptor Frederick Hart, who sued Warner Brothers several years ago for including a reproduction of his renowned sculpture, *Ex Nihilo,* in the movie *The Devil's Advocate.* The sculpture at issue depicts the creation of mankind out of the torrential void, and it adorns the tympanum over the main entrance to the Washington National Cathedral.[29] For Hart, *Ex Nihilo* was the product of a thirteen-year spiritual quest, which preceded his conversion to Catholicism.[30] The movie features a near-exact duplicate of *Ex Nihilo* that hangs in the apartment of the movie's main character, John Milton. Milton, portrayed by actor Al Pacino, is actually Satan, and he appears on Earth in the guise of a corporate lawyer. In the movie's climactic scene, the carved bodies of the sculpture come alive and erotically grope one another, as Milton encourages his offspring to participate in an incestuous relationship.[31]

Hart observed that the movie "promoted themes which are the antithesis of the spiritual meaning" of his work. His narrative of pain is tellingly real:

They've poisoned my whole body of work. There's a degradation taking place here. Somebody was sloppy. They just figured that since it was in a public place, it may be public. It is a wholesale dissemination of perversion. What started out as an intellectual search turned into a spiritual discovery. Everything I did at the cathedral evolved from a spiritual conviction and awakening.

I've had people call me and say how could I let my work be degraded to such a degree, let it be demonized in this fashion. I feel absolutely outraged that a work that was meant to express the great majesty and beauty and mystery of God's creation has been radically perverted.[32]

Hart's lawsuit was limited to video rentals of the movie since it was initiated after the movie's theatrical release. Ultimately, Hart's story ended rather happily for the artist, as Warner Brothers agreed to a settlement in which it would change portions of the film to eliminate any perceived confusion in the future distribution of the movie.[33] This happy ending, however, was not mandated by any existing law governing the nature of information that must be provided by those who use the works of others in order to dispel misperceptions of the original author's meaning and message.

Similarly, composer Carl Perkins and singer Connie Francis confronted objectionable contextual uses of their music. Perkins's song "Honey Don't" was used as the background music for a scene depicting the rape of a child in the movie *Prince of Tides*. Unfortunately for Perkins, the licensing of the song was beyond his control. Perkins observed: "[P]eople are asking me, 'Carl, why would you have a song in such a filthy place in a movie?' They are shocked, especially since they all know I started [a] child-abuse center. I am very damaged by this and very hurt."[34] Connie Francis sued Universal Music Corporation for licensing her music to be used in films featuring homosexuality, suicide, prostitution, and rape—topics Francis finds particularly disturbing in light of her own experience with rape and torture in 1974. Although her songs were not altered or deformed in the films, she objected to their very usage in this context.[35] The court denied

Francis's claim, in part based on her having transferred her rights without reservation. On one level, the situations involving both Perkins and Francis are distinguishable from that involving Frederick Hart because the latter involved an unauthorized use whereas Perkins and Francis arguably could have attempted to protect themselves from such textual integrity violations through carefully negotiated contracts. As Chapter 3 shows, however, in cases where the law completely fails to afford any measure of relief to creators in situations involving such objectionable contextual uses of their works, the ability of contract law to protect authors' integrity interests is severely compromised.[36]

Sometimes the text in danger of being violated is an individual's persona rather than a conventional work of authorship. For example, suppose a well-known actress appears in a film, a clip from which is posted on the Internet for promotional purposes. The digital clip is then downloaded, and the actress's image is copied into a program that can manipulate and animate it, thereby creating a new piece of digital film containing a perfect copy of the actress's image. Now imagine that the new work is a screen saver in which the actress's clothing has been digitally removed. In that screen saver, the actress is animated to be posing in a series of suggestive and lewd positions.[37] This kind of image theft already has occurred with still photographs and as technology advances, we will see an increasing number of such thefts of both still and moving images.[38]

Although the narratives explored herein differ with respect to the nature of the violation and the type of work in question, they all illustrate assaults to textual integrity for which the United States maintains relatively few remedies. Societies that care about fostering the creation of works of authorship should take seriously the idea that authors are concerned about safeguarding the textual integrity of their works. A principal reason the United States values authorship is its recognition that authorship as a construct fosters personal self-expression, a quality prized in free democratic societies. Underlying this view is the idea that the freedom to be an author promotes individual dignity. In short, compelling reasons exist for introducing noneconomic, or inspirationally based, motivations into the dialogue on authors' rights.

CHAPTER 2

The Intrinsic Dimension of Human Creativity

PSYCHOLOGICAL TEXTS explicating theories of creativity place a tremendous importance on the intrinsic dimension of creativity. Carl Jung once observed that "the creation of something new is not accomplished by the intellect but by the play instinct acting from inner necessity."[1] The idea of "play" suggests that many authors create in an imaginary world much like a child in a sandbox where the rewards for creation may be nothing more than personal satisfaction and perhaps a complimentary nod from passers-by. "Play" remains an important aspect of the act of creation for many authors who remain "masters" of their works in their alternative universe.

Renowned social psychologist Teresa Amabile's work focuses on the Intrinsic Motivation Principle as a "cornerstone" of the social psychology of human creativity. She defines intrinsic motivation as "any motivation that arises from the individual's positive reaction to qualities of the task itself; this reaction can be experienced as interest, involvement, curiosity, satisfaction, or positive challenge."[2] In contrast, Amabile explains extrinsic motivation as arising "from sources outside of the task itself," including "expected evaluation, reward, [and] external directives."[3] Amabile's early work concluded that intrinsic motivation is conducive to creativity, whereas extrinsic motivation is detrimental to creative enterprise. Although subsequent research resulted in her modified view that in certain instances extrinsic motivation can enhance creativity, her more recent work still recognizes "the critical importance of intrinsic motivation to creativity."[4]

Amabile's insights are confirmed by substantial anecdotal evidence establishing the existence of a deeply held belief that many artists create for the sake of the creative process rather than to generate profits.[5] For example, Susan Scafidi has discussed the published survey results contained in a working paper for MIT's Sloan School of Management that examines the motivations of those who contribute to open-source projects. The paper's authors found "that intrinsic motivations such as intellectual stimulation and enjoyment of the creative process outweighed extrinsic motivations like career advancement."[6]

Other scholars have proposed a nuanced view of human creativity that combines examining creativity on an individual level with an analysis of how individual creativity is impacted by cultural factors.[7] My perspective assumes individuals are the products of their cultural environments and therefore, the intrinsic dimension characteristic of any one creator necessarily subsumes these cultural influences. In other words, an author's particular internal dimension of creativity is a product of her own individualistic perspective and personality, her cultural environment, as well as the interaction between an author's individualism, and her external cultural milieu.[8]

The internal nature of the creative process has been discussed by numerous authors representing a broad spectrum of artistic interests. Individual creators attest to the "gestational period" underscoring creativity—that timeframe in which the creative juices flow internally, almost imperceptibly. Henry Miller's observation is characteristic of this view: "The best thing about writing is not the actual labor of putting word against word, brick upon brick, but the preliminaries, the spade work, which is done in silence, under any circumstances, in dream as well as in the waking state."[9] This inner labor—termed "the unconscious machine" by mathematician Henri Poincaré—is what creators underscore as the pivotal component of creativity.[10] Poet Amy Lowell similarly noted that a poet "is something like a radio aerial—he is capable of receiving messages on waves of some sort; but he is more than an aerial, for he possesses the capacity of transmuting these messages into those patterns of words we call poems."[11] Similarly, Bertrand Russell has emphasized "the fruitless effort he used to expend in trying to push his creative work to completion by sheer force of will before he discovered the necessity of waiting for it to find its own subconscious development."[12] These observations from creators representing varied disciplines demonstrate belief in the universality of "hidden organic development at some stage of the creative process."[13] This inner labor embodies a drive to create emanating from powerful forces within the soul of the author.

It is possible to better understand these internal forces by examining a wide range of narratives that depict the creative process as inspirationally motivated. The narratives featured in this chapter suggest many common insights regarding inspirational motivations that are critical to understanding the intrinsic nature of human creativity. The parental metaphor of authorship provides one of the most compelling examples of the inspirational motivation characteristic of the intrinsic dimension of creativity. The basis for this metaphor can be traced back to the Creation narratives found in Genesis, which probably are the most celebrated stories about creativity in Western society. As such, these narratives reveal a set of shared societal norms that are reflective of Western society's understanding of human creative enterprise.[14] Interestingly, sculptor Frederick Hart began the process of creating *Ex Nihilo* by consulting the Creation narratives in Genesis as "purely pragmatic research" for his own creative endeavor.[15]

Chapter 1, verse 27 of Genesis can be translated as: "God created man in His image, in the image of God He created him."[16] Historian and former Librarian of Congress Daniel Boorstin credits this language with furnishing a path leading man to regard himself as a potential creator, thus underscoring an unprecedented parallel between God and humanity.[17] According to Rabbi Joseph Soloveitchik, a leading modern authority on the meaning of Jewish law, the term "image of God" in this narrative underscores "man's striving and ability to become a creator."[18] This perspective sees creativity as rooted in the inspirational element of mirroring both God's creative capacity and His parental connection with His works. The word *create* actually derives from the Latin verb *creo*, which means "to give birth to."[19] Although the Hebrew word used in the Genesis narratives for Divine creativity, *bara*, literally means "cut out" and is reserved only for God,[20] Rabbinic scholars regard the Creation narratives in Genesis as "challeng[ing] man to create, to transform wilderness into productive life."[21]

Indeed, it does not require a tremendous degree of imagination to see that the opening verses of Genesis reveal a description of the womb: "the deep, unformed darkness is the womb, ripe with potential . . . the water is the amniotic waters that protect the fragility of life."[22] The concept that an author "gives birth" to her artistic creations provides the foundation for the insurmountable connection between an author and her work. This vision of authorship completely pervades our perceptions about creativity. In testifying before Congress regarding the issue of film colorization, Elliot Silverstein, representing the Directors Guild of America, remarked:

Our compensation . . . lies in very large part in love of the art of bringing [art] to life—in the satisfaction of realizing visions that we love—visions that have been carried in the wombs of our imaginations. . . . So our sensibilities are acutely bruised when we see *our children* publicly tortured and butchered . . . by the various instruments of the new technologists. . . .[23]

Author Madeleine L'Engle, in her book about artistic creativity and Christianity, *Walking on Water: Reflections on Faith and Art*, also affirmed this idea when she described works of authorship coming to the author and saying: "Here I am. Enflesh me. Give birth to me."[24] The parental metaphor of authorship is evident even in how we contemplate unauthorized uses of creative works. As early as 1710, Daniel Defoe referred to literary theft as a kind of child snatching.[25] Moreover, the word *plagiarism* is derived from the Latin term for "kidnapping."[26]

Another critical motivation characteristic of the intrinsic dimension of creativity is the "gifted" theory of the creation process that emphasizes inspiration as emanating from an external source beyond that of the author herself. Numerous authors have attested to the "gifted" or endowed theory of human enterprise. For example, Roger Sessions embraced this view by positing that a composer is "not so much conscious of his ideas as possessed by them."[27] Sessions observed that "very often he is unaware of his exact processes of thought till he is through with them; extremely often the completed work is incomprehensible to him immediately after it is finished."[28] Writer Lewis Hyde, in his book *The Gift*, explicitly spoke of inspiration as a gift, noting that although all artists may not emphasize the "gifted" phase of the creation process, all feel it.[29] This notion is epitomized by the following observation Hyde attributes to poet Gary Snyder: "You get a good poem and you don't know where it came from. 'Did I say that?' And so all you feel is: you feel humility and you feel gratitude."[30] Thomas Wolfe made a similar observation in the context of writing a novel: "It was something that took hold of me and possessed me, and before I was done with it—that is, before I finally emerged with the first completed part—it seemed to me that it had done for me."[31] Such sentiments validate Lewis Hyde's global point: "[s]piritually, you can't be much poorer than gifted."[32]

The Creation narratives in Genesis also illuminate the idea that the human ability to engage in expression, including through artistic skill, is endowed by an external source. Chapter 2, verse 7 of the text tells us that "the Lord God formed man from the dust of the earth. He blew into his nostrils the breath of life, and man became a living being."[33] According to the Rabbinic tradition, the phrase "the breath of life" is understood to mean that God blew his own breath into Adam's nostrils, thus infusing man with a human soul.[34] Moreover, the purpose of this special human soul was to enable man to speak and express himself. Rashi, the celebrated eleventh-century French Biblical commentator, explains that the soul of man is more alive than the soul of animals because man's soul contains the powers of speech and reasoning.[35] Although the classical Jewish tradition, as would be expected, views God as the external source of expression and creativity, the more generalized idea is that creative expression is gifted in that it comes from a source beyond the author's control.

Current psychological theories about creativity endorse a multifaceted explanation of human creativity but maintain a connection between the "gifted" aspect of the creative process, the concept of faith, and the state of self-transcendence.[36] Modern scholars of creativity believe self-transcendence is critical to the development of an artistic soul because it reaffirms that, to maximize creative output, an artist must get beyond herself and back to the source of her gift if true artistic creation is to occur. Contemporary psychologists and creativity scholars John Dacey and Kathleen Lennon emphasize this aspect of the creative process: "Being spiritual means striving to enlarge one's connection to that force lying within, a force that can make it possible to transcend the ordinary self and reach one's fullest potential."[37] Similarly, writing in the middle of the twentieth century, Erich Fromm believed that creativity stemmed from self-transcendence, a state allowing man to perceive God's immanence by doing something greater than himself.[38] Lewis Hyde observed that whereas the narcissist believes that her creative gifts come from herself, the true creative spirit is aware of an "abiding sense of gratitude" moving her "to labor in the service of her genius."[39] C. G. Jung once remarked: "The work in process becomes the poet's fate and determines his psychic development. It is not Goethe who creates Faust, but Faust who creates Goethe."[40] Thus conceived, creativity "often defines itself as no more than a sense of self-surrender to an inward necessity inherent in something larger than the ego."[41]

Accounts of creativity by artists support these psychological theories regarding the connections between faith, self-transcendence and the state of giftedness. A powerful testimonial of these connections appears in a narrative by Pamela Travers, the creator of Mary Poppins:

C. S. Lewis, in a letter to a friend, says, "There is only one Creator and we merely mix the elements he gives us"—a statement less simple than it seems. For that "mere mixing," while making it impossible for us to say "I myself am the maker," also shows us our essential place in the process. Elements among elements we are to shape, order, define, and in doing this we, reciprocally, are defined and shaped and ordered. The potter, molding the receptive clay, is himself being molded.

But let us admit it. With that word "creative," when applied to any human endeavor, we stand under a mystery. And from time to time that mystery, as if it were a sun, sends down upon one head or another, a sudden shaft of light—by grace one feels, rather than deserving—for it always comes as something given, free, unsought, unexpected.[42]

Another example of the relationship between self-transcendence and the "gifted" phase of artistic creation is provided by Alan Durham in his description of artist Jean Arp. Durham explains that by "eliminating all volition" in favor of the workings of chance, Arp believed that he could summon quasi-Divine forces to his aid.[43] According to Arp, the most successful artist is one who is most attentive to these external influences and allows himself to be restored "to an attitude of humility vis-à-vis man's experience of the world and his role as a creator within that world."[44] Dancer Anna Halprin echoes these observations: "To me, a performer is simply a vehicle, a submergence of the ego."[45] Similarly, painter Max Ernst has written that "[t]he author is present as a spectator, indifferent or impassioned, at the birth of his own work."[46] Lewis Hyde captures the essence of these sentiments by observing: "For a creative artist, 'feeding the spirit' is as much a matter of attitude or intent as it is of any specific action; the attitude is, at base, the kind of humility that prevents the artist from drawing the essence of his creation into the personal ego."[47]

Author Madeleine L'Engle also emphasizes the concept of self-transcendence in the creative process. She writes that the work "comes to the artist and demands to be served," and notes how the artist must get outside of herself, or get "on the other side" of herself in order to complete her task.[48] Thus, "[w]hen the work takes over, then the artist is enabled to get out of the way, not to interfere."[49] Again, the relationship between faith, self-transcendence, and the state of giftedness is manifest in L'Engle's conception of creativity. All artists, according to L'Engle, regardless of their external propensity for religious observance, are of necessity "in a condition of complete and total faith."[50] This faith may be in their vision as artists or in their work, but faith is what underscores and supports the pivotal moment of creation.[51] Artistic creation necessitates an abandonment of complete control.[52] Regardless of whether the artist professes a formal religious faith or creed, the very process of artistic creation necessitates a conscious state of self-transcendence, with a concomitant awareness of the emergence of a greater force at work.

Interestingly, the classical Rabbinic interpretation of the Creation narratives in Genesis also reflects the importance of self-transcendence in creativity. Jewish theology teaches that man's capacity for speech mirrors God's, and that man's speech is reflective of his creative potential in the same way that God's speech reveals His creative capacity.[53] In describing the Divine act of creation, the Old Testament does not say that God *made* a world, but rather that He *spoke* the world into existence by preceding every creative act with a declaration. For example, "God said, 'Let there be light,' and there was light."[54] According to the Jewish tradition, for both God and man, speech is singularly reflective of the ability to transcend the self and relate to someone or something else.[55]

Scholars of artistic creation theory also have emphasized the importance of yet another motivation regarding creativity—the concept of stewardship. Stewardship blends an awareness of both externally endowed inspiration and the cyclical dimension of creative enterprise. The cyclical nature of creativity is again apparent in the early narratives in Genesis, as Genesis 3:19 maintains the view that God created man from the dust, and to the dust he returns.[56] Drawing from the "dust to dust" cycle of Divine creativity in these narratives, the idea here is that humans also must continually keep their creative gifts in a state of motion. The poet Rainer Rilke articulated this cyclical journey, beginning at a state of "primal innocence" with every new work:

I will shuffle slowly ahead, each day moving forward but a half-step, and often losing ground. And with each step will I seem to leave you farther behind, for where I am going no name has any value, no memory can remain; one must reach it as one reaches the dead, in consigning all one's forces to the hands of the Angel who leads you. I am leaving you behind—but *as I will be making full circle*, I will again draw nearer with each step.[57]

Similarly, Lewis Hyde remarked that some artists "take their gifts to be bestowals of the gods or, more often perhaps, of a personal deity, a guardian angel, *genius*, or muse—a spirit who gives the artist the initial substance of his art and to whom, in return, he dedicates the fruit of his labor."[58] Hyde also wrote of myths "of closing the circle, of artists directing their work back toward its sources."[59] As an example, Hyde depicted the work of Ezra Pound as being "animated by a myth in which 'tradition' appears as both the source and ultimate repository of his gifts."[60] He also discusses the Chilean poet Pablo Neruda, who took great pride when he discovered that an unknown worker had heard his poems because that was a sign that his gift was being directed back to the "brotherhood," to "the people," whom he believed to be the source of his gift in the first place.[61] Narratives such as these persuaded Hyde that "[t]he only essential is this: *The gift must always move*."[62] By this he means that "the primary commerce of art is a gift exchange, that unless the work is the realization of the artist's gift, and unless we, the audience, can feel the gift it carries, there is no art."[63]

Over time, the notion of stewardship, which assumed a prominent theological focus, particularly in Christianity, embraced this cyclical view of creativity. From a theological standpoint, stewardship reaffirms that gifts are endowed by a Divine power, beyond that of the artist. Also, stewardship embraces a temporary view of possession to the extent it conceives of gifts returning to their original source.[64] The stewardship doctrine became crystallized in the medieval period, during which time ownership of private property was premised on the idea that it served as a temporary status, one designed to operate exclusively in this world. Since ownership was conceived on the model of a stewardship of God's order, property was regarded as inalienable because it ultimately belonged to God.[65]

Applying this perspective to works of authorship, the idea is that an author who deems herself to be God's servant believes that God "claims every aspect of an author's creativity."[66] Central to this concept of ownership based on stewardship theory is the idea of possessing something originally obtained as a gift—an unearned benefit "bestowed" upon the recipient.[67] Thomas Wolfe captured this concept fittingly in describing the mindset of sculptor Frederick Hart, who "became a Roman Catholic and began to regard his talent as a charisma, a gift from God. He dedicated his work to the idealization of possibilities God offered man."[68] Stewardship also is consistent with the idea of the author as the guardian of her meaning and message during her lifetime. For example, Hart viewed God as the source of his gift, and during his lifetime, he fought to safeguard the original meaning and message of *Ex Nihilo* since that work embodied his intrinsically motivated message to the world.[69]

The narratives discussed throughout this chapter are concerned with motivations for creativity that, taken together, form a compelling intrinsic dimension of human innovation. This intrinsic dimension focuses on creativity as a response to an inherent drive rather than simply as a quest for economic reward. The insights derived from these narratives about creativity reinforce two broader, but related, points. First, creativity is spurred largely by incentives that are noneconomic in nature. Intuitively, we know this to be true, and history supports the importance of noneconomic motivations for creation. Consider, for example, the intrinsic creativity present in children. The innate nature of the urge to create is also suggested by the works of authors lacking any expectation or hope of remuneration such as the cave drawings of prehistoric man, the artistic creations of inmates on death row,[70] and the works of authorship produced by the inhabitants of the Nazi death camps during World War II.[71] Elisabeth Kübler-Ross, the psychiatrist who outlined the five stages of grief in her groundbreaking work on the emotional components of dying, often spoke of her experience volunteering in a concentration camp after World War II as the catalyst influencing the course of her research. Specifically, she was struck by the beautiful butterflies carved all over the walls of the barracks housing the prisoners about to be put to death. She contemplated those butterflies for the rest of her life, as they helped her realize that even in the midst of tragedy, human beings still can find beauty.[72] This point was underscored more recently by the publication of the book *Art Against the Odds,* which features works by inmates and other artists who were isolated, self-taught, and not motivated by profiting from their creations.[73] Art made the worlds of these artists more comforting and tolerable. Thus, a perspective grounded in such inspirational motivations emphasizes creativity as fulfilling an inalienable responsibility to others as well as to the creator's own substantive personality. This paramount responsibility is what drives the intrinsic dimension of innovation. The narratives discussed in this chapter support this view of creativity by elevating noneconomic motivations for creativity such as personal satisfaction, challenge, or even stewardship.

A second point drawn from these narratives is that an inspirationally driven explanation of creativity seeks to unify the intrinsic drive and its external embodiment, so that the external is understood as a reflection of the author's inner cognitive processes. This explanation, by emphasizing the intrinsic process of creativity, recognizes that the value of expression derives from the *effort* to communicate as much as from the tangible result. The intrinsic dimension of creativity is not necessarily concerned with the commodity's ultimate economic worth, but instead values the commodity as a reflection of its creator and an embodiment of the creator's message and the work's intended meaning. According to this perspective, the commodity that embodies the author's work serves as a testament to the author's beliefs and inspirational motivations. During the time the author is in possession of her endowed gift, she seeks to ensure that her subjective meaning and message are appropriately attributed and presented to the public. Thus, the intrinsic dimension of innovation emphasizes the creator's responsibility in serving as the guardian of her meaning and message.

The concepts of the author's meaning and message are integral to appreciating the importance of an author's ability to safeguard the integrity of her texts. The theoretical framework developed in this book emphasizes the author's subjective view of the meaning and message of her work, as opposed to how the work might be reinterpreted by either the audience or other users. Again, the point is that the author's external work embodies the author's intrinsic creative process. Of course, the view of creativity I propose may not comport with the manner in which creativity is expressed in all instances. For example, creativity can involve random, accidental, or "eureka-like" moments that arguably conflict with the idea that the ultimate product is an expression of the author's intrinsic creative dimension. Some commentators have attempted to reconcile such unintended creative occurrences with a personality or personhood interest in the final product. Thus, Justin Hughes has posited that personhood interests justifying protection of some type "can arise from simply being the human source of an intellectual property *res*."[74] Alan Durham has argued that authorship should be defined to include at least certain indeterminate works.[75] Others such as Henri Poincaré have questioned the very foundation of a eureka-like moment, instead maintaining that "sudden illumination" is "a manifest sign of long, unconscious prior work."[76] Regardless of how some unintended creative works come into being, it must be acknowledged that there are instances in which a seemingly very creative work lacks an inspirationally driven process of development. This reality does not, however, detract from the relevance of the vision of creativity I develop.

An explicit understanding and recognition of the creative process and the connection between art and inspiration is important for it enables us to better comprehend the struggle creators face in navigating the conflict between the intrinsic dimension of creative enterprise and the commodification of its end products. An exclusive focus on commodification at the expense of the intrinsic dimension of creativity denudes the beauty and value of the "inner labor."[77] Lewis Hyde has observed that "every modern artist who has chosen to labor with a gift must sooner or later wonder how he or she is to survive in a society dominated by market exchange."[78] Indeed, evidence provided by both authors and creativity theorists indicates that too much of a focus on the commodification of one's art can diminish creative enterprise. Teresa Amabile has demonstrated that some authors have experienced blockages of their creativity upon receiving substantial monetary rewards.[79] English professor Mark Rose also has discussed the dichotomy between art and its commodification by questioning how "to negotiate the gap between creativity and commerce, between the notion that copyright is grounded in personhood and the need for a property law to regulate trade in vendible works."[80]

Absent appropriate consideration of inspirational motivations in the authors' rights dialogue, the resulting legal protection for authors' rights may be skewed and incomplete.[81] Such is the case in the United States. The following chapter examines the governing legal framework.

CHAPTER 3

The Current Legal Framework

ALTHOUGH COPYRIGHT LAW would seem to be the most natural avenue for authors seeking to redress violations of the integrity of their texts, such protections historically have been noticeably absent from the statutory scheme. Rather than afford protection for the personal rights of authors with respect to their works, copyright law in this country predominantly safeguards the pecuniary rights of the copyright owner (who may or may not be the actual author). The 1976 Copyright Act affords the copyright owner the exclusive rights to reproduce and distribute the original work, to prepare derivative works, and to perform and display publicly certain types of copyrighted works.[1] As all of these rights are assignable, either individually or collectively, the author may not be the one ultimately entitled to enforce these rights.[2] Thus, the primary objective of our copyright law is to ensure the copyright owner's receipt of all financial rewards to which she is entitled by virtue of copyright ownership. Authorship and copyright ownership, pursuant to the statutory scheme, are two distinct categories.

A review of the history of copyright law in this country and the philosophies that have shaped its direction are useful in understanding the current scope and coverage of the law. Utilitarianism is the predominant copyright justification in the United States, as evidenced by the Copyright Clause's provision of limited temporal protection as an economic incentive to create. The Framers adopted a copyright model that vested authors, perceived as less powerful than publishers, with authority because they were mindful of how concentrated power has the potential for undermining liberty. In reality, the United States had inherited from England a set of conflicting messages regarding authors' rights, in which economic protections were closely intertwined with personal rights.[3] Several of the state copyright statutes adopted shortly after the American Revolution, and before the enactment of the Constitution, emphasized heavily the personal claims of authors.[4] Nonetheless, the scant history of the Copyright Clause[5] fails to reflect an explicit concern with recognizing the personal rights of authors as an independent end. On the contrary, the evidence suggests that the Framers' primary policies were influenced heavily by the utilitarian goals of promoting progress, safeguarding public access, and protecting the public domain as the mechanism ensuring access to information and facts in expressive works.[6]

The vote on the Copyright Clause was not accompanied by any recorded debate at the Constitutional Convention, and it was approved unanimously.[7] Intellectual property historian Edward Walterscheid notes that the Clause was "an afterthought," and therefore the delegates "gave it less thought than perhaps they should have."[8] We do know, however, that the Framers feared monopolistic concentrations of power and had a desire to foster an atmosphere of intellectual fluidity. James Madison, one of the primary forces behind the inclusion of the Clause, believed that both patents and copyrights were monopolies and therefore had to be circumscribed. Moreover, the central focus on preventing monopolies accounted for the need, absent recourse to any explanations, for a durational limit for copyrights and patents.[9] At the same time, the Framers were motivated by concerns regarding dissemination of knowledge and preservation of a public domain necessary to ensure access to necessary information. Relevant to these concerns was the Framers' desire for the United States to be "culturally competitive" with other nations, a goal that could only be achieved through the enactment of copyright laws that would encourage authorship activity.[10] It has been suggested that the Framers, many of whom were lawyers, were especially persuaded of the value of literature and therefore "when the chance came to simplify the task of protecting literature and to secure authors their property rights, the [F]ramers eagerly jumped on this opportunity."[11]

Under the utilitarian model, the operative goal is the widespread dissemination of intellectual works. Moreover, the traditional utilitarian justification for copyright law in this country is supported by a functionalist, economically based analysis that views works of authorship as fungible commodities and thus equivalent to consumer goods. This perspective is one that departs substantially from the holistic approach toward artistic creation that emerges from the narratives explored in the prior chapter.

Natural law theory, though not the predominant philosophical justification for copyright law in the United States, also has played a role in shaping the law.[12] Natural law theory, particularly as developed by John Locke,[13] espouses the God-given right to acquire *external* things, either through exerting labor or by initial possession, and to dispose of such items as desired.[14] Along with this focus on the acquisition of property, however, Locke maintained that the gifts bestowed by God upon man are held by man in stewardship, and as such are inalienable and subject to strict limitations on human conduct.[15] According to this view, an individual cannot dispose of her life and personal autonomy. In contrast, Locke conceived of a person's labor and actions as alienable "private" property.[16] Thus, a Lockean theory of copyright law maintains that an author's expression, having been created with her mental labor, is an ideal object for commodification.[17] Moreover, Locke's view of labor is that of an unpleasant necessity—something that must be done to ensure a return of private ownership.[18] Locke's perspective thus underscores that "the passion for material appropriation is viewed as fundamental, even primary, in motivating the creation acts of the individual."[19] Thus, a Lockean theory of copyright law defines labor, and the external product in which it results, in terms of potential commodification.[20] Moreover, once something becomes externalized, the part of it characterized by personal autonomy as a gift from God is lost because the object itself is capable of commodification.

Thus, in light of the utilitarian and Lockean underpinnings of copyright law in the United States, the prevailing law and policies de-emphasize the intrinsic process of creation in favor of a narrative favoring dissemination, commodification, and economic reward. According to this interpretation of copyright law, the importance of the product and its external validation are paramount. This perspective differs significantly from one which emphasizes the product's importance as a reflection of the author's meaning and an embodiment of her message.

Copyright law in the United States fails to afford authors, in an explicit fashion, comprehensive moral rights such as the right to have their works attributed to them or the right to have their works maintained and presented in a manner consistent with their artistic vision. The 1976 Copyright Act, in its original form, contains only one provision that explicitly recognizes, in a limited context, an interest protected elsewhere by the moral rights doctrine. Section 115 allows the reproduction in phonorecords of a musical composition that has been distributed previously, provided the copyright owner is notified and receives a specified royalty. Section 115(a)(2) stipulates that a compulsory license includes the privilege of making a musical arrangement of the work that conforms to the style of the concerned performance, as long as the arrangement does not "change the basic melody or fundamental character of the work."[21] To date, no pertinent litigation has arisen with respect to this provision, and currently the Register of Copyrights is proposing legislation to eliminate it.[22]

More recently, when Congress enacted the Digital Millennium Copyright Act in 1998, it included a de facto right of attribution through the copyright management information provisions. Section 1202(a) of the statute prohibits the provision of false copyright management information (CMI) that will "induce, enable, facilitate, or conceal" copyright infringement.[23] Section 1202(b) prohibits the removal or alteration of CMI, as well as the distribution and public performance of works if the CMI has been removed or altered, with knowledge that the removal of such information will "induce, enable, facilitate, or conceal" copyright infringement.[24] Further, § 1202(c) defines CMI broadly to include the title of the work, the author, copyright owner, and in certain instances the writer, performer, and director of a work. The net effect of these provisions is the preservation of the names of authors and other artists in connection with their works. This "quasi-moral rights" protection potentially can impact a large category of works, particularly since both the statutory language and the legislative history suggest that CMI can pertain to analog as well as digital forms of copyright.[25] Still, given the need for a plaintiff to prove that the defendant was contemplating copyright infringement in connection with the removal or alteration of the CMI, § 1202 is tied to the traditional economic copyright model rather than "independent authorial interests in proper attribution."[26] Moreover, as

Justin Hughes has observed, "because the CMI content would be decided by the copyright holder, section 1202 does nothing for the *author* vis-à-vis the *copyright holder*, a common fact pattern in attribution disputes."[27] Thus, the provision probably has the greatest applicability with respect to third-party copiers.

The copyright provision with the greatest potential to safeguard authors' integrity interests is § 106(2) of the Copyright Act, which grants to the copyright owner the exclusive right to prepare and to authorize the preparation of "derivative works based upon the copyrighted work."[28] Section 101 defines a "derivative work" as one that is "based upon one or more preexisting works."[29] Section 106(2) can provide limited recognition of integrity interests when a party uses an author's preexisting work to create a derivative work without permission, and the modified work violates the author's textual integrity. In such instances, the author can sue for copyright infringement and simultaneously redress the integrity violation as part of that lawsuit. There is another way in which § 106 can facilitate safeguarding authors' integrity interests, although to date it has not been tested in the judicial system. Suppose that a party is authorized by the author to make a derivative work but, in the course of exercising this right, makes changes that the author deems to be violative of her artistic spirit, intended meaning or message. Further, assume the derivative work is billed as "based upon" the author's underlying work, despite the existence of these objectionable changes. A strong argument can be made that the original author should be allowed to maintain a copyright infringement action against the author of the derivative work, based on the adapting party's violation of the scope of the license agreement. Under this approach, the adapter's mutilating changes and resulting false attribution conceivably constitute copyright infringement under § 106(2).[30]

Aside from these provisions, the only explicit adoption of moral rights on a federal level in the United States derives from a 1990 amendment to the 1976 Copyright Act known as the Visual Artists Rights Act (VARA).[31] VARA was passed two years after the United States joined the Berne Convention for the Protection of Literary and Artistic works.[32] The Berne Convention is the oldest multilateral treaty governing copyright protection, and as a result of the United States' adherence to Berne, American authors enjoy increased copyright protection internationally.[33] Article *6bis* of the Berne Convention recognizes the moral rights of attribution and integrity.[34] When the United States joined Berne, the entertainment and publishing industries vehemently opposed the adoption of specific moral rights legislation as part of the United States' adherence to the Convention. When Congress eventually passed VARA following our adherence to Berne, there was little debate or discussion. Significantly, on the last day of the 101st Congress, a major bill was passed that authorized eighty-five new federal judgeships. Sponsors of this bill had to include several unrelated measures in order to appease senators who would otherwise oppose the federal judgeships bill. One such measure was VARA, which had already been passed by the House of Representatives but had been blocked in the Senate Judiciary Committee by some Republican senators. Thus, VARA was passed by the full Senate only because those Republican senators acquiesced in light of their desire to pass the federal judgeships bill.[35]

VARA provides very circumscribed federal statutory protection for the moral rights of certain visual artists by prohibiting unauthorized, intentional modifications to their works that will prejudice their honor and reputation.[36] In addition, VARA safeguards an artist's right of attribution in situations not limited to intentional changes, but still does not guarantee an author the ability to exercise the rights of anonymity or pseudonymity.[37] VARA additionally provides, in the case of works of visual art of "recognized stature," the right to prevent their destruction, either by intentional or grossly negligent acts.[38] The statute also contains special provisions for works of visual art that have become part of buildings.[39] One significant problem with VARA is that the statute only applies to a very narrow category of visual art such as paintings, drawings, prints, and sculptures.[40] VARA also specifically excludes protection for reproductions of works, and fails to provide any remedy when works are used in a context found objectionable or distasteful by the author. Additionally, the statute fails to define critical terms such as *prejudice, honor,* or *recognized stature.*[41] A waiver is permitted pursuant to VARA if the author expressly agrees to waive in a signed, written instrument.[42]

In addition to numerous flaws inherent in VARA, one of the main difficulties with the statute is widespread ignorance of its existence even today. When VARA was enacted, Congress directed the Copyright Office to commission a report on the impact of its waiver provisions.[43] As part of this undertaking, the Copyright Office mailed a survey to visual artists, art lawyers, agents, dealers, and others working with visual artists. It mailed about 6,800 questionnaires nationally and received 1,061 responses from forty-seven states. Nine hundred and fifty-five respondents categorized themselves as "visual artists" within the meaning of the copyright law.[44] Significantly, 73 percent were aware that visual artists had moral rights, but only 41 percent were aware that those rights could be waived. Artists who were represented by an agent or who derived a larger annual gross income from their artwork had a greater awareness of the waiver's operation. Those artists from states with moral rights statutes enacted prior to VARA had a higher degree of general moral rights awareness, but no greater awareness of waiver.[45] More recent evidence suggests that there has been little change in artists' awareness of VARA since the Copyright Office Report was issued in 1996.[46] It is telling that a defendant city's ignorance of VARA justified a court's refusal to award a plaintiff artist enhanced damages for the city's violation of VARA by destroying her sculpture. Since the city did not know about VARA, its actions were not deemed "willful" as required by the copyright provision regarding enhanced statutory damages.[47]

Prior to VARA's enactment, California, Connecticut, Louisiana, Maine, Massachusetts, Nevada, New Jersey, New Mexico, New York, Pennsylvania, and Rhode Island provided specific statutory moral rights protections for certain types of works, notably visual art. One particularly complicated problem raised by VARA is its preemptive effect with respect to these state statutes. For example, VARA provides that state laws are not preempted if they "stem from activities violating rights that are not equivalent" to those provided under VARA.[48] With respect to activities covered under VARA, however, that statute governs their application exclusively. Not only does the specific content of the state statutes vary among the states, but the respective state statutes also differ from VARA. For example, some of the state statutes extend protection to visual and graphic works in any medium, and thus maintain a more expansive definition of "fine art" than does VARA.[49] In general, state provisions that provide more comprehensive protection to works covered by VARA probably would be deemed preempted by VARA because the broader protections would not be seen as providing different or nonequivalent rights. This view is consistent not only with VARA's legislative history[50] but also with the law according to the 1976 Act under which courts frequently adopt a strict standard regarding what type of elements negate preemption.[51] In fact, at least one district court has already held that the New York moral rights statute was preempted by VARA.[52]

When the United States originally joined the Berne Convention, one of the reasons Congress believed that no additional moral rights protections were needed was the existence of measures such as § 106(2) of the Copyright Act and the state moral rights statutes just discussed. In addition, however, moral rights opponents cited § 43(a) of the Lanham Act, which often was invoked as a substitute measure for moral rights protection.[53] Section 43(a) provides a federal remedy for the use of either a "false designation of origin" or a false description or representation in connection with any goods or services.[54] Thus, to the extent that an author's works are published in an altered state, with her name attached, such publication can implicate § 43(a). The seminal case, *Gilliam v. American Broadcasting Companies, Inc.*,[55] was very favorable for authors and illustrates the operation of § 43(a) in this context. In *Gilliam*, the Second Circuit determined that the plaintiffs, the group of British writers and performers known as "Monty Python," stated a cause of action under § 43(a) based on the defendant network's broadcasting of a program truthfully designated as having been written and performed by the plaintiffs but which had been edited, without plaintiffs' consent, into a mutilated and distorted form that substantially departed from the original work.[56]

Even when § 43(a) has been stretched to incorporate protections for moral rights, the underlying focus of this cause of action is reputation damage deriving from a "false designation of origin." In contrast, moral rights' focus on the author's dignity, spirit, meaning, and message of the work encompasses much more than reputation damage. Yet, the United

States has been reluctant to adopt even limited legislative measures under § 43(a) that would provide some increased moral rights protection. In the early 1990s, the Film Disclosure Act was introduced before Congress as an amendment to § 43(a) in order to address the issue of film colorization. This amendment would have required labeling of a materially altered film if the artistic author, defined in the statute, objected to the alterations. Representatives of the powerful motion picture industry opposed the bill, speaking of the chilling effect of the proposed amendment on those other than directors and writers.[57] Ultimately, the bill was not adopted.

The Supreme Court recently considered § 43(a) as a substitute for moral rights in the specific context of a case invoking this provision to redress "reverse passing off." Express reverse passing off occurs when an infringer removes the name or trademark on another party's product and sells that product under a name chosen by the infringer, resulting in a likelihood of consumer confusion.[58] In *Dastar Corp. v. Twentieth Century Fox Film Corp.*,[59] the plaintiff brought a reverse passing-off action under § 43(a) based on the defendant's copying and modifying tapes of the original version of a television series about General Dwight Eisenhower's European campaign during World War II. The defendant copied and edited the tapes, which were in the public domain, and manufactured for sale as its own product a video set called "World War II Campaigns in Europe." The defendant's tapes did not refer to the original television show, or to the book upon which the original show was based. In rejecting the plaintiff's claim that the defendant's sale of the tapes absent appropriate attribution violated § 43(a) of the Lanham Act, the Supreme Court pointed to the confined nature of the right of attribution in VARA, and cautioned against invoking § 43(a) as a "cause of action for misrepresentation of authorship of noncopyrighted works."[60]

Dastar clearly was the "origin" of the tapes it produced but the question presented to the Court was whether "origin" under the Lanham Act refers to the actual producer of the end product or to the creator of the underlying work that served as the starting point of the end product. The Court interprets "origin" to mean "the producer of the tangible product sold in the marketplace," rather than to "the person or entity that originated the ideas or communications" embodied in the product.[61] In so holding, the Court refused to apply a different test for "origin" under the Lanham Act for communicative products, as opposed to tangible goods. A different resolution would, according to the Court, cause conflict between the Lanham Act and copyright law. The court was especially concerned with problems of line-drawing in determining the identity of a work's "origin."[62]

At least two issues are open following *Dastar*. First, *Dastar* involved the use of a work that was in the public domain, but subsequent lower courts have relied upon the decision in holding that § 43(a) cannot be invoked as a substitute for the right of attribution in cases involving copyrighted works not in the public domain.[63] These courts have applied *Dastar* absent explicit analysis of the implications of the Court's opinion for nonpublic domain works. Second, the Court's language appears to leave open the possibility that an author can preserve a claim for misattribution when the infringer merely repackages the author's work,[64] or for misrepresentation under § 43(a)(1)(B) rather than reverse passing off under § 43(a)(1)(A).[65] As Jane Ginsburg notes, however, these options "prove strained or insufficient" due to a variety of requirements including the need for the misrepresentation to occur in commercial advertising or promotion that is concerned with the alleged false representation.[66]

Aside from § 106(2) of the Copyright Act, state moral rights laws, and § 43(a) of the Lanham Act, United States courts have relied upon existing common law doctrines to protect an author's moral rights such as breach of contract, defamation, and invasion of privacy. Unfortunately, for reasons discussed below, none of these areas of law function as sufficient substitutes for moral rights. Some courts have articulated a willingness to interpret ambiguous contracts to vindicate an author's interests. For example, in *Gilliam v. American Broadcasting Companies, Inc.*,[67] the Second Circuit held that the extensive unauthorized editing of a work protected by common law copyright constituted copyright infringement at least in the absence of a governing contractual provision. In general, however, United States courts are reluctant to afford extensive protections to authors against objectionable modifications absent express contractual provisions.[68] There is the additional problem that the author may lack privity of contract with the defendant.[69] Further, relatively unknown authors face a disparity of bargaining power that frequently results in a loss of valuable protections. Authors are unlikely to be successful by resorting to contractual measures since, as Yochai Benkler aptly observed, people "contract against the background of law that defines what is, and what is not, open for them to do or refrain from doing."[70] Indeed, the very purpose of moral rights laws is to "alter the bargaining power between the authors and artists and those who use their works."[71]

The law of defamation offers creators an avenue for relief if their works are disseminated to the public in such a manner as to injure their professional reputations. The injury might take the form of the publication of a mutilated version of the creator's work under the author's name,[72] or a false attribution of authorship with respect to a work of poor quality with which the author was not associated.[73] The key to any successful defamation action, however, is the author's showing that the unauthorized acts exposed her to contempt or public ridicule, thus injuring her professional standing.[74] Therefore, the use of this theory will be of no avail for an author who believes the integrity of her work has been impaired but who cannot show damage to her professional reputation. Moreover, an author also must be sufficiently well-known to have a reputation before this theory can be invoked.[75]

Alternatively, an author whose works have been published without her authorization or who is the victim of a false attribution may seek to redress her injuries by suing for invasion of privacy.[76] This theory also is of limited assistance to authors seeking redress for violation of their moral rights. For one thing, the scope of the right of privacy varies from state to state and some formulations contain exceptions that are fatal to invasion of privacy actions based on moral rights violations. For example, the New York statute does not make actionable the use of an author's name, portrait, or picture in connection with any production sold or disposed of by the author.[77] Such a provision fails to recognize moral rights' fundamental premise that there must be accountability for the interests protected by the doctrine following a grant of the right to use the work.

The right of privacy sometimes is confused with another doctrine, the right of publicity, which potentially represents a vital avenue for safe-guarding textual integrity when the text at issue is an individual's persona rather than a conventional work of authorship. The right of publicity is a legal theory that enables individuals, particularly celebrities, to protect themselves from unauthorized, commercial appropriations of their personas. The right of publicity case law reveals instances in which an individual's persona is appropriated in an objectionable context or for an objectionable purpose. For example, in *Waits v. Frito-Lay, Inc.*,[78] singer Tom Waits sued Frito-Lay and its advertising agency for using a soundalike who imitated Waits' distinctive voice in a commercial for Doritos. Waits has a firm public policy against doing commercials because he believes that commercials undermine the artistic integrity of musicians. The jury awarded damages to Waits not only for the economic value of his voice, but also for injury to his mental well-being and professional reputation. The Ninth Circuit affirmed the propriety of the entire damage award and specifically noted that a violation of a plaintiff's right of publicity can induce humiliation and embarrassment.[79]

The right of publicity will be explored in greater depth in Chapter 8 but for now, it is worth noting that whereas the United States lags woefully behind other countries in its adoption of moral rights, it is a leader among nations in protecting publicity rights. This situation is curious because moral rights protections are analogous to publicity rights in at least two ways. First, as the *Waits* case indicates, although the right of publicity often is viewed as an economic right, some decisions actually are more concerned with redressing the injured feelings and mental anguish of publicity plaintiffs. Second, both doctrines seek to protect the integrity of texts by rejecting fluidity of textual interpretation by the public in favor of the author's interpretation. On a theoretical level, both the right of publicity and moral rights contradict the view that members of the public have the unconditional right to interpret texts according to their own cultural needs. As the right of publicity safeguards individuals' abilities to control the public presentations of their personas in commercial contexts, moral rights allow authors of artistic works a comparable measure of control regarding the substantive presentations of their works.

It is interesting to speculate as to why there exists a difference between the United States' treatment of publicity rights and moral rights,
given the parallels between these doctrines. The answer probably resides
in the relative value our society places on celebrity texts as opposed to
other artistic works. In general, any system of ownership rights encourages people to devote time to the things that are most valued by society.[80]
Regarding intellectual property specifically, "[t]he history behind the recognition (or non-recognition) of protection afforded a particular form of
intellectual property often reflects the philosophical and cultural role
that form of intellectual property plays in a country's heritage."[81] In
France, for example, where moral rights protections are among the strongest, a cultural tradition exists in which artists are elevated as a special
class of laborers who possess almost spiritual qualities, and their works
are treated as a special category of property. As a result, in France and
other countries with a civil law tradition, artists' rights often are protected against other parties' contract or property interests. The following
chapter explores these themes more closely by examining the operation
of moral rights in the international sphere.

CHAPTER 4

International Norms

AS OF THE CLOSE OF THE FIRST DECADE of the twenty-first century, the United States appears to be rather isolated in its failure to recognize explicitly adequate moral rights.[1] The existence of more substantive moral rights protections in both civil and common law jurisdictions not only creates a disparity between the law in the United States and many other countries,[2] but also results in situations in which American authors find substantially more protection for violations of their moral rights abroad than at home.[3]

Moreover, there is the stark reality that we may not be in compliance with our obligations under the Berne Convention.[4] Berne binds its adherents to a unitary copyright law system that is administered by the World Intellectual Property Organization (WIPO). Since 1928, Berne has recognized the rights of attribution and integrity with the following language:

Independently of the author's copyright, and even after the transfer of the said copyright, the author shall have the right to claim authorship of the work, as well as the right to object to any distortion, mutilation or other modification of the said work which would be prejudicial to his honour or reputation.[5]

Berne also provides that these moral rights are to be maintained "at least" until the expiration of the economic rights and "shall be exercisable by the persons or institutions authorized by the legislation of the country where protection is claimed."[6] Significantly, Article 6bis(3) clarifies that the Convention relies upon the specific legislation of the nations adhering to the treaty to govern substantive applications of its provisions within each of the member nations.[7] Although the 1994 Agreement on Trade-Related Aspects of Intellectual Property Rights (TRIPs) incorporates the Berne Convention and provides for sanctions for noncompliance, the United States insured that Article 6bis was excluded from the "rights and obligations" TRIPs delineates.[8] Thus, trade sanctions and other penalties cannot be imposed under the World Trade Organization's mandatory dispute resolution process for noncompliance with Berne's moral rights provisions.[9] Moreover, the European Union has excluded moral rights from its overall copyright harmonization efforts.[10]

In 1996, Article *6bis* was incorporated by reference into WIPO's Copyright Treaty, resulting in the adoption of moral rights for performing artists by the WIPO Performances and Phonograms Treaty (WPPT). Article 5(1) of WPPT provides:

Independently of a performer's economic rights, and even after the transfer of those rights, the performer shall, as regards his live aural performances or performances fixed in phonograms, have the right to claim to be identified as the performer of his performances, except where omission is dictated by the manner of the use of the performance, and to object to any distortion, mutilation or other modification of his performances that would be prejudicial to his reputation.[11]

The WPPT incorporates a right of integrity and attribution and tracks Berne's duration, and implementation, although it requires contracting parties to adopt enforcement mechanisms.[12] One commentator has noted that because the original purpose of this treaty was to protect performance of underlying works, it may be inconsistent with protection for the right of publicity for personas.[13] Even though performers in some countries such as France and Germany enjoy aspects of moral rights,[14] more widespread adherence to the WPPT may change the landscape of moral rights for performers in the future.[15]

Thus, on the international level, the only existing protections for moral rights are Article *6bis* of Berne for authors of works and the WPPT provision for performers.[16] Moral rights therefore remain "chiefly a matter of national law."[17] Historically, there has been a divergence in moral rights protection between the civil and common law traditions, although recently the majority of common law jurisdictions have enacted moral rights protections to some degree.[18] This chapter focuses initially on the civil law tradition given that moral rights originated in this system.

Mark Rose, in his historical account of authors and owners, argues that the author was regarded as an individual with an interest in "the status of his name and reputation before he was recognized as a fully empowered figure in the marketplace."[19] As early as the sixteenth and seventeenth centuries, in England, France, and elsewhere, a general feeling for the author's personal interests had developed based on the concepts of honor and reputation, rather than on property theories rooted in an economic foundation.[20] Still, the development of a crystallized notion of authors' rights, from both a personal and an economic standpoint, was a long way off at this time.

Curiously in France, which is among the most sympathetic jurisdictions to authors' personal rights, the earliest recognition for authors was dominated by a concern for economic, rather than personal rights. Prior to the emergence of moral rights, the view of copyright around the time of the French Revolution was substantially similar to the Anglo-American perspective.[21] Beginning in the nineteenth century, however, a growing acceptance of the notion of the Romantic author impelled French courts to recognize explicitly authors' personal interests and their authorial dignity.[22] During this time, authors such as Alphonse de Lamartine, Honoré de Balzac, and Victor Hugo passionately appealed to the French legislature to endorse more substantial legal protections for authors.[23] Hugo particularly objected to the notion of the public domain as a violation of authors' natural property rights and a concept at odds with principles of individual liberty.[24]

French law ultimately embodied a view of moral rights that assumes the author's personal and economic interests are protected by conceptually distinct sets of rights. This is known as the "dualist" theory, which is ultimately attributable to philosopher Georg Hegel. He believed the labor component of a work represents an inalienable part of the author, and perceived that its embodiment in an external medium transformed such a work into an alienable commodity.[25] Hegel thus rejected the protection of pure ideas because "the purpose of a product of mind is that people other than its author should understand it and make it the possession of their ideas."[26] Hegel viewed mental accomplishments and talents as appropriate subjects for business transactions but believed they also manifest "something inward and mental."[27] Under this conception, although intellectual works are capable of commodification, the author retains general rights of personality that survive market exploitation of the external work.[28] Hegel's philosophy thus incorporates a concern for the intrinsic dimension of human creativity as well as the ability to alienate the externalized product. In fact, in France, the commentators address the interdependence of moral and economic rights, although they stress that the moral ones predominate over the economic.[29]

Other countries such as Germany relied on an equally strong set of entitlements deriving from Immanuel Kant and Otto von Gierke. According to Kant, authors' literary works represent a complete embodiment of the internal self,[30] and therefore he understood such works as part of the author's being rather than as commodified objects.[31] This conception of authors' rights greatly influenced Gierke, the major figure in the development of the monist copyright theory characteristic of German law.[32] According to the monist theory, intellectual works belong exclusively to "the internal, personal sphere."[33] This perspective sees the author's economic interests as a component of the personal interests.[34]

Thus, the civil law view of artistic creation embodies a strong concern for the intrinsic dimension of creativity. Both the monist and dualist theories emphasize this dimension, although the dualist perspective also recognizes the external work as an entity capable of being severed from its creator. Even so, the dualist theory emphasizes both the connection between the creator and her external work, and the idea that the tangible product cannot be understood without reference to the intrinsic creative process. These philosophies are markedly distinct from those which have shaped the United States' laws governing authors' rights.

It should be emphasized that almost everywhere, moral rights apply to works that are copyrightable, or in the context of civil law systems, to works that are capable of giving rise to economic rights. Moral rights typically are contained in the copyright statutes of particular jurisdictions.[35] Also, moral rights protect the original author of a work, as opposed to assignees, licensees, or those who commission a work. Further, at least in most civil law jurisdictions, authors are almost always regarded as the initial copyright owners because the work for hire doctrine is not recognized.[36] Still, as Henry Hansmann and Marina Santilli have noted, civil law jurisdictions may reach similar results even absent the application of a formal work for hire doctrine.[37] For example, under

Italian law, a court might find that one who was otherwise considered an employee for hire in another jurisdiction is not considered an "author" of a particular work, and thus denied moral rights on that basis.[38]

Film presents an interesting example of authorship that might be considered as part of an employment relationship. Although there are certain limitations with respect to the exercise of moral rights in connection with film,[39] the civil law countries generally extend moral rights to the authors of films.[40] Thus, when the heirs of John Huston sued Turner Entertainment Company and a French station for colorizing and broadcasting *The Asphalt Jungle*, they prevailed in France.[41] More recently, an Italian court held that a television company in Italy violated the moral rights of the deceased film director Fred Zinnemann when it broadcast a colorized version of *The Seventh Cross*. Zinnemann deliberately elected to make the film, which concerned the horrors of prewar Nazi Germany, in black and white, and the court ruled that the colorized version of the film damaged his honor and reputation. The television company was precluded from repeating a showing of the colorized version, required to destroy all colorized versions of the film, and ordered to pay damages.[42]

In the civil law tradition, the right of attribution typically enables authors to claim authorship as well as remain anonymous or use pseudonyms.[43] The controversial Dead Sea Scrolls case, litigated in Israel, raises an interesting example of an attribution violation.[44] Although the roots of Israeli law derive largely from the common law tradition, it also incorporates some aspects of the civil law tradition through strong protections for authors' moral rights.[45] The case involved the defendants' unauthorized publication in the United States of the deciphered reconstructed text of a particular Dead Sea Scroll. Harvard professor John Strugnell was among those scholars who were initially allowed access to the scrolls pursuant to a policy of exclusivity promulgated first by Jordan and subsequently by the Antiquities Authority of Israel. At first Strugnell worked alone, but eventually he required the assistance of someone with greater knowledge of linguistics and Jewish law. Professor Elisha Qimron joined Strugnell in 1981 and spent eleven years deciphering the scroll. From the sixty to seventy fragments Qimron received from Strugnell, Qimron compiled a text of about 120 lines, referred to in the court's opinion as "the deciphered text."[46] In 1990, Qimron and Strugnell reached an agreement with the English Oxford University Press regarding publication of the deciphered text, along with photographs of the scroll's fragments and interpretation. Prior to the appearance of this publication, however, defendants Hershel Shanks and the Biblical Archaeological Society published in the United States a book called *Facsimile Edition of the Dead Sea Scrolls*. This book contained the 120-line deciphered reconstructed text of the scroll and a set of nearly 1,800 photos of unpublished scroll fragments. Shanks gave the credit for the reconstruction and decipherment to Professor Strugnell, working "with a colleague." The unnamed colleague was Professor Qimron, who at the time was a junior untenured academic.[47]

Qimron's complaint, filed in an Israeli court, raised whether the defendants violated Qimron's right of attribution by publishing the text without mentioning his name.[48] The court found that the defendants violated Qimron's moral right of attribution and that the deliberate omission of Qimron's name was "contemptuous and mockery."[49] The significance of the attribution violation to Qimron is evidenced by his admission following the Israeli Supreme Court's ruling that had Shanks listed his name in the defendants' publication, Qimron probably would not have initiated the lawsuit. Qimron's observation underscores the importance of professional reputation and artistic dignity with respect to his endeavor. The moral nature of the harm is underscored by the Israeli Supreme Court's observation that "[a] person is entitled that his name be attributed to the 'children of his spirit,' "[50] and therefore, the defendants' actions violated not only Israeli law, but also the "human-moral duty."[51]

With respect to the right of integrity, although Berne and other countries[52] require that actionable modifications must negatively impact the author's honor or reputation, some countries such as France and Germany do not explicitly incorporate this caveat.[53] Still, there are certain limitations to the right of integrity even in jurisdictions that maintain the strongest moral rights protection. In Germany, for example, the right of integrity with respect to film and works included in film only protects against distortions or mutilations that are gross in nature.[54] Moreover, in France, the right of integrity is applied more narrowly with respect to certain types of works such as computer programs, architectural works, and other works with minimal originality.[55]

The right of integrity applies to both actual and contextual modifications.[56] Thus, in Italy, a composer and singer well-known for his stance on the environment successfully relied on the right of integrity to prevent an assignee of the copyright in his songs from selling cassettes with his music in conjunction with environmentally harmful detergent.[57] Another case involving an objectionable contextual use was brought by several prominent Russian composers who sought injunctive relief against the defendant's use of their music in a film that, in the plaintiffs' view, had an anti-Soviet theme. In addition to the use of the plaintiffs' music, which was in the public domain, the defendant used the plaintiffs' names on the credit lines. The plaintiffs brought simultaneous actions in both the United States and in France. The United States court refused to award the plaintiffs any relief[58] but the French court, not surprisingly, concluded that there was undoubtedly a moral damage. It awarded the plaintiffs damages and ordered the film seized.[59]

An interesting case concerning the appropriate balance between the original author's right of integrity and the freedom to create enjoyed by all authors has been the subject of litigation in France in recent years. Pierre Hugo, the heir of Victor Hugo, sued the publisher of two books that were presented as sequels to *Les Miserables*. In France, even works in the public domain are protected by moral rights.[60] Hugo was objecting to the content of the books on the ground that they resurrected an original character, Inspector Javert, in an inappropriate manner inconsistent with his original personality, and presented what Hugo considered to be disrespectful and scandalous treatments of the original.[61] The Cour de Cassation, the highest court in France, determined that an author's freedom to create, which is a consequence of the freedom of expression provided for in Article 10 of the European Convention on Human Rights,[62] precludes an author's heirs from banning the creation of sequels after the original author's economic rights have expired. The court did, however, emphasize that the freedom to create enjoyed by the author of a sequel is limited by respect for the original work's integrity and the original author's name. The court held that infringement of the moral right of integrity requires "evaluating the litigious works themselves" and specifically whether they "have altered Victor Hugo's work" or "have created confusion on the work's attribution."[63] Thus, the court remanded to the appellate court for a determination of whether the sequels respect the "spirit" of the original work.[64]

In jurisdictions with well-developed moral rights laws, other rights exist in addition to the right of integrity and the right of attribution. For example, some jurisdictions maintain a right of disclosure and a right of withdrawal. Underlying the right of disclosure is the idea that the author, as the sole judge of when a work is ready for public dissemination, is the only one who can possess any rights in an uncompleted work. An inalienable right of disclosure can be problematic with respect to works such as film because a director or screenwriter can block the distribution of a film that was already largely completed. For these reasons, "civil law countries have adopted special statutory provisions excepting film from rigorous application of the right of disclosure."[65]

The right of withdrawal, which is maintained in countries such as France, Germany, and Italy, is connected to the right of disclosure in that the author also enjoys the right to determine whether a work should be withdrawn from the public if it no longer reflects the author's convictions or spirit.[66] The right of withdrawal is best understood as a means of allowing authors to "retract the economic rights that they may have assigned or licensed to a third party in order to enable that third party to exploit the work."[67] This right is rarely exercised for two reasons. First, the author must have serious moral reservations with respect to the ongoing ability of the work to represent her personal convictions.[68] Thus, an author must affirmatively show severe harm.[69] Second, the right is applicable only to published works rather than works of visual art, and the right therefore is difficult to exercise as a practical matter.[70]

Interestingly, civil law countries typically do not protect an author against complete destruction of her work.[71] One partial exception is the provision found in the Swiss statute that requires an owner of artwork to offer, before the work's destruction, to sell the work to its creator for the "material value of the work."[72] Perhaps the underlying rationale for the failure of most countries to prevent destructions of works of art is that a work that has been destroyed completely cannot reflect adversely upon the creator's honor or reputation.[73] Of course, this explanation is not relevant to those instances where a work is destroyed in a manner that subjects the creator to shame or embarrassment.[74]

The issues of alienability and waiver are the most troublesome for civil law countries due to potential interference "with the principle of freedom of contract between authors and users of copyrightable works."[75] The Netherlands takes an approach to waiver that is unusual among the civil law countries in that authors are allowed to waive their moral rights, although they cannot waive the right to object to prejudicial distortions or mutilations.[76] Even in France, where the right of integrity is considered inalienable in theory, there are limitations, at least in practice, regarding the extent to which it is inalienable. For example, an author may consent to acts that would violate her right of integrity, although she cannot bind herself to a waiver through an "enforceable agreement not to change [her] mind in the future and seek a judicial remedy for the violation."[77] In adjudicating the validity of waivers as a defense in actions for alleged right of integrity violations, the French judiciary tends to enforce contracts allowing reasonable alterations that do not distort the spirit of the author's work, particularly with respect to adaptations and contributions to collective works.[78] This inclination on the part of French courts illustrates the inherent infeasibility of truly inalienable moral rights. In Italy, blanket waivers are prohibited but authors can enter into agreements to waive their moral rights with respect to specific alterations performed by specific individuals.[79] Overall, the interests of creators in safeguarding their reputations and professional standing must be balanced against the interests of those who perform adaptations. As a general matter, courts apply what amounts to a "reasonableness" criterion in assessing whether particular modifications are infringing, but distinct applications of this criterion can differ according to national tradition.[80] For example, playwright Samuel Beckett successfully opposed an all-female production of *Waiting for Godot* in France, but was unsuccessful in a comparable action in The Netherlands.[81]

Moreover, courts tend to rule against authors if they agree to specific modifications "either before or after the fact and then try to rely on their inalienable moral rights to reverse their previous decisions to the detriment of the other party to the contract."[82] Cyrill Rigamonti discusses a case in which the author of a literary figure popular in France entered into a contract with a motion picture company for several films based upon the author's novels. The author agreed to a lump sum payment when he learned that the protagonist of his novels had been altered in a manner to which he objected. Moreover, the credit line in the movie was modified to say that the movie version was only "inspired by" as opposed to "based" upon the author's work. Eventually the author sued to have the contract annulled on the ground that it violated his moral rights. The court upheld the contract because the author had accepted the modifications in exchange for money and the disclaimer was sufficient to inform the public about the modifications. Moreover, the court ruled that moral rights do not afford authors the ability to unilaterally abrogate freely concluded contracts where authors have full knowledge of the situation.[83]

With respect to waiver-related issues in connection with the right of attribution in the civil law tradition, authors generally "always preserve their right to disclose the fact of their authorship, even if they previously agreed to publish their work anonymously or under a pseudonym."[84] The topic of waiver of the right of attribution necessitates consideration of the status of ghostwriters. France permits ghostwriters to renege upon their waivers and insist upon attribution,[85] whereas in Italy, ghostwriters often are not considered authors according to their contracts and therefore do not enjoy moral rights.[86] In Germany, typically a ghostwriter's waiver of attribution is binding absent special circumstances in which an author can assert a legally protectable interest in attribution. The provision for such special circumstances reveals "the core of an author's moral rights that may not be fully alienable or waivable."[87]

Regarding the appropriate duration for moral rights, there are two perspectives. Many countries follow the minimum standard mentioned in the Berne Convention and simultaneously terminate a creator's moral rights and economic rights.[88] In contrast, the French view is that moral rights last indefinitely.[89] In France, an author's moral rights always have been regarded as a separate body of protections, rather than as a doctrine that is intertwined with the creator's pecuniary rights.[90] Thus, pursuant to French theory no logical inconsistency results from protecting an author's moral rights indefinitely, despite the limited duration of the economic rights.

In some countries, moral rights can be inherited or can be exercised by the spouse and next of kin upon an author's death absent a specific provision in an author's will.[91] Some countries, however, provide an alternative form of protection by entrusting a deceased author's moral rights to an official body designated to protect the nation's creative works. The circumstances under which such a public body can exercise a deceased author's rights are quite varied, however. Hansmann and Santilli note that in Italy, the government's rights of enforcement coexist with those of the artist's heirs.[92] Moreover, in virtually all countries with legislation providing for the exercise of moral rights by a public authority, the enforcement powers always extend to works within the public domain.[93]

Now that a foundation has been provided for civil law jurisdictions, it is instructive to compare the common law regimes. In general, moral rights have been adopted by the common law countries more recently than by their civil law counterparts.[94] Although Canada adopted moral rights in 1931,[95] other common law countries acted decades later. The United Kingdom legislated moral rights in the 1988 Copyright, Designs, and Patents Act (CDPA),[96] and New Zealand borrowed the United Kingdom statute and enacted its version in 1994.[97] Australia enacted comprehensive moral rights legislation in 2000,[98] and recently considered the enactment of a groundbreaking concept that would afford indigenous communities a form of moral rights.[99] Ireland's moral rights law became effective in 2001.[100] Although the particulars of these moral rights statutes vary to a significant extent, as a whole they stand in contrast to the United States' "minimal compliance" approach to Berne.[101]

There is some variability in the common law countries as to who qualifies as an author capable of enjoying moral rights. For example, in Canada, the Act does not define "author" but it excludes performances, sound recordings, and broadcasts from moral rights protection.[102] In the United Kingdom, the CDPA provides that the author of a sound recording or film is "the person by whom the arrangements necessary for the making of the recording or film are undertaken."[103] Therefore, producers have authorship status in the United Kingdom, but the statute also specifies that the "director of a copyright film" is entitled to moral rights.[104] In contrast, authors of computer programs do not enjoy moral rights in the United Kingdom.[105] Further, the CDPA substantially diminishes the attribution and integrity rights of employed authors.[106] The Australian statute does not define "author" although it adopts a presumption that the author is the person named as such on publicly distributed copies.[107] Although films were not among the covered works under the Australian Copyright Act of 1968, the 2000 amendment codifying moral rights granted them to the "maker" of the film, defined as "the director of the film, the producer of the film, and the screenwriter of the film."[108] These authors do not, however, have moral rights until the film is in final form.[109]

There is also variability in the applicability of the right of attribution. For example, in Canada, the right to be attributed—either by name or a pseudonym—is conditional on being "reasonable in the circumstances."[110] The Canadian Act does not, however, define reasonableness so courts consider each situation individually. The Canadian statute also is relatively unique in that it appears to incorporate a subright of anonymity within its right of attribution.[111]

The right of attribution in the United Kingdom does not explicitly cover the right to prevent misattribution of an author's work to another, which has prompted a lack of clarity as to whether this aspect of attribution exists.[112] Moreover, the statute includes a right to pseudonymous attribution but not anonymity.[113] Interestingly, there is no requirement that the author's designated form of identification must be reasonable.[114] Perhaps the most significant feature of the CDPA is that the right of attribution must be "asserted" by the author or other designated beneficiary.[115] In other words, the right of attribution can only be infringed if the author has previously asserted this right, in which case the infringer is deemed "bound" by the prior assertion.[116] The assertion requirement can be satisfied by a statement in a written instrument and is binding only on those who receive actual or constructive notice of the assertion.[117] According to Jane Ginsburg, the assertion requirement derives from the language of Article *6bis* in Berne that "the author shall have the right to claim authorship of the work,"[118] but in her view the conversion of this language into a requirement of an affirmative assertion of authorship not only tortures the language of Berne but also "may well violate the Berne Convention's rule that '[t]he enjoyment and exercise' of authors' rights, including moral rights, 'shall not be subject to any formality.' "[119]

The CDPA also is somewhat unique in that it expressly provides that an individual has a right against false attribution, meaning a right not to have a work "falsely attributed to him as author."[120] Versions of this right existed in the United Kingdom as early as 1862.[121] Infringement of the right against false attribution occurs when a work containing a false attribution is issued, exhibited, performed, or communicated to the public.[122]

The Australian law of attribution[123] differs from the law in the United Kingdom in that it does not mandate an assertion requirement in order for an author to exercise the right of attribution.[124] With respect to both attribution and integrity, the Australian law provides a defense of "reasonableness," and the statute gives content to this concept by enumerating a number of factors.[125] The specified reasonableness factors include industry practice as well as the voluntary codes of practice of the relevant industries for the work. Another distinguishing feature of the Australian statute is that it places the burden on the infringer to show that the omission of attribution was reasonable, and thus differs from the statutes in the other common law jurisdictions.[126]

As for the substance of the right of integrity in common law jurisdictions, the prevailing view is that authors enjoy the right to object to "derogatory treatment" of their works but there are numerous exceptions to this general position. For example, the CDPA reveals several caveats with respect to the exercise of the right of integrity. The CDPA defines derogatory treatment as a "distortion or mutilation of the work *or is otherwise prejudicial to the honour or reputation of the author or director.*"[127] The italicized language has created confusion as to whether an author or director always must demonstrate prejudicial impact in order to bring a cause of action alleging "derogatory treatment."[128] Moreover, the right of integrity in the CDPA does not appear to extend to objectionable contextual modifications.[129] This feature of the CDPA makes it considerably narrower in scope than the moral rights statutes in the civil law tradition. From a remedial standpoint, an interesting aspect of the CDPA is that it suggests courts applying the right of integrity may limit relief to a disclaimer indicating that the illegally modified work was not the product of, or approved by, the author.[130]

In Canada, the right of integrity provision does seem to require a showing of prejudice to the author's honor or reputation, but the statute also specifically provides that prejudice is "deemed" to occur when a painting, sculpture, or engraving has been distorted, mutilated, or otherwise modified.[131] Thus, the right of integrity appears to be applied more broadly to a confined class of fine art. Another interesting feature of the Canadian statute is that it seems to make objectionable contextual uses actionable at least to some extent in that it covers uses "*in association with* a product, service, cause, or institution."[132] Moreover, the right of integrity in Canada is not subject to the "reasonableness" requirement, unlike the right of attribution.[133]

In Australia, the author's right not to have her work subjected to derogatory treatment is uniquely limited by the definition of "derogatory treatment," which requires that distortions and alterations be "material."[134] In addition, infringement can be proved only by showing that the defendant's action was prejudicial to the author's honor or reputation.[135] The "reasonableness" defense operates similarly for integrity as it does for attribution, except that the statute incorporates the additional factor of "whether the treatment was required by law or was otherwise necessary to avoid a breach of any law."[136]

The rules regarding waiver operate in a similar manner in the context of both attribution and integrity. In light of the relevant waiver regimes, the default rule is that unless these rights have been waived specifically in whole or in part, it is assumed that the author retains the right to object to infringing uses of her work even if there has been an assignment of the copyright.[137] As for the specific waiver regimes, in Canada, moral rights generally cannot be assigned but can be waived. Moreover, the waiver does not need to be in writing and can be implied.[138] With regard to alienability and the right of attribution specifically, Canadian law provides that in situations involving ghostwriters or employees, the determination of whether attribution is appropriate is on a case-by-case basis, and therefore, is linked to the issue of waiver. The case law suggests that courts use the reasonableness standard and the waiver provision allowing implied waiver to dismiss claims involving attribution infringement.[139]

The CDPA also maintains a broad waiver provision.[140] Authors in the United Kingdom also can fully waive their moral rights prospectively with a signed written instrument.[141] The distinguishingly broad feature of the CDPA waiver provision is that the statute expressly provides for unconditional blanket waivers for future works.[142] Cyrill Rigamonti has observed that it is questionable whether the United Kingdom statute can be said to provide for "moral rights at all because the statutory validity of unconditional blanket waivers extinguishes any trace of inalienability, which is one of the key features of the concept of moral rights in a contractual setting."[143]

In contrast, the Australian Copyright Act mandates a "considerable specificity for effective waiver of attribution rights in nonemployee works."[144] The Australian statute does not contain express language regarding "waiver" but incorporates "consent" provisions into the Act.[145] The statute essentially provides that no infringement exists if the act in question is within the scope of a written consent "genuinely" given by the author or her representative.[146] With respect to works produced by employees, however, the waiver requirements in Australia are very lenient[147] in that employees can give a blanket consent with respect to all works produced during the period of employment.[148] Jane Ginsburg has observed that whereas the waiver standards of Canada and the United Kingdom do not entail the requisite specificity to comply with Berne, the Australian statute "offers a better model because it gives exploiters the opportunity to contract out of attribution rights in writing in specific contexts, but (apart from employee works) bars the blunderbuss approach."[149]

Having established both the theoretical groundwork for moral rights and the landscape of protection in the United States and elsewhere, it is time to explore in more depth the contours of an appropriate moral rights regime. Such a system should strengthen protection for authors' attribution and integrity rights in a manner that is compatible with our particular legal system. The following chapter begins this analysis by exploring the unique impact of the public domain in the United States' copyright law.

CHAPTER 5

Ownership of the Author's Message and the Public Domain

THE DOMINANT NARRATIVE surrounding both the enactment of the Copyright Clause and its interpretation has always been the provision of economic incentives to promote the creation of subject matter deemed important to our society. The United States' capitalist culture and its classical utilitarian tradition also contributed to the development of a copyright doctrine more concerned with commodification than the creation process. Equally significant, the First Amendment bolstered the United States' emphasis on the importance of society's ability to recycle material. These influences are apparent in the United States' depiction of the public domain as the mechanism that ensures everyone access to information and facts in expressive works.

As Diane Zimmerman has observed, the legal academy contains numerous defenders of the public domain who base their arguments on "pragmatic judgments about what will best promote a healthy intellectual property policy" or on normative perspectives of the philosophical justifications for private property rights.[1] As of 2006, Pamela Samuelson identified and insightfully analyzed thirteen different conceptions of the public domain.[2] The functions of the public domain appear to be as diverse as the academic models that seek to define its essence. In this regard, Samuelson has articulated the following functions mined from the ever-growing array of scholarship on the topic: "as a building block for the creation of new knowledge, and as an enabler of competitive imitation, follow-on creation, free or low cost access to information, public access to cultural heritage, education, self-expression and autonomy, various governmental functions, or deliberative democracy."[3] The complexities of the public domain have spawned several recent substantial publications treating the subject in comprehensive detail.[4] In light of these multifaceted conceptions and functions, it has become increasingly difficult to articulate, much less apply, a concise yet viable theory of the public domain.[5]

At the risk of vast oversimplification, the concept of the public domain in intellectual property law entails common ownership by the public as a whole of the property comprising the public domain. This means that each member of the public has a "property interest" and "an equal right to adapt and transform the material in question."[6] I invoke the practice of some scholars in using the terms *public domain* and *commons* interchangeably, although not all scholars endorse this view.[7] As Pamela Samuelson's nuanced analysis of current conceptions of the public domain clarifies, scholars' definitions "cluster around three main foci: the legal status of information resources, freedoms to use information resources, and the accessibility of information resources."[8] The issue of legal status arises by virtue of the fact that different scholars have distinct conceptions of what material ought to be in the public domain.[9] The "freedom to use" conceptions of the public domain are concerned with available uses of information resources even if the material in question is protected by intellectual property rights.[10] Other scholars emphasize the importance of access to information in their public domain theories.[11] The distinct conceptions of the public domain in the scholarly realm is mirrored in the reality that those who produce and use information products also may have divergent concerns and needs with respect to the public domain. These variations may arise from the differences inherent in various user communities. Thus, artistic communities may have needs in this regard that are distinct from scientific communities.[12] Similarly, certain audience members might prefer a legal structure that maximizes the chance that a given work will enjoy a stable meaning,[13] whereas others might desire a climate in which users can freely borrow and adapt prior works.

This chapter underscores that in developing appropriate moral rights protection for the United States, it is critical to consider how these protections will impact the public domain. Initially, in addressing the interface between moral rights protection and the public domain, it is important to emphasize that the concern here is with textual integrity violations that currently do not violate copyright law. In other words, the restraints that arise by virtue of moral rights protection would operate with respect to interests that largely are free from enclosure in the United States at this point in time. For example, recall that an individual does not violate copyright law by failing to attribute authorship of a work. In this regard, the question for purposes of this chapter is whether, notwithstanding this application of copyright law, the enactment of moral rights protections would inappropriately encroach upon the public domain.

In approaching this issue, consider that the burgeoning interest in the public domain is driven by concerns regarding an increasingly expansive copyright law.[14] Many scholars believe that copyright law inappropriately allocates speech entitlements to "highly organized, amply funded, and politically influential speech industries."[15] Indeed, widespread apprehension exists among both legal scholars and artistic creators that expanding copyright protection adversely impacts smaller, less powerful creators at the expense of large conglomerates.[16] Yochai Benkler has observed that "enclosure is likely to have the most adverse effects on amateur and other non-commercial production" and "tends to benefit organizations with large owned-information inventories."[17]

These concerns, while perhaps valid from the standpoint of copyright law, should not be invoked automatically to bar the development of legal protections designed to allow an author to safeguard the integrity of her texts. With respect to the concern for inappropriate allocation of speech entitlements favoring large corporations, these considerations are not necessarily relevant to moral rights because individual creators, as opposed to large corporations, frequently may be the beneficiaries of stronger moral rights protections. For example, Congress's decision to confine moral rights protection pursuant to VARA was the result of its desire to avoid conflict with politically savvy entities that expressed concern about the ability of their industries to continue to derive profits and remain powerful in the face of expanded moral rights protection.[18] In contrast, those groups desiring stronger moral rights protection were handicapped by limited financial resources and their inability to unite. Although Congress heard the testimony of some artists and individual film directors urging a broader scope of coverage for moral rights, in the end their stories were drowned out by those who were more politically powerful.[19]

Moreover, moral rights are distinguishable from copyrights based on the theoretical predicate supporting the respective doctrines. Moral rights are aimed at preserving an author's dignity, honor, and autonomy;

copyrights afford economic protection. Moral rights laws embrace inspirational motivations for creativity whereas copyright law, as it has been designed in the United States, has been shaped by justifications based on economic incentives. A viable approach to the implementation of moral rights in this country should reflect both a complete view of creativity as well as the realities of the laws already in place.[20] Despite the legitimate concern with the shrinking public domain and its impact on the future of creativity in this country, it should not be assumed that enhanced protections for authors' attribution and other integrity interests will undermine the future of the public domain or contradict constitutional norms.

On the contrary, a compelling case can be made for the proposition that enhanced moral rights protections can foster the objectives of the Copyright Clause to the extent they "promote the progress of science and useful arts, by securing for limited times to authors and inventors the exclusive right to their respective writings and discoveries."[21] The Clause is unique in that it is the only one incorporating a grant of power with a specific prescription of how best to accomplish this grant.[22] A question exists as to whether the primary directive is the one incorporating the "to promote progress" language or the one securing to authors and inventors the exclusive rights to their works "for limited times."

There is debate regarding the appropriate interpretation of the two critical phrases contained in the Clause.[23] Some commentators assert that the "to promote" language functions as a statement of purpose, and that the real power inherent in the Clause is in the phrase "by securing for limited times to authors and inventors the exclusive right to their respective writings and discoveries."[24] Other scholars believe that promoting progress is the primary grant, with the ability to secure a limited exclusive right to authors and inventors as an illustrative example of how to best accomplish this objective.[25] A comprehensive historical study of the Copyright Clause by Dotan Oliar instead suggests that each component of the Clause functions as a limitation upon the other. Specifically, he argues that "[t]he Framers wished to vest in Congress an intellectual property power that would be limited to the promotion of progress of science and useful arts, and they also wished to exclude Congress from using other means to exercise this limited power."[26]

Moral rights are neither explicitly prohibited nor sanctioned by the Copyright Clause.[27] Most likely, the Framers did not specify attribution or integrity rights because they were not fully cognizant of these specific rights given their subsequent emergence in Europe years later. Mark Rose has documented how the development of copyright law in England was framed in terms of property theory despite the fact that some of the early decisions under the Statute of Anne focused on authors' personal interests.[28] His careful look at the rhetoric of Lord Camden, whose published speech was a determinative factor in the vote against perpetual copyright in *Donaldson v. Beckett*,[29] shows that Camden's objection was to the notion of authorship as an economically based enterprise.[30] The dignity interests of the author were not really a part of this discourse. Although France began to recognize explicitly authors' personal and dignity interests in the nineteenth century,[31] the Anglo-American copyright tradition began somewhat too early to embrace these concepts.[32] Despite the lack of explicit authorization of moral rights by the Framers, I argue that they fit within the scope of the constitutional grant of power on two accounts. First, they can be understood as "promoting progress" within the meaning of that term as it was used historically. Second, they can function as a "limited right" to authors and thus can be viewed as within the scope of the means delineated by the Clause.

There is no reason to conclude that the law governing authors' rights in this country cannot incorporate moral rights. On the contrary, the very objectives of the Copyright Clause might be furthered if the laws governing authors' rights embraced appropriately tailored moral rights protections. Recall from Chapter 3 that the Framers were most concerned with the concept of promoting progress and their primary objective in enacting the Copyright Clause was to stimulate an open culture steeped in knowledge and education.[33] In the early republic, the conventional understanding of promoting progress appeared to be equivalent to the utilitarian conception of dissemination of knowledge.[34] These objectives are best achieved through a legal framework that promotes the public's interest in knowing the original source of a work and understanding it in the context of the author's original meaning and message. Indeed, knowledge is fostered if works of authorship are evaluated by the public in this manner, at least as a starting point for the further contemplation of such works. For an author's meaning and message to be conveyed accurately, both the choice of attribution and integrity of her work must be respected. Thus, moral rights protections that are narrowly crafted to promote public education regarding the authorship and original artistic meaning and message of the work represent appropriate measures to achieve the very objectives of the Copyright Clause.[35]

The history of the Copyright Clause also illustrates that certain means of "promoting progress" were clearly rejected by the Framers. For example, Oliar's study emphasizes that Congress excluded other means to accomplish the "promotion of progress" such as "the founding of a university and the grant of encouragements."[36] Although moral rights are distinct from copyright law conceptually, they have always been understood historically as related to copyright law in that they pertain to copyrightable works and are incorporated into national copyright laws.[37]

Further, moral rights are measures that, conceptually speaking, should last for the lifetime of the authors, and thus comport with the "limited times" constitutional requirement. As discussed in Chapter 3, the Framers were concerned with preventing monopolistic control and so they circumscribed both patent and copyright protection for defined periods to safeguard this interest.[38] The underlying theoretical components of the intrinsic dimension of creativity supporting moral rights protections are consistent with a duration lasting for the author's lifetime. For example, the concept of stewardship, to the extent it encourages dedication of creative work back to its original, inspirational source,[39] is consistent with the Framers' intentions of preventing monopolistic control over intellectual works in perpetuity. Further, the guardianship aspect of stewardship has particular significance under a framework in which the work is conceived as a testament to the author's beliefs, inspirational perspective, and intrinsic dimension of creativity.[40] It is, therefore, during the author's lifetime that her need to safeguard the message and meaning of her work is most acute.[41]

If stronger moral rights protections demonstrably comport with the objectives of the Copyright Clause, the Supreme Court would be likely to uphold such measures as long as it was satisfied they did not violate any other Constitution mandate.[42] As an initial matter, the history of Supreme Court copyright jurisprudence manifests the Court's marked deferential posture regarding the substance and operation of copyright law. Beginning in *Wheaton v. Peters*,[43] the Court adopted the view that it is the legislature's prerogative to determine the specific manner in which the law in this area should be formulated and administered.[44] By holding that Congress created a new right for authors in enacting copyright legislation rather than sanctioning an existing right,[45] the Court began a pattern of deference to the legislature that still continues.[46]

Further, the question involving the constitutionality of moral rights protections likely would be resolved by asking whether the Court would consider such measures to represent a "rational exercise of the legislative authority conferred by the Copyright Clause."[47] In a telling footnote in *Eldred v. Ashcroft*, which upheld the constitutionality of Congress's retroactive extension of the duration of copyright protection, the majority opinion reaffirmed the Court's reluctance to subject Congressional judgment involving copyright to heightened judicial scrutiny.[48] According to the Court, the "stringent version of rationality" advocated in Justice Breyer's dissent "is unknown to our literary property jurisprudence."[49] Moreover, the Court observed that because the Copyright Clause "empowers Congress to *define* the scope of the substantive right . . . [j]udicial deference to such congressional definition is 'but a corollary to the grant to Congress of any Article I power.' "[50]

Thus, as long as stronger moral rights laws remain within the parameters of Constitutional authority, Congressional discretion is likely to be upheld by the Court. The First Amendment, unique to the United States,[51] often is cited as the basis for objections to stronger moral rights protection in this country.[52] In general terms, these objections are usually grounded in the notion that an unbounded right of integrity preventing unauthorized modifications and alterations will prevent creators subsequent to the original author from expressing their own speech. Significantly, however, with respect to the conflict between moral rights and the First Amendment, there are important free speech issues on both sides. The free speech interests of subsequent users must be balanced against those of original authors not to have their works distorted or modified in objectionable ways with implicit or explicit attribution, resulting in a coerced use of their expression.

This analysis assumes that moral rights must be applied consistently with the First Amendment.[53] Pursuant to the Supreme Court's recent decision in *Eldred* as interpreted in *Golan v. Gonzales*,[54] the operative inquiry is whether moral rights protection would alter "the traditional contours of copyright protection."[55] In *Gonzales*, the court held that § 104A of the Copyright Act, which restored copyright protection to certain foreign works that are still protected under foreign copyright law but which have fallen into the public domain in the United States,[56] "altered the traditional contours of copyright protection in a manner that implicates plaintiffs' right to free expression" and therefore had to be subjected to First Amendment review.[57] In contrast, moral rights protection always has been within the purview of copyright law as discussed above.[58] Moreover, several of the state copyright statutes adopted shortly after the American Revolution and before the enactment of the Constitution emphasized heavily the personal claims of authors.[59] *Golan* also emphasized that the existence of "built-in free speech safeguards" typically will insulate legislation from First Amendment review.[60] As will be discussed in more detail below, I am proposing moral rights legislation with substantial cabining mechanisms that furnish operative free speech safeguards.[61]

If moral rights protections were subjected to First Amendment scrutiny, however, the paramount questions are the appropriate level of scrutiny and whether moral rights protections would survive the designated scrutiny.[62] Classic First Amendment jurisprudence suggests that the choice of scrutiny is dependent upon whether moral rights are seen as content-based or content-neutral.[63] In theory, content-based restrictions on speech "suppress, disadvantage, or impose differential burdens upon speech because of its content,"[64] whereas content-neutral restrictions serve "purposes unrelated to the content of expression" even if they have "an incidental effect on some speakers or messages but not others."[65] Still, in many instances the practical distinction between these two types of regulations is unworkable.[66] For example, if a given regulation impacts the communicative nature of expression, it might be deemed content-based, and therefore subject to strict scrutiny.[67] Thus, it could be argued that copyright law concerns "communicative impact" given its preoccupation with the choice of the expression involved.[68] On the other hand, copyright law might be seen as not involving communicative impact at all since "it does not turn on the communication of any particular idea."[69]

Although the majority of scholars believes that copyright law is content-neutral,[70] moral rights necessitates a distinct analysis. My argument is that appropriately tailored moral rights protections that do not proscribe speech and are enacted for a legitimate purpose other than discriminating on the basis of the message conveyed should not be deemed content-based and subjected to the strictest form of scrutiny.[71] Such moral rights protections are viewpoint-neutral because they do not suppress speech based on distaste for the content of the speech.[72] All uses of an author's work that are deemed objectionable by the original author are treated equally, regardless of viewpoint or content. Therefore, although these moral rights protections may be deemed "content-sensitive," they should be evaluated pursuant to intermediate rather than strict scrutiny, requiring that they be "narrowly tailored to serve a significant governmental interest,"[73] and "leave open ample alternative channels for communication of the information."[74] A key component of such an analysis is balancing the competing interests on each side.

Applying an intermediate type of scrutiny, moral rights protections that are narrowly crafted and effectively balance the free speech interests on both sides should be able to withstand a First Amendment challenge. Chapter 10 explores in greater detail the parameters of moral rights protection that I am advocating but for purposes of this discussion, I offer some preliminary observations. I believe that for moral rights to be viable in the United States, attribution should be mandated in most circumstances,[75] whereas the right of integrity must be more cabined. Specifically, I recommend that the right of integrity be enforced by requiring public disclaimers acknowledging variations inconsistent with the original author's meaning and message when a work is used in a manner deemed objectionable by the original author during the author's lifetime.[76] The form of such disclaimers can vary, depending on the work at issue and the nature of the objectionable use. At base, even a general disclaimer signals to the public that a subsequent creator has taken the original author's work and modified it in ways that are not in keeping with the author's meaning and message.

Moral rights protections of the type I contemplate will not hamper creativity, significantly impact a creator's choice of content, or impinge on public access to material.[77] For example, even organizations devoted to a vibrant pubic domain believe in the importance of attribution.[78] The freedom to speak embraced by the First Amendment does not necessitate permitting those who use others' expression to omit attribution of original authorship, to misattribute authorship, or to modify another's work and still represent it as that of the original author.[79] Nor will free speech be thwarted if people are barred from using others' expressions in a manner deemed objectionable by the original author absent a public disclaimer that their work does not represent the original author's meaning and message. To the contrary, such moral rights protections are narrowly tailored to promote public education regarding the authorship and original artistic meaning and message, and therefore foster compliance with the public dissemination objective of the Copyright Clause.[80]

Significantly, the type of moral rights protection I am proposing also comports with the free speech theories that have been developed by leading scholars in this area whose work manifests an appreciation for the dual nature of free speech interests. For example, Edwin Baker has proposed a "liberty" model for First Amendment protection according to which speech is protected "because of the value of speech conduct to the individual."[81] He sees "individual self-fulfillment and participation in change as the key First Amendment values."[82] Martin Redish has developed a somewhat similar theory according to which he maintains that the only true value served by the First Amendment is "individual self-realization."[83] He understands the self-realization concept as including an instrumental value that safeguards "the development of the individual's powers and abilities" in order to realize her full potential, as well as an intrinsic value that guarantees individual control over one's destiny.[84] Both of these First Amendment theories emphasize the importance of an individual's autonomy, which is indeed the very interest protected by moral rights. As Baker asserts, "people's choices, their definition and development of *themselves*, must be respected—otherwise they become mere objects for manipulation or means for realizing someone else's ideals or desires."[85]

Although these two theories differ from one another in important ways that are outside the scope of this treatment,[86] with respect to moral rights protections the application of both theories results in the anomaly that the liberty or self-realization of the original author may impinge on the liberty or self-realization of those who seek to use the original author's expression. The key to the successful application of these free speech theories to moral rights protection lies in the recognition that balancing is essential.[87] In striking the appropriate balance, consideration must be given to whether a given use of an author's expression is considered coercive because "to the extent that speech is involuntary," it "does not involve the *self*-realization or *self*-fulfillment of the speaker."[88] In developing his theory of free speech, Baker recognizes that "respect for the integrity and autonomy of the individual usually requires giving each person at least veto power over the use" of her own speech.[89] Therefore, speech is subject to control when it is "designed to disrespect and distort the integrity of another's mental processes."[90]

These free speech theories support moral rights protections requiring an appropriate disclaimer that negates the coercive element of the user's speech. My proposal for moral rights achieves a balance with a "thumb on the scales" in favor of free speech.[91] Moreover, the inherent flexibility of the disclaimer remedy "places a good deal of faith in the ability of judges to exercise their authority with wisdom and discretion, both in establishing and applying general rules of First Amendment construction and, where necessary, in engaging in *ad hoc* balancing."[92]

Moreover, there is a consistency between the narrowly tailored rights I advocate and several current theories of the public domain. David Lange has articulated one of the broadest conceptions of the public domain, conceiving of it proactively as "an affirmative source of entitlements" capable of thwarting "the encroachments upon the creative imagination threatened by intellectual property."[93] To Lange, the function of the public domain is to confer upon individuals the "status" necessary to exercise creative imagination.[94] As such, the public domain should afford affirmative protection for creative appropriations, and consequently the law should presumptively privilege such appropriations.[95] Notwithstanding this broadly conceived standard, however, Lange acknowledges that his conception of the public domain is consistent with a concern for attribution.[96] Moreover, although he would allow appropriation regardless of the "reputation or sensibilities" of the author, his public domain model also would allow for suitable disclaimers and acknowledgments in "appropriate cases."[97]

Malla Pollack's conception of the public domain is one that possesses an "inherently feminist" character.[98] She argues that by enlarging the public domain, "society would move towards a more feminine" or "humanist" culture.[99] In her view, the feminine public domain is the source of fertility that gives rise to creativity. Her feminine theory of the public domain relies on a sense of artistic "giftedness" and a cyclical sharing of creative enterprise. Pollack contends that in western society, gift exchange is a "female commerce" that stands in opposition to male-driven market exchange.[100] Therefore, the "free sharing" and "giving forward to an audience" characteristics of a nurturing public domain make it feminine.[101] The theoretical grounding for Pollack's feminine public domain has strong parallels to the "gifted" and cyclical dimension of creativity discussed in Chapter 2 and therefore supports the theoretical predicate for moral rights protection.[102]

Pollack's concern for recognition of the "feminine" character of the public domain relates on a theoretical level to those conceptions of the public domain focusing on the democratic goal of equal access to material regardless of one's wealth or social status.[103] Such democratic visions of the public domain emphasize the need for a public domain that is inclusive and equally participatory. Edward Lee argues that in our democracy it should be the province of the people to act as "the ultimate keepers of the common culture and knowledge."[104] A framework for moral rights that incorporates narrowly tailored protections for the creator in effect only during the creator's lifetime is consistent with this objective. Anthony Reese's work on a public domain that is composed of private, unpublished materials provides further direct support for this consistency.

The public domain Reese identifies is the result of our copyright law placing unpublished works into the public domain when their ordinary copyrights expire.[105] A detailed discussion of the relevant copyright law is beyond the scope of this chapter, but for clarity it must be noted that Reese's "private" public domain derives from the enormous deposit into the public domain in January 2003 of every unpublished work ever created by an author who died prior to 1933.[106] Ironically, although many of these unpublished works previously have been kept private, they are now theoretically accessible to the public assuming those who are holding these materials will make them available.[107] In contrast, in civil law countries with well-established moral rights protections, the use of unpublished works can be restricted by the author's successors even after the copyright terms expire. For example, in France, a perpetual and descendible moral right of disclosure allows an author's executor or heirs to determine whether to disclose a work to the public.[108] The vision of moral rights I am proposing, however, would not hamper access to unpublished works in the public domain in the United States because it would only allow moral rights to be exercised by the author, the person whose intrinsic dimension of creativity is most clearly connected to the work. This framework promotes a democratic public domain.

With respect to both the attribution and the disclaimer remedy I advocate, these constraints upon use also are consistent with a "governance" or contractually constructed[109] model of the public domain that emphasizes freedom to use information resources despite the presence of intellectual property protections.[110] For example, Lawrence Lessig's conception of the public domain is that of a commons that is "within the reach of members of the relevant community without the permission of anyone else."[111] Lessig does not equate the absence of permission characteristic of the commons with the ability to use material in the commons at a cost of zero. In contrast to other accounts of the public domain that mandate a use that is both free of exclusive rights and available at a zero cost,[112] Lessig's somewhat controversial view of a commons essentially contemplates licensed uses.[113] Included subject matter is available for use at a cost, as long as the payment is nondiscriminatory.[114] This vision embraces liability rule protection[115] of the commons pursuant to which parties are not prohibited from using the material as long as they pay, or otherwise satisfy procedural requirements, for this ability. Although there is ambiguity in how Lessig is using the term *liability rule*, probably the most important aspect of his analysis for purposes of this discussion is that the commons may require a degree of governance in order to be successful.[116] Governance may take the form of a mandatory payment or satisfaction of some other requirement for usage. The narrowly tailored moral rights protections I am advocating are completely consistent with a conception of the commons that allows for governance procedures. My approach is consistent with the nature of liability rule protection because the user's conduct is allowed as long as the appropriate attribution and disclaimers are provided. Under this approach, users can build upon the original author's work, subject to designated conditions.

An even more global conception of a governance-oriented commons would recognize that the commons may be built not only on legal restraints such as liability rules but also on community norms.[117] There are several examples of injunctive norms that are explicitly adopted by certain groups and individuals for the purpose of reshaping and modifying the effects of copyright law.[118] Robert Merges sees the emergence of such norms as a private-ordering response to the strengthening of intellectual property protections.[119] Some of these injunctive norms even address attribution and integrity interests. Thus, the ethical injunction against plagiarism furnishes a set of norms regarding attribution for journalists, writers, and scholars that is so "commonplace and pervasive that they seem almost unworthy of comment."[120] Moreover, several of the current governance models such as Creative Commons and the GNU software license agreements incorporate textual integrity interests to some degree. As discussed in Chapter 1, the Creative Commons recently changed its default license to include attribution.[121] In addition, the Creative Commons agreement is consistent with the right of integrity by allowing authors to select a license option that precludes modifications of their works. The current version of the GNU software license continues the practice of the prior versions by allowing a creator to supplement the terms of the license with author attribution.[122] The creator may prohibit misrepresentations of origin of material added by authors, require that modified versions of material be marked "in reasonable ways as different from the original version," and limit the use of authors' names for publicity.[123] All of these public domain models built upon community norms illustrate the compatibility between moral rights protections and a vibrant public domain.[124]

In sum, our commitment to the public domain does not preclude the adoption of moral rights protections. It is possible to design a framework for moral rights that not only will satisfy, but also advance, the Constitution's requirements and objectives. In light of this conclusion, a more detailed examination of the interface between our existing copyright law and a proposed system of moral rights is now in order.

CHAPTER 6

Marginally Original and Functional Works of Authorship

COPYRIGHT LAW, at least in the United States, sets a particular floor for the standard of originality required for covered works. It does not make sense to discuss the application of moral rights to works that do not possess at least this minimal level of originality. On the other hand, in light of the theoretical differences underlying copyrights and moral rights, and their distinct applications, there may be sound reasons for recognizing moral rights as part of our copyright law generally but nonetheless confining their application to a smaller category of works than are covered by copyright law. The conventional justifications for applying moral rights only to works we label "fine art" rather than to the products of all authors embrace the view that such works are unique, entail substantial skill and effort, and are "generally acquired principally for their expressive or decorative character, and not for functional or utilitarian uses."[1] In many instances, such works may be less likely to need modifications that may ultimately conflict with the creator's artistic vision in order to serve their intended functions.[2] Recall that even in France, limitations exist regarding the enforcement of the right of integrity depending on the nature of the work: "[O]bviously, a [French] court is going to be less scrupulous about an editor's polishing up a set of instructions for use of a home appliance than his reworking the text of a poem."[3]

It is necessary to determine, as a normative matter, whether moral rights should be applicable to fewer types of works than currently are eligible for copyright protection, and if so, how the law can make viable distinctions. In approaching this question, it is helpful to return to the history of copyright generally in the United States. Edward Walterscheid has speculated about the precise intent of the Framers in using the term *writings* in the Copyright Clause, concluding they most likely intended to cover forms of literary expression other than just books.[4] Yet, it is far from clear what the Framers meant by "writings" in light of the absence of discussion at the federal convention of the final language of the Copyright Clause.[5] Over time, Congress has extended copyright protection to an increasingly broader category of works, and the courts have acquiesced in these determinations.[6] The first copyright statute in 1790 covered only books, charts, and maps. Walterscheid posits that although it required a significant stretch to fit maps and charts within the scope of "writings," such a result was justifiable on the ground that extending copyright protection to such works would promote learning and knowledge.[7] In contrast, President Washington refrained from asking Congress to extend protection to fine art because he did not believe the Clause provided the basis for such authority.[8] Yet, fine art categories were added beginning in 1802.[9]

The 1909 Copyright Act seemingly broadened copyright's coverage even further by providing that "the works for which copyright may be secured . . . shall include all the writings of an author."[10] By stipulating that copyright protection applies to "works" and includes "all the writings of an author," the statute neither confined copyright protection to "writings" nor included any limit on the types of works eligible for protection.[11] The 1976 Copyright Act circumvented these problems by stipulating that copyright protection instead extends to "original works of authorship."[12]

In 1991, the Supreme Court in *Feist Publications, Inc. v. Rural Telephone Service Co.*[13] declared originality to be a constitutional requirement in a case denying copyright protection to the plaintiff telephone company's white page listings. In elaborating upon the standard for originality, the Court held that it requires "only that the work was independently created by the author (as opposed to copied from other works), and that it possesses at least some minimal degree of creativity."[14] *Feist* thus defines originality as requiring two elements: first, independent selection, and second, at least minimal creativity, and thereby merges the concept of originality with that of creative authorship.[15] In *Feist,* independent selection was not at issue because there were no allegations that the plaintiff copied its listings from any other work, so the focus of the Court's opinion is on whether the plaintiff's listings possessed the requisite degree of creative authorship.

Prior to *Feist,* some courts and commentators drew a distinction between originality and creativity, positing that originality refers to whether the creator made an independent contribution, whereas creativity is a more subjective concept that is concerned with the nature of that contribution.[16] Other courts viewed the subjective element of originality as a requirement that the author contribute "more than a 'merely trivial' variation."[17] Still, *Feist's* adoption of a subjective, even if very minimal, "creativity" requirement for copyright has been severely criticized on the ground that it is at odds with the legislative history of the 1976 Act, and furnishes an ambiguous and inappropriately high standard for protection.[18] On the other hand, Diane Zimmerman has observed that *Feist* suggests the Court may believe a degree of genuine, recognizable creativity is a constitutionally mandated part of the originality inquiry.[19] In any event, copyright law now is clear that a copyrightable work must manifest a contribution that is both independent and creative in order to satisfy the originality requirement.

As discussed, the necessary degree of creativity is minimal according to *Feist.* Distinguishing originality from novelty, the court emphasized that "the requisite level of creativity is extremely low; even a slight amount will suffice," and "[t]he vast majority of works make the grade quite easily."[20] Thus, factual compilations may possess the requisite originality in light of the author's selection and arrangement of the otherwise unprotectable material.[21] The Court does caution, however, that "[t]here remains a narrow category of works in which the creative spark is utterly lacking or so trivial as to be virtually nonexistent."[22]

Significantly, *Feist's* elevation of the originality requirement to a constitutional magnitude signifies the importance of Congress's role in determining the parameters of how the originality standard should be applied. As William Patry has observed: "The *Feist* Court did not strip Congress of its voice on all originality issues; instead, the Court only set a threshold standard. Congress is free to set a higher standard, or, in protecting particular types of works, to declare how the originality requirement must be satisfied."[23]

Despite the broader scope of coverage for copyright law, it is clear that Congress has discretion not only to enact moral rights but also to confine their application to more limited types of works. As previously discussed, moral rights can function as "limited" rights granted to authors for the purpose of promoting progress.[24] Moreover, the Supreme Court has long deferred to Congress's judgments regarding the specific implementation of copyright legislation.[25]

A compelling argument can be made that moral rights protections should apply to more narrow categories of works of authorship than are currently eligible for copyright protection. Pursuant to such a framework, only works satisfying a heightened standard of originality, as manifested by substantial rather than "a modicum" of creativity,[26] would qualify for protection. The current low standard for creativity should not be imported unthinkingly as the standard for a work's eligibility for moral rights protection. Copyright's standard of originality arguably fulfills the goals of the Copyright Clause with respect to works whose incentive for creation depends completely, or even primarily, upon an economic motivation. There are, quite simply, copyrightable works with fairly low degrees of originality such as arrangements of databases or specific computer programs that might not be created at all if their authors did not have the guarantee of some economic reward. *Feist* recognizes this difficulty by setting a low standard for originality, and suggests that the level of originality in a particular work will determine the scope of copyright protection such work receives.[27] Works containing large amounts of unprotected expression will have more thin copyright protection than works containing greater amounts of truly expressive material. For example, *Feist* instructs us that "copyright in a factual compilation is thin . . . [A] subsequent compiler remains free to use [such] facts . . . to aid in preparing a competing work, so long as the competing work does not feature the same selection and arrangement."[28]

In contrast, for works whose creation also is rooted in the inspirational realm of authorship, economic incentive is not the only relevant factor[29] since this perspective of creativity emphasizes the intrinsic dimension of the creative process. The focus of an inspirational perspective is on the author's relationship to her work and her sense of personal satisfaction or fulfillment resulting from the act of creativity itself. Moreover, the external product of creativity is seen as the embodiment of the author's meaning and message. Moral rights are designed to recognize this intrinsic dimension of creativity and therefore works should be required to manifest "substantial" creativity in order to be protected.

The type of differentiation suggested here would require courts to become involved in determining whether a particular work possesses the requisite degree of creativity to qualify for protection. At first blush, this may seem to be a controversial suggestion based on "'the doctrine of avoidance' of artistic determinations,"[30] which represents "one of the most stable and explicitly stated doctrines across art law."[31] This position has a strong pedigree, dating at least as far back as Justice Holmes's famous statement in *Bleistein v. Donaldson Lithographing Co.* that "[i]t would be a dangerous undertaking for persons trained only to the law to constitute themselves final judges of the worth of pictorial illustrations, outside of the narrowest and most obvious limits."[32] This language has "become a refuge for judges who do not want to engage with aesthetic questions."[33]

A distinction can be drawn, however, between a work's artistic merit and its artistic rank. That is to say, Justice Holmes's discussion in *Bleistein* seems directed toward judicial assessment of a work's artistic merit. In contrast, the concepts of heightened originality and substantial creativity also can be applied to assess a work's artistic rank. If Congress were to enact expanded moral rights protection, it could provide some assistance in these matters by excluding certain ranks, or categories of works, from the scope of coverage. A straightforward way to accomplish this result legislatively is to preclude completely moral rights protection for certain types of works that are essentially functional in their totality and therefore lacking in any significant artistic characteristics. In contrast, for categories of works that incorporate both functional as well as artistic qualities, courts will have to assess whether to accord these works moral rights protection on an individual basis. As this chapter discusses shortly, copyright law contains adequate guidance for facilitating such judicial evaluations.

As a practical matter, an outright statutory exclusion of the type contemplated would eliminate the possibility of moral rights being asserted in *particular types of* subject matter such as databases, building codes,[34] office memos,[35] cabinets,[36] and software.[37] On the other hand, it would leave the door open for works such as architecture and even the type of pictorial advertising at issue in *Bleistein*[38] that combine functionality with artistry. Such cabined requirements for protection not only comport with the underlying theory of moral rights but also avoid potential criticisms that stronger moral rights will open the door to covering a multitude of "creative" enterprises with little significant artistic value.[39]

By analogy, it is helpful to consider the extent to which VARA has provided guidance with respect to what constitutes "a work of visual art" covered under the statute. VARA explicitly excludes any "poster, map, globe, chart, technical drawing, diagram, model, applied art, motion picture or other audiovisual work, book, magazine, newspaper, periodical, data base, electronic information service, electronic publication, or similar publication" as well as merchandising, advertising, or promotional material.[40] Leaving aside the statute's problematic exclusion of highly original works other than visual art, the list of statutory exclusions suggests that the statute intends to exclude more functional types of visual art.[41] This intention is reinforced by the statute's provision that with respect to the right to protect against the destruction of a covered work, the work must meet the additional requirement of possessing "recognized stature."[42] Although the statute fails to define "recognized stature," one court has interpreted this requirement as "a gate-keeping mechanism" affording protection only to artwork "that art experts, the art community, or society in general views as possessing stature."[43]

Indeed, in enumerating those works of visual art covered by VARA, the statute establishes some basic parameters with respect to the requisite originality, creativity, and aesthetics of the eligible works. Thus, the statute covers only paintings, drawings, prints or sculptures, existing in single copies, or in limited editions of 200 copies or fewer that are signed and consecutively numbered by the author.[44] Photographic images also are covered but only those produced for "exhibition purposes," signed by the author, and existing in a single copy or a limited edition of 200 or fewer copies.[45] The legislative history contains the testimony of Jane Ginsburg observing that there is a unique value inherent in the original or limited edition of a copy of a work of art because these objects "embody the artist's 'personality' far more closely than subsequent mass produced images."[46] I question VARA's "limited edition" and "exhibition purposes" requirements on the ground that they bear no relationship to the level of originality of the underlying work, which I see as the operative issue in connection with the scope of coverage for moral rights. Still, by offering a circumscribed definition of "visual art," VARA provides a model for how legislation can delineate limited coverage.

Predictably, courts applying VARA have denied moral rights protection in cases involving mass-produced posters[47] and original drawings used as the basis for the design of a trophy.[48] In another case, the question was whether a public sculpture park with a nautical theme should be considered a work of visual art within the meaning of VARA. The district court declined to consider the plaintiff's contributions to the park as an integrated piece of "sculpture" covered by VARA, based on the judiciary's tendency to construe the definitions in VARA narrowly and the fact that "a park does not fit the traditional definition of [a] sculpture."[49] The First Circuit affirmed the judgment against the artist, but predicated its holding on the view that VARA does not protect site-specific art.[50] On the other hand, a district court held that an intermediate clay model of the head of Queen Catherine that would have been used to create a large bronze statue qualified as a work of visual art as it was analogous to other protectable preliminary work such as "certain photographic negatives" or a painter's drawings and sketches.[51] As these cases show, the scope of VARA's coverage is narrowly crafted and interpreted so as to ensure, to the extent possible, that protected works manifest a high degree of artistic originality and creativity.[52]

Photography presents a particularly interesting study of the application of originality and creativity, both with respect to VARA and copyright law generally. Recall that in order to be protected under VARA, a photograph must be made "for exhibition purposes only."[53] In *Lilley v. Stout*,[54] a district court considered the applicability of VARA in a controversy arising from the collaboration of photographer Lilley and his one-time girlfriend, Stout. Lilley sued Stout under VARA as a result of Stout's incorporation of Lilley's photographs, without attribution, in *Red Room at Five*, a work consisting of the photographs placed in a binder with a red cover and illustration.[55] In her defense, Stout argued that the photographs were not produced for "exhibition purposes only" because they were taken as studies for potential paintings. The court sided with Stout, denying Lilley his right of attribution, based on its view that in taking the photographs, the plaintiff's purpose was to assist Stout with her project rather than to exhibit the works.[56]

Apart from VARA, copyright determinations are more complex with respect to fine art photography given that this medium straddles "the boundaries between technology and artistic expression."[57] Although photography was included in the copyright statute as protectable subject matter as early as 1865,[58] the Supreme Court did not have occasion to consider the scope of protection in photographs until 1884. In *Burrow-Giles Lithographic Co. v. Sarony*, the Court looked to the findings of fact with respect to the photograph in question and concluded that copyright protection was warranted due to it being a "useful, new, harmonious, characteristic, and graceful picture, [which the plaintiff created] entirely with his own original mental conception."[59] The Court gave the following examples of the plaintiff's original conception: the subject's pose and arrangement, the selection and arrangement of the costume, draperies, and other accessories used in the photograph, and the arrangement and disposition of the lighting, which resulted in the "desired expression."[60] Based on these findings, which focused on the photographer's staging of the process as the justification for originality, the Court held that the photograph was "an original work of art, the product of the plaintiff author's intellectual invention."[61]

Christine Farley explains the Court's decision in terms of both the artistic view of photography prevalent at that time, and the need for preserving the notion that post-shutter activities are free of artistic choice, and thus remain author-free and objective.[62] Due to photography's inherent mechanical nature, at the time of *Burrow-Giles*, "very few photographers, and even fewer artists, considered photography to be within the realm of art."[63] The "artistry" of photography at this time understood "arranging" or "picture-making" as the primary component of the art.[64] Moreover, there was a prevailing view that the image produced by photography was free of human intervention and therefore well suited as objective evidence in legal disputes. A focus on the photographer's input as consisting of pre-shutter activity facilitated this conception.[65]

Significantly, the holding in *Burrow-Giles* was extraordinarily narrow, extending only to the particular photograph before the Court,[66] and thus reserved the more difficult question of the copyrightability of "ordinary," as opposed to "high art" photographs.[67] The Court's limited holding rendered later courts without adequate guidance[68] and even today, determining originality in the context of photographs raises complicated questions. For example, sometimes the photograph in question is not the result of deliberate artistic decisions being made by the photographer. There have been documented instances of photographers shooting in a deliberately haphazard manner, without any creative choices being exercised with respect to the work.[69] Contemporary methods of photography such as surveillance cameras and satellite images take this problem to a new level.[70]

Moreover, the theoretical premise of *Burrow-Giles* is consistent with the idea, invoked even in modern cases, that unless a photograph is actively staged, it is lacking in originality on the ground that it simply duplicates that which already exists.[71] For example, in *Bridgeman Art Library, Ltd. v. Corel Corp.*,[72] the court held that there was insufficient originality with respect to color transparencies of paintings in the public domain. When the subject matter in question is that of nature itself, this issue is especially relevant. In *Dyer v. Napier*, a federal district court observed that "it is well-settled that when a live creature commonly appearing in nature is reproduced, the only elements protected by copyright are those original aspects which are not required in the depiction of the creature as expressed in nature."[73] In that case the court determined that the photographer of a "mother mountain lion perched on a rock with a kitten in her mouth"[74] enjoyed a "thin" layer of copyright protection with respect to his original elements such as the choice of location, background, lighting, shading, timing, angle, and framing.[75] Nevertheless, the court granted summary judgment to the defendant who had created a bronze sculpture of a mother mountain lion in the same pose as the lion in the plaintiff's photograph. According to the court, any similarity between the two works was the result of non-protectable elements of the plaintiff's copyrighted photograph.[76]

The artistry of photography can inhere not only in the pre-shutter staging process, but also in both the creative choices associated with the timing of the click of the shutter and in post-shutter activity. With regard to timing, creative choices include "the precise timing to click the shutter, the angle of the shot, the frame, the focus, the distance from the subject, [and] the centering of the subject."[77] As for post-shutter activity, actions such as retouching, cropping, framing, redeveloping, and coloring seem obvious exercises of creative decision making.[78] Moreover, digital technology has multiplied the opportunities for post-shutter creativity. For example, the well-known photographs of Depression-era, southern tenant-farmers taken by Walker Evans have now been digitally reproduced by two of his former colleagues.[79] Evans worked on assignment for the Farm Security Administration, and so his photographs are public property in the Library of Congress and capable of being reproduced by anyone.[80] The new prints "modulate and unify the midranges of grays in [the original] pictures to soften contrasts and give a warmer ambience to [the] photographs."[81] The resulting prints are "seductive and luxurious," qualities that stand in sharp contrast to both the subjects themselves and to Evan's original "gelatin silver prints."[82]

Despite the challenges presented by photography to the application of the originality requirement,[83] the medium's potential to express substantial degrees of individual creativity is clear. A compelling example of this point is furnished by the unique role photography plays in art therapy. As a medium that does not require knowledge of drawing, painting, or sculpting, photography has lowered the barriers to entry. In midtown Manhattan, for example, the International Center of Photography encourages poor, urban, teenage girls with few other positive outlets for their energies to develop their self-awareness and gain control of their lives through digital photography.[84] Moreover, as the digitization of the Evans prints shows, now more than ever, photographs are potentially subject to unauthorized modifications that may be out of keeping with the original meaning and message of the author's work. The Evans prints were digitized by two individuals who had "the authority of first-hand experience with Evans and an obvious devotion to him."[85] Yet, even here, the author of a newspaper article discussing an exhibit of the digitized prints was critical of the resulting prints, and worried that "[s]omebody looking at one of these new Evans prints is likely to assume it is by Evans, which it is of course only up to a point."[86]

Thus, photography as a category should be accorded moral rights protection under a standard requiring heightened originality with substantial creativity but judges will need to draw lines in assessing how this standard should apply to particular works in question. As discussed, historically courts have had to make these same types of determinations with respect to whether photographs manifest the requisite originality for copyright protection.[87] Other types of works will also raise these same line-drawing issues regarding the application of an originality standard requiring substantial creativity. For example, music scholars have argued that popular music is far less original and creative than the classical genre because its market orientation necessitates little variation between songs. In this regard, Professor Simon Frith explains that popular music is "music produced commercially, for profit, as a matter of enterprise not art."[88] Classical music, in contrast, is far more artistically driven and thus displays much greater diversity in composition. As music critic Tim Smith has observed: "[T]he great composers didn't follow the rules, but made the rules follow them."[89]

The foregoing discussion supports the idea that although certain functional types of works should be excluded per se from moral rights protection,[90] other works such as art, literature, music, and even architecture presumptively should qualify if a sufficient showing of originality can be made with respect to the particular work at issue. For many works, the requisite level of originality likely will not be an issue. For works at the margins, however, courts will have to decide whether a heightened originality standard with substantial creativity has been met.[91] Any originality determination thus will necessitate at least some judicial evaluation of the artistic rank of a given work.

Realistically, if a heightened standard of originality with substantial creativity were to be embraced in moral rights legislation, the judicial line-drawing that would result will not be much different from that which currently takes place in applying the *Feist* standard for copyright originality. In *Burrow-Giles*,[92] the Supreme Court recognized that because copyright law lacks the patent system's safeguard of a prior examination by an authoritative tribunal, it is more important in a copyright case for the author to prove "the existence of those facts of originality, of intellectual production, of thought, and conception on the part of the author."[93] So from an early point in time, courts were sensitive to the importance of how to prove originality in copyright law.[94] In discussing the legality of piracy, David Lange has stated that courts need to determine whether they are dealing with "appropriation unmotivated by any creative exercise."[95] In advising how to do this, he writes: "There is no escaping: we must decide," a decision that, in his view, "ought to be grounded in fact-finding affected by law."[96] That same reasoning applies to the determination of heightened originality with substantial creativity for purposes of applying moral rights protections.

Under copyright law, there is precedent in the Second, Seventh, and Ninth Circuits for applying a heightened standard of originality when derivative works, defined in the statute as original works of authorship that are "based upon one or more preexisting works," are at issue.[97] The Second Circuit has held that with respect to reproductions of artistic works, a higher degree of skill, "true artistic skill," may be required to make a reproduction copyrightable.[98] Although courts following this approach might be somewhat inclined to evaluate the artistic merits of a given work, the Seventh Circuit's case law clarifies that the purpose of this heightened standard of originality for derivative works is to ensure that a sufficiently pronounced difference exists between the underlying and derivative works so that subsequent artists are not faced with copyright problems if they depict the underlying work.[99] In other words, courts need to determine originality under copyright law to ensure adequate differentiation among multiple works created subsequent to the original work. Although this determination may seem more objective in theory than one involving subjective creativity, in practice, subjectivity will be a factor when courts are faced with the paramount question of whether a given work is sufficiently distinguishable from the work upon which it is based. Thus, the case law reveals an inclination and ability to endorse different levels of originality where appropriate.

In elucidating different levels of originality, *Burrow-Giles* is an important precedent not only because the Court elevated art photography above ordinary photography, but also because the Court elected to mark this distinction by focusing on the artistic process as narrated by the artist in addition to the final product.[100] According to the Court, although authorship was evident in the photograph itself, the narrative supplied by the photographer was vital in assisting the Court's perception. The photographer's narrative emphasized his actions taken in furtherance of pre-shutter, "composition-making" activity.[101]

This emphasis on the author's decision making during the artistic process has a parallel in the case law concerning whether subject matter constitutes copyrightable applied art or non-copyrightable industrial design. As will be discussed, relevant cases consider the author's narrative with respect to the design process in making this determination. By way of background, according to the 1976 Copyright Act, copyright protection does not extend to "useful articles" that have "an intrinsic utilitarian function."[102] The legislative history accompanying the definition of a "useful article" speaks of physical and conceptual separability as the appropriate litmus tests in determining whether a particular useful article constitutes copyrightable art.[103] Thus, courts have recognized that a work can obtain copyright protection when the artistic features are physically or conceptually separate from those that are utilitarian.[104] Although the application of the physical separability test is rather clear in that it simply asks whether the ornamental nature of the object in question can be physically separated from the object,[105] it is unlikely to be of much aid when the object under consideration is two-dimensional rather than three-dimensional.[106]

The conceptual separability test is more complex than the physical separability test and courts have used a variety of approaches in determining whether the artistic components of a work are conceptually separate from the work's utilitarian function.[107] In *Brandir International, Inc. v. Cascade Pacific Lumber Co.*,[108] the test adopted by the court looks to whether the design process reflects the creator's artistic judgment, as exercised independently of functional considerations. *Brandir* affirmed the Copyright Register's denial of copyright for a bicycle rack originating from a wire sculpture on the ground that it is a useful article and the artistic aspects of the work were not conceptually separable from its utilitarian function pursuant to the test invoked by the court. In evaluating whether the design of the bicycle rack should be protected as a "sculptural work,"[109] or denied protection as a useful article, the court noted that the application of its "design process" test will require the parties to present evidence relating to the "design process and the nature of the work."[110] According to the majority, such a test would not be difficult to apply since "[t]he work itself will continue to give 'mute testimony' of its origins."[111]

Although *Brandir* was a case about copyrightable subject matter rather than the originality requirement, the test it adopts for determining the copyrightability of applied art is relevant to determining how a requirement of heightened originality with substantial creativity can be applied in the context of moral rights. The test in *Brandir* seeks to determine the author's creative intent and relies upon the sequences of the author's actions or decisions in the design process. The *Brandir* model thus relies on evidence regarding the design process and the nature of the completed work. This same type of evidence also can facilitate a judicial determination of heightened originality requiring substantial creativity based on the creator's conscious artistic choices as manifested in the design process and the nature of the work itself. Such a test for the applicability of moral rights makes particular sense since, according to the theoretical predicate for moral rights, the external product of creativity embodies the author's personal meaning and message.

Thus, the case law involving the conflict between copyrightable art and non-protectable industrial design[112] furnishes a helpful path for contemplating the operation of a standard for determining whether particular works in question manifest heightened originality with substantial creativity. Rather than making these determinations according to the judiciary's individual perceptions of an author's creativity, courts should take the author's own narrative of creativity into account. Thus, courts should ask whether, in light of the author's articulated narrative, her design choices reflect heightened originality with substantial creativity. Random actions by the artist that are not the result of artistic decision making in furtherance of her meaning and message would militate against a work satisfying this test.

The advantage of such a test is that it would free courts from having to ascertain unilaterally the nature and significance of a creator's meaning and message. Instead, the court would determine whether, based upon the author's narrative, the design process reflects heightened originality with substantial creativity in furthering the author's articulated meaning and message. In terms of its operation, this test would be similar to the one invoked in *Brandir* in terms of its reliance on the design process in determining whether a particular work was so influenced by artistic design so as to qualify as copyrightable art. Thus, heightened originality requiring substantial creativity will be measured by the process itself, with the evidence being provided by the author.

In addition, some courts have augmented *Brandir*'s focus on the design process with a consideration of whether "the artistic aspects of an article can be 'conceptualized as existing independently of their utilitarian function.' "[113] This approach would be especially useful for judicial determinations of whether a particular work manifests heightened originality with substantial creativity for purposes of moral rights protection because it would additionally incorporate a consideration of the degree to which reasonable observers perceive the object as creative. Thus, an appropriate test also should consider evidence bearing upon the perceptions of the reasonable beholder. Such evidence could include the extent to which the object has been used or displayed, custom and usage within the art world, expert opinion, and survey evidence including the object's marketability as art.[114] As noted by Judge Newman in his renowned dissent in *Carol Barnhart Inc. v. Economy Cover Corp.*, the "ordinary, reasonable observer" is a good standard and in fact has been entrusted "to decide other conceptual issues in copyright law, such as whether an allegedly infringing work bears a substantial similarity to a copyrighted work."[115] In approaching the issue of heightened originality with substantial creativity from this standpoint, perhaps some "courts will inevitably be drawn into some minimal inquiry as to the nature of art," but realistically "some threshold assessment of art" cannot be avoided in these inquiries.[116]

Another advantage of this test is that it comports with the reality that certain works may not manifest heightened originality with substantial creativity according to a reasonable observer even if they possess specific meanings and messages from the author's standpoint. Appropriation art is one such example in that it borrows from common images in the media and advertising and places them in new contexts, with the objective of attempting to change society's thinking about these images.[117] The creativity inherent in this practice stems from "the selection of the texts and their recontextualization."[118] Thus, in the 1980s, postmodern artist Sherrie Levine created a series of photographs in which she intentionally rephotographed famous photographs in order to comment on the concept of originality.[119] The work of appropriation artist Jeff Koons has produced several reported cases, and recently in *Blanch v. Koons*,[120] the Second Circuit held that his use of a part of a copyrighted photograph of a pair of women's legs in a collage painting was a fair use. The painting by Koons in that case consisted of "four pairs of women's feet and lower legs dangling" over images of sweets with Niagara Falls and a grassy field in the background.[121] One of the pairs of legs featured in Koons's painting was from the plaintiff's work. A particularly interesting facet of this case is the court's reliance on the message of the work as articulated by Koons himself. The court concluded that Koons not only possessed a genuine creative rationale for borrowing the plaintiff's work, but also that his work possessed a sufficient transformative value such that it altered the borrowed work "with new expression, meaning, or message."[122] The opinion emphasized Koons's message of this particular work with the following observation: "By juxtaposing women's legs against a backdrop of food and landscape . . . he intended to 'comment on the ways in which some of our most basic appetites—for food, play, and sex—are mediated by popular messages.'"[123]

Although Koons's work in *Blanch v. Koons* might have satisfied both components of the proposed test, other works of appropriation art could possess a particular meaning or message personal to the author but still fail to satisfy ordinary reasonable observers that heightened originality with substantial creativity is present. The benefit of the proposed test is that it incorporates a dual standard that, taken together, is a useful measure of a work's originality for purposes of determining whether it should be entitled to moral rights protection. A standard for heightened originality with substantial creativity is preferable to one that requires the trier of fact to discern independently the creator's meaning and message. Thus, reliance on the author's narrative with respect to the design process and on evidence concerning the perceptions of ordinary reasonable observers is a viable way for courts to assess whether a work possesses the requisite originality to be within the scope of moral rights protection.

One final point should be made with respect to the application of the coverage standards I advocate in this discussion. In Chapter 5, I introduced the idea that moral rights should be applied more broadly to the right of attribution than the right of integrity. I will continue this discussion in Chapter 10, but at this juncture it is fair to question whether the standard of coverage I am proposing should apply equally to attribution and integrity. Granted, there are certain norms that have developed that suggest the proprietary of attribution even for functional works. A good example is open-source software, which is discussed in the following chapter.[124] Although I endorse these norms because they are consistent with affording authors recognition, I do not believe they support requiring attribution for functional works as part of a statutory moral rights law given the theoretical predicate for moral rights. If a work is purely functional, it simply does not make sense to talk about its meaning and message even if attribution is otherwise desirable. Moreover, as a practical matter, differentiating covered works based on which right is at stake would introduce unnecessary complications into the application of moral rights. Therefore, I would apply the standards for coverage developed in this chapter equally to attribution and integrity.

CHAPTER 7

Authors in Disguise and Collaborative Works

A LARGE NUMBER OF COPYRIGHTED WORKS are produced outside the framework of an individual author whose identity is known to the public. Such works include those produced by authors who write anonymously or under a pseudonym, and ghostwriters. Copyright law in the United States also maintains a provision, the work for hire doctrine, which transfers both the copyright and authorship rights to the employer of a creator in certain instances. Moreover, an increasingly large number of works are the product of collective authorship. These works reinforce the observation of the court in *Follett v. New American Library, Inc.* that "the concept of authorship is elusive and inexact."[1] All of these works present particular challenges for the development and implementation of a moral rights system. If the primary objective of moral rights is to safeguard the meaning and message of an author's work, it would seem as though the true author's identity should be publicly known. Yet, for many of the works discussed in this chapter, this knowledge may not be readily available. Although the application of moral rights to works produced by "authors in disguise" presents challenges from the standpoint of both objectionable textual modifications as well as appropriate attribution, the attribution problem perhaps is the most readily understood issue in this context.

Recent legal scholarship has evaluated the practices of anonymity, pseudonymity, and ghostwriting from the perspective of consumer deception. Laura Heymann has proposed "a doctrine or moral rights for readers," and invokes the concept of an "authornym" as a branding choice offered by the author to the consuming public in the form of the author's trademark.[2] She does not see appropriate "authornymic attribution" as grounded in authorial "justice," but rather as a method of preserving organizational integrity so that reader responses will be informed and consumer confusion minimized with respect to creative works.[3]

Writing primarily in the context of employment law, Catherine Fisk also has documented the branding function of attribution as a trademark. She observes that "readers of Nancy Drew novels expect them to be authored by 'Carolyn Keene' even though she does not exist and the books were written by a number of different people according to specifications established by the publisher."[4]

Greg Lastowka also calls for recognition of the trademark function of authorship and has recommended that attribution interests be regulated so as to prohibit "deceptive misattributions of authorship that result in consumer harms."[5] Although attribution interests are not formally regulated by trademark law, the more egregious situations still can wind up in court. One example is the case involving the acclaimed novel *Sarah* that was the subject of a federal trial culminating in a jury verdict of fraud, and an award of $116,500 in damages and $350,000 in legal fees to the plaintiff movie company.[6] The allegedly autobiographical book was a dark story of dysfunctional family dynamics and prostitution set in an Appalachian truck stop. The real author—a Brooklyn mother named Laura Albert—not only used the pseudonym JT LeRoy as her fictional literary name but also deceptively developed a public persona to go along with the pseudonym. Ultimately, Albert contracted with the plaintiff, under her pseudonymous identity, to make a movie based on the book. Notwithstanding the potential for extreme cases such as this, Henry Hansmann and Marina Santilli have observed that pseudonymous works present "at most a modest fraud on the public," because the use of this practice does not deceive the public as much as it does deny them the information of the real author's identity that they might otherwise like.[7] In their view, this argument applies with even greater force to anonymous works because here there is "no offsetting concern that the public will be deceived into believing that there is some person other than the true author who has written the work in question."[8]

Despite the appeal of treating attribution and other integrity interests within the framework of trademark law, I suggest that trademark law is not analytically consistent with the theoretical basis for moral rights protection. Trademark law is concerned with preventing consumer confusion, a concept totally unrelated to the authorial interests encompassed by moral rights. Whether consumers are confused by a particular party's actions with respect to a work of authorship is a completely separate inquiry from whether a party has, through lack of attribution, misattribution, or other modifications, distorted the meaning and message of an author's work. Thus, in contemplating the difficulties presented by anonymous, pseudonymous, and even works that are the product of ghostwriters, the starting point is not determining whether the public is deceived by these attributions but rather ascertaining exactly whose meaning and message the work at issue reflects. From this standpoint, works that are written anonymously or under a pseudonym present different considerations from works that are the product of ghostwriters.

Although VARA does not specifically include the negative rights of anonymity or pseudonymity,[9] these rights do comport with the Berne Convention. David Nimmer has observed that although the language of Berne on this point is "sparse," the semiofficial guide published by WIPO recognizes this aspect of the right of attribution as being within the scope of the Convention.[10] There is good reason for this view in that an author's decision to write anonymously or under a pseudonym can be viewed as a branding choice that is a fundamental part of the author's meaning and message. Hansmann and Santilli have observed that an "artist may have good reasons to exist in the public's mind as two different artists" and this analysis, in their view, applies "even more strongly to works published anonymously."[11] I suggest that more often than not, the reasons underlying an anonymous or pseudonymous attribution choice relate to how the author understands both the personal meaning of her work and her intended externalized message.

A compelling example of this phenomenon is Laura Heymann's observation that in certain instances, an author may choose to subordinate her own identity to the "broader purpose of the text," as in the case of a Holocaust survivor who wishes her work to represent the voices of all of the victims.[12] Heymann catalogues other motivations as to why someone would select various expressive identities that include gender morphing, and masking of particular cultural, racial, or ethnic identification. Such authors are experimenting with different modes of authorship so as to, in effect, reflect a personal meaning and facilitate the communication of a particular message to their readers. In this regard, consider also the facts of the Supreme Court's decision in *McIntyre v. Ohio Elections Commission*,[13] in which the defendant distributed some leaflets opposing a proposed school tax levy with the attribution "Concerned Parents and Tax Payers." Heyman observes that what motivated McIntrye to use this designation was "not the fear of retribution but a deliberate construction of identity, a desire to have the viewpoints in her handbill attributable to an identity other than her 'true' identity."[14] In fact, she posits that in *McIntyre*, the defendant may have been motivated to take advantage of a perceived audience tendency to give more weight to joint authorship than to an individual writer.[15] Catherine Fisk provides another telling example when she discusses the practice of newspaper writers electing a byline strike as a means of publicly protesting "objectionable workplace policies."[16] Fisk maintains that in such instances, the reporters are hoping that the absence of their bylines will alert readers to their complaints.[17] As these examples pointedly show, an author's choice to write either anonymously or under a pseudonym can be understood as a component of the work's essential meaning for the author and its intended message to the public.

If, as the previous discussion shows, the practices of anonymity and pseudonymity can be reconciled with moral rights protections for the actual author on the ground that these attribution designations function as part of the author's meaning and message, the situation is very different when it comes to ghostwriting. For one thing, the scenarios in which ghostwriting occurs are quite varied. Perhaps there are instances in which it is appropriate to conclude, based on the theoretical justifications for moral rights, that a ghostwriter should be completely denied attribution credit. This is a supportable result where the final product is far more representative of the named author rather than the ghostwriter. Hansmann and Santilli conclude that "there is less reason to extend to ghostwriters than to other writers or artists the protection of moral rights" since a "ghostwriter's skill is, in important degree, to be able to suppress her own personality when writing and to capture, instead, the style and character of the nominal author for whom she is working."[18] Therefore, a person serving as a ghostwriter "is typically not the kind of person whose works as a group have special value connected with the personality of their creator."[19] Political speechwriting represents one particular example of this type of situation. Moreover, the norms of politics also operate to preclude credit for the speechwriter. As Catherine Fisk has remarked, we have a tradition "of keeping speechwriters well in the background" in order "to preserve the cult of the personality in contemporary American politics."[20] Perhaps we do engage in voluntary deception when we attribute the words of a politician as a window into her mind and soul,[21] but the norms of the political world are far too strong to dismantle. For better or worse, we can allow the politician to retain the attribution on the theory, even if somewhat fictional, that the speech embodies her particular message.

In many other instances, however, it seems far more objectionable when ghostwriters do the lion's share of the truly creative work without any attribution. The degradation inherent in the process for both the attributed author as well as the ghostwriter has been documented in a recent memoir by "professional" ghostwriter Jennie Erdal.[22] Erdal compares ghostwriting to prostitution in the following graphic description: "[T]here is more than a random connection between the two; they both operate in rather murky worlds, a fee is agreed in advance and given 'for services rendered,' and those who admit to being involved, either as client or service-provider, can expect negative reactions—anything from mild shock and disapproval to outright revulsion."[23] As this comparison illustrates, in contrast to the political speechwriter scenario, in many instances there seems something wrong and unseemly about an individual taking credit for work that has been written by someone else, even if the ghostwriter has agreed to these terms. On the topic of ghostwriting, Greg Lastowka has observed: "[a]ckowledgement may be granted to a ghostwriter, but since the whole premise of ghostwriting seems to be about the misattribution of authorship, the more credit the ghostwriter gets, the less the activity appears like ghostwriting and the more it appears like collaboration."[24] One of the most egregious ghostwriting narratives discussed by Lastowka is the story of Virginia Cleo (V.C.) Andrews, whose publisher opted to reproduce best-selling books such as *Midnight Flight* in her name even after her death.[25]

The operative inquiries in assessing how ghostwriters should fare with respect to moral rights in the United States should be whose meaning and message does the work in question convey, and what are the relevant norms governing the particular type of work at issue? Most likely, any such determinations would have to be made on a case-by-case basis, which may present a potential problem from the standpoint of desired predictability in legal applications. One area worth exploring is the imposition of more visible credit notices when a very creative work is written by a ghostwriter with minimal input or assistance from the accredited writer. For example, *Line of Control*, one of celebrated author Tom Clancy's *Op-Center* books written by ghostwriter Jeff Rovin,[26] contains on the bottom of the front cover a declaration that it was written by Jeff Rovin, although this declaration is in very small type. This accreditation is preceded, however, with the statement that the book was "Created by Tom Clancy and Steve Pieczenik."[27] Leaving aside the issue of whether this form of accreditation is sufficient to forestall consumer confusion, I suggest that the theoretical predicate of moral rights protection still is well served by requiring these types of notices. Jeff Rovin's authorial interests are recognized and for those who care to look carefully enough, the promotion of knowledge also is well served by these designations.

Although ghostwriting is limited in its application to literary works, the practice of hiring someone to create a work of authorship for which no attribution credit will be given has had a long and distinguished history in the United States in the form of the work for hire doctrine. This work for hire doctrine operates to vest authorship status in the employer of the creator, or in certain instances, in the party who commissions the work. Work for hire is the only aspect of our copyright law that essentially conflicts with an explicit right of attribution for all authors. Although variations of this doctrine appear in other countries such as the Netherlands and Russia, for the most part the United States is rather unique in its explicit embrace of this position.[28] According to Adolf Dietz, the work for hire doctrine as applied "takes away with one stroke of the pen the constitutional guarantee for the initial and true author."[29] The work for hire doctrine perhaps can be justified when it operates to divest an author of copyright ownership given the economic quid pro quo she receives. On the other hand, by allowing an author to relinquish her authorship status and all that such status entails, the work for hire doctrine arguably undermines authorship dignity in a fundamental way.[30]

From the outset, the approach underlying the work for hire doctrine in the United States was very focused on economic realities. Significantly, the work for hire doctrine originally was codified as a default rule invoked to determine copyright ownership in the absence of a contractual stipulation on this point.[31] With respect to works for hire, the employer is regarded as the author in a legal sense, as compared to the creator of a work, whom Judge Learned Hand once termed "the 'author' in the colloquial sense."[32] Thus, the work for hire doctrine fails to distinguish between colloquial authorship in the sense of physically rendering a work and legal ownership of the copyright in which the creative work is embodied. This is a significant distinction because the dignity interest pertinent to the authorship norms discussed earlier applies to "authors" as that term is understood colloquially rather than legally. Regardless of whether an author transfers any or all of her copyrights, the creative work continually manifests the colloquial author's subjective meaning and message. The author's dignity is tied to the accurate presentation and attribution of this object, despite the transfer of the object itself or the copyrights to the work. In her study of the norms of attribution, Catherine Fisk has stated that "[t]o most employees most of the time, what matters is not that you own your . . . copyright, but that you can truthfully claim to be the . . . author of it."[33] By simply positing that the employer becomes the author, no consideration is given to the consequences of deeming the employer to be the physical source of the creation.

The work for hire doctrine has been in place in the United States, at least in theory, for over a century.[34] The 1909 Copyright Act failed to include a definition of "work made for hire," but stipulated that "the word 'author' shall include an employer in the case of works made for hire."[35] The 1976 Act attempted to create more certainty in work for hire determinations to preclude employees from claiming an after-the-fact copyright interest in such works.[36] Section 201(b) of the 1976 Act specifically embraces the work for hire doctrine by providing that "[i]n the case of a work made for hire, the employer or other person for whom the work was prepared is considered the author for purposes of this title, and, unless the parties have expressly agreed otherwise in a written instrument signed by them, owns all of the rights comprised in the copyright."[37] Further, the 1976 Act invokes a two-pronged definition of a "work made for hire" as "a work prepared by an employee within the scope of his or her employment; or a work specially ordered or commissioned" for specified types of uses.[38] To satisfy the specially commissioned prong of the definition, the parties also must "expressly agree in a written instrument signed by them that the work shall be considered a work made for hire."[39]

The legislative history accompanying the codifications of the work for hire doctrine under both the 1909 and 1976 Acts does not reveal an explicit appreciation for the personal rights of authors as distinct from their ownership interests. Additionally, the history does not specifically address the implications of vesting authorship, as opposed to ownership, rights in an employer.[40] In fact, the language of § 201(b) suggests that a signed written agreement can transfer copyright ownership, but not authorship status, to the hired party, or colloquial author, with respect to works made for hire.[41] It would have been reasonable to expect that the text and history of VARA, which represents the primary codification of moral rights in the United States, to recognize the distinction between ownership and authorship. The reality is otherwise.[42] In defining "visual art" for purposes of stipulating the scope of VARA's application, VARA explicitly excludes works made for hire from coverage, thus avoiding examination of the entire issue.[43] Similarly, six of the eleven state moral right statutes exclude works made for hire from their statutory protections.[44]

For the most part, the work for hire case law similarly fails to consider the distinction between authorship and ownership because ownership of the copyrighted property typically is what is at issue in work for hire disputes.[45] Between 1978, the effective year of the 1976 Act and 2007, the specially commissioned prong of the work for hire doctrine[46] has been the subject of roughly thirty-five cases. The employee prong[47] has given rise to nearly double this number since 1989, the year the

Supreme Court provided guidelines for determining whether an individual should be considered an employee or an independent contractor in *Community for Creative Non-Violence v. Reid*.[48] Taken together, these decisions total roughly 100 cases, but only a handful involve facts that could even potentially give rise to attribution or other textual integrity violations. Despite the relative lack of precedent on this point, however, it is instructive to examine these decisions because they demonstrate how the operation of the work for hire doctrine has the potential to conflict with the dignity interests of authorship that are the predicate of moral rights protection.

In *Community for Creative Non-Violence v. Reid*,[49] a nonprofit organization, the Community for Creative Non-Violence (CCNV), sued James Earl Reid, an artist whom it had commissioned to do a sculpture of a homeless family for a Christmastime pageant. Reid wanted the work to be cast in bronze so that it would be more durable, but CCNV rejected this idea due to time and financial constraints. Ultimately, Reid suggested that he cast the sculpture in a synthetic substance that would be more economical but still durable, a compromise accepted by CCNV. No written agreement was signed and no mention was made of the copyright. During the creation process, members of CCNV visited Reid to discuss the project. After the completion of the sculpture, it was displayed for about a month and then returned to Reid's studio for minor repairs. Upon hearing of CCNV's plans to take the sculpture on a major tour, Reid refused to return the sculpture because he believed it could not withstand such an ambitious tour. Reid urged CCNV to cast the statue in bronze or create a master mold, but CCNV declined to spend additional sums of money on the sculpture. Reid then refused to return the sculpture and filed a certificate of copyright registration in his own name. He proposed to take the sculpture on a more modest tour than the one contemplated by CCNV. CCNV then filed a competing certificate of copyright registration and instituted a lawsuit, seeking the sculpture's return and a declaration of copyright ownership. The Supreme Court held that Reid was an independent contractor rather than an employee of CCNV, and therefore, ownership of the copyright did not belong to CCNV pursuant to the work for hire doctrine.[50]

The *Reid* court concluded that the general common law of agency should govern whether an individual is an employee under the work for hire definition, with the focus on whether a hiring party has the "right to control the manner and means by which the product is accomplished."[51] To decide whether an agency relationship exists, courts should balance a variety of factors derived from the common law as outlined in the Restatement of Agency.[52] A review of these factors reveals that the Restatement's emphasis is on "the relationship between the person performing the work and the person paying him to perform the work,"[53] as is evidenced by the following factors: "the source of the instrumentalities and tools; the location of the work; the duration of the relationship between the parties; whether the hiring party has the right to assign additional projects to the hired party; . . . the method of payment; the hired party's role in hiring and paying assistants; whether the hiring party is in business; the provision of employee benefits; and the tax treatment of the hired party."[54] These factors are largely irrelevant when evaluating a situation involving a potential work made for hire in the context of a violation of authorship dignity. In these instances, the focus should be on whether the work itself conveys the hired party's meaning and intended message, and if so, whether misattributions or presentations of the work by the hiring party or anyone else distort these communicative qualities.[55]

Reid did not involve an application of the specially commissioned prong, for which the relevant categories of covered works are limited to those specified in the statute. For some of these categories, such as parts of motion pictures or other audiovisual works, it may be logical to approach a work for hire and moral rights conflict by asking whose meaning and message the work embodies.[56] Justin Hughes has discussed the characteristics of a commissioned work.[57] Initially, he notes the prevalence of the economic focus in applying this factor based on the cases' concern with the extent to which a commissioning party has undertaken the financial risk.[58] Yet, he suggests that the "commission test" also reflects noneconomic concerns indicative of the "intentionality" of the commissioning party as "a measure of whether the patron's intentions imbue and control the artistic endeavor."[59] His discussion of these "personhood" interests reinforces the view that in certain instances, it is appropriate to evaluate a specially commissioned work from the standpoint of whose meaning and message the work reflects—the creator's or that of the hiring party.[60] Nonetheless, several of the categories in the specially commissioned prong such as instructional texts, tests, or answer materials for tests[61] would not meet the heightened originality standard discussed in the foregoing chapter. It simply does not make sense to discuss meaning and message in connection with such works. Moreover, in practice, the "specially ordered or commissioned" work for hire cases yield little relevant information on how to approach a work for hire and moral rights conflict because in many of these decisions the focus is on compliance with the provision's additional requirement of a written instrument signed by both parties stipulating that the work is one for hire.[62]

Although the facts of *Reid* did not involve an express moral rights violation, they certainly raise the potential for such a claim. Specifically, CCNV, as the commissioning party, owned the sculpture at issue but did not own the copyright. As a legal matter, *copyright* ownership and authorship remained with Reid because the work did not satisfy the requirements of the court's work for hire test.[63] Therefore, the case resulted in ownership of the artwork in one party, and the copyright to the artwork in another.[64] Under such a scenario, textual integrity issues can arise when the owner of the artwork fails to attribute authorship or desires to take some action that will modify, or perhaps even destroy, the work's meaning and message as conceived by the author. Thus, CCNV's desire to take the sculpture on a tour that would have been too ambitious for the work could have been the basis for a right of integrity claim by Reid had VARA been in effect at the time of the decision.[65] With respect to the governing law, however, presumably CCNV had the right to take the sculpture on a tour, even if that tour would damage or destroy the work.[66] Similarly, the law at that time would not have required CCNV to attribute authorship of the work to Reid although on remand, the district court ordered that any two-dimensional reproductions of the sculpture must credit Reid as the creator.[67]

These issues would not have been resolved any more satisfactorily had the court concluded that the sculpture was a work for hire. If the court had held that CCNV owned the copyright, CCNV also could have taken actions with respect to the sculpture that would have obliterated the meaning and message of Reid's work. For example, as the copyright owner, CCNV would have been able to reproduce the work but would not be required to attribute authorship. CCNV also would be able to modify or even destroy the work, actions that surely would impact the work's meaning and message as determined by Reid.

More recently, the facts pertaining to the Supreme Court's decision in *Dastar Corp. v. Twentieth Century Fox Film Corp.*,[68] discussed in Chapter 3, provide another example of the potential problems the work for hire doctrine can present with respect to preserving the colloquial author's textual integrity. Subsequent to the Supreme Court's decision on the § 43(a) claim, the Ninth Circuit held that the book upon which the original television series was based was a work for hire and therefore, Doubleday, the book's publisher, owned the copyright as a result of its exercise of the copyright renewal provisions in effect under the 1909 Act.[69] Although this case did not involve a dispute between the colloquial author, General Eisenhower, and the book's publisher, a different factual scenario could be envisioned in which General Eisenhower had a dispute with his publisher regarding a matter involving the integrity of the book in its published form. If the work was considered a work for hire, Doubleday, as the legal author, would not be accountable to the colloquial author for any such problems absent a contractual arrangement to the contrary. Leaving aside the sufficiency of contract law to address such issues, the fact remains that the work for hire doctrine has the capacity to be applied in such a way as to effect a change in the meaning and message of a work from the standpoint of the colloquial author. According to the court, Doubleday had "sufficient supervisory powers" over General Eisenhower's authorship,[70] but the facts of the case still show that General Eisenhower's authorship dignity is embodied in the work, imbuing it with his personal meaning and message. Indeed, an endorsement of the book by historian Allan Nevins appearing on the book's dustcover states that the book "expresses the personality of the author" and that the audience "will feel this is General Eisenhower speaking . . . with the heartiest desire to tell the truth about himself and others."[71] The point is that work for hire status does not necessarily eviscerate the colloquial author's meaning and message.

The only case to examine directly VARA's exclusion of works made for hire from the definition of "visual art" is *Carter v. Helmsley-Spear, Inc.*,[72] in which the Second Circuit concluded that the plaintiff artists' "walk-through" sculpture, which occupied the majority of the lobby of the defendant's building, was a work made for hire. This determination precluded the application of VARA to the plaintiffs' lawsuit seeking to enjoin the defendants from removing, modifying, or destroying the artwork.[73] The facts of *Carter* involved a situation in which the artists enjoyed substantial creative control over the work.[74] Thus, the real issue presented in this case is whether and how an author's moral rights should be applied in a situation in which the author is technically employed by another entity but nonetheless engaged in a highly creative enterprise over which she has maintained substantial creative control. More recently, the court in *Martha Graham School and Dance Foundation, Inc. v. Martha Graham Center of Contemporary Dance*,[75] relied on the analysis in *Carter* in concluding that certain of Martha Graham's dances were works for hire despite the high degree of artistic freedom and creative control enjoyed by the famous choreographer. According to the court, "[t]he fact that Graham was extremely talented understandably explains the Center's disinclination to exercise control over the details of her work, but does not preclude the sort of employee relationship that results in a work-for-hire."[76]

The foregoing discussion demonstrates that work for hire is concerned with authorship in the legal sense, which essentially implicates the question of copyright ownership. Not surprisingly, the incompatibility between the work for hire doctrine and the concept of authorship dignity supporting moral rights fails to capture the attention of the courts. Some commentators explain this result by positing that perhaps no conflict exists because when works made for hire are at issue, the work's tangible expression essentially is controlled by the employer or commissioning party.[77] As such, no authorship dignity violation realistically occurs because the work in question does not reflect the colloquial author's meaning and message but rather that of the hiring party.[78] Henry Hansmann and Marina Santilli even suggest that the work for hire doctrine "constitutes a waiver of moral rights, in recognition by the artist and the commissioning party that the latter's need for flexibility in the use of the work exceeds the artist's subjective and reputational interests."[79]

These assumptions do not necessarily reflect the realities of the process of human creation in employment situations. Therefore, they do not furnish a basis upon which to justify the work for hire doctrine's trumping a creator's attribution and integrity interests without concern for violating the colloquial author's autonomy and dignity interests. Receipt of a monetary benefit, even pursuant to an employment relationship, does not necessarily destroy the author's desire for attribution and for the preservation of the meaning and intended message of her work. The norms of authorship that underscore moral rights operate at a level distinct from the economically focused inquiry mandated by the work for hire analysis. No inconsistency exists between the hiring party retaining the economic rights and the hired party retaining moral rights in cases where the hired party is largely responsible for the meaning and intended message of a work. Thus, in order to determine whether and how moral rights and the work for hire doctrine should coexist, it is important to examine the extent to which a particular creator "for hire" imbues the work with her own subjective meaning and intended message reflective of her dignity as an author, as opposed to merely executing orders dictated from the hiring party. In this regard, works made for hire present parallels to the ghostwriting situations discussed previously.[80]

The portraits created by Dina Gottliebova Babbitt while a prisoner at Auschwitz poignantly illustrate the general point that an author can maintain a powerful attachment even to works produced under circumstances completely beyond her control. While in Auschwitz, Babbitt's artistic abilities came to the attention of Josef Mengele, the infamous Nazi doctor known as the Angel of Death. Mengele sought scientific evidence for his racial theories and demanded that Babbitt paint portraits of the Gypsies incarcerated at the camp because, in his view, photography did not accurately portray their skin tones. Babbitt's condition for complying was simple—either both she and her mother would be saved from death or she would commit suicide by touching an electrified fence. Her portraits survived and are now on display at the Auschwitz–Birkenau Memorial and Museum in Poland. The Museum considers the portraits to be its property rather than Babbitt's "personal artistic creations" because they were "documentary work done under direct orders from Dr. Mengele and carried out by the artist to ensure her survival."[81] Babbitt saw the situation differently because to her, these works represented her life and the life of her mother. Her narrative is clear: "Every single thing . . . was taken away from us. And now finally, something is found that I created, that belongs to me. And they refuse to give it to me. This is why I feel the same helplessness as I did then."[82] Babbitt's portraits were not exactly works made for hire in the conventional sense, although the parallels are stark. Her payment was her survival and the directives to which she was forced to respond were clear. Nonetheless, even in this situation, she retained a compelling authorship dignity interest in her work.

The majority of work for hire cases decided under the employee prong of the statutory definition involve quasi-functional copyrightable material such as computer programs that realistically lack the ability to convey an author's meaning and message.[83] Nevertheless, cases such as *Carter v. Helmsley-Spear, Inc.*[84] and *Martha Graham School and Dance Foundation, Inc. v. Martha Graham Center of Contemporary Dance*[85] involve works made for hire that are capable of embodying an author's meaning and conveying her message. These cases illustrate that even if one is considered an employee for purposes of a work for hire analysis, the works produced still can manifest the colloquial author's meaning and intended message rather than that of the hiring party.

Ultimately, Congress will have to make vital categorical determinations regarding the applicability of both moral rights generally and their interface with the work for hire doctrine specifically. In order to embrace both the theoretical basis for moral rights and the certainty regarding copyright ownership sought by Congress in crafting the 1976 work for hire provision,[86] it would seem that any work that is categorically eligible for moral rights protection should not be made to forfeit automatically this protection just because it was created for hire. In this regard, VARA's exclusion of works made for hire is problematic. A much better approach would be to provide that authors of works otherwise subject to moral rights protection retain their rights as colloquial authors, even if their works are created for hire, absent compelling reasons for divesting them of their rights. Among the reasons that might support failing to accord moral rights to a particular work for hire are that the work in question was created under someone else's direction or control to such a degree that it does not represent the colloquial author's meaning and intended message, or that public policy militates against applying attribution and other integrity interests in a given situation. For example, in the case of speechwriters who are considered employees rather than independent contractors, or newspapers that disallow bylines so as to speak with a collective voice,[87] it may not be desirable on public policy grounds to mandate a right of attribution. One way to get around this problem from a legal standpoint is to conclude that such writers are independent contractors rather than employees, and as such, their works are not governed by copyright law but rather by contract law. Where this is not possible, however, the public policy caveat may be operative. Although considering public policy as a factor in determining whether an author retains her moral rights may appear similar to an implied waiver in certain instances, it is important to keep in mind that an author's moral rights may be subject to limitations even in jurisdictions with the strongest moral rights protections.[88]

Until now, the discussion has focused primarily on works that are authored by one individual in a colloquial sense but whose true identity is not attributed. Collaborative works also raise their own variety of the "authors in disguise" problem. Initially, it should be noted that collaborative works also can be created in a work for hire context.[89] The application of moral rights to collaborative works is further complicated by how the judiciary currently applies copyright's provision for joint authorship. The story of Lynn Thomson, the plaintiff dramaturg in *Thomson v. Larson*,[90] the high-profile joint authorship case involving the hit play *Rent*, illustrates the legal problem here. The New York Theater Workshop hired Thomson, a dramaturg and stage director, to help playwright Jonathan Larson clarify and transform the storyline of *Rent*. Their revised version of the play was "characterized by experts as 'a radical transformation of the show.' "[91] The agreement Thomson signed stipulated that she agreed to provide "dramaturgical" assistance and research to the playwright and director in exchange for $2,000 and billing credit as "dramaturg."[92] According to Thomson, her collaboration with Larson resulted in a new script that incorporated only half of the previous text.[93]

Hours after the final dress rehearsal, Larson died. Subsequently, *Rent* opened on Broadway and was a smashing success. Thomson approached Larson's heirs and requested a percentage of the royalties from the play. When negotiations broke down, Thomson brought suit, alleging that she is a coauthor of the play and entitled to 16 percent of the author's share of the royalties.[94] Thomson's complaint alleged that "she developed the plot and theme, contributed extensively to the story, created many character elements, wrote a significant portion of the dialogue and song lyrics, and made other copyrightable contributions to the Work."[95] Thomson initiated her lawsuit to receive, on a personal level, both credit and compensation. In this regard, she has observed: "I can only repeat that everyone acknowledged what I did until I asked to be paid for it. The producer's response to why he wouldn't put me on the title page was simply, 'I don't have to.' "[96]

The 1976 Copyright Act defines a *joint work* as "a work prepared by two or more authors with the intention that their contributions be merged into inseparable or interdependent parts of a unitary whole."[97] Neither the statute nor its legislative history defines *inseparable* or *interdependent*. Yet, appellate courts influential in the copyright arena such as the Second,[98] Seventh,[99] and Ninth[100] Circuits adhere to a test for joint authorship that requires both independent copyrightability of each contribution and intent by all putative authors at the time of the collaboration that they be coauthors. Using this test, the Second Circuit affirmed the district court's denial of Thomson's joint authorship claim. Yet, the "intent to be coauthors" standard reflects a narrative distinct from the language of the Copyright Act and its legislative history.[101] The decisions in these circuits evince concern with the prospect that, notwithstanding the provision of a relatively minor contribution, a party can be deemed a joint author under the statutory definition as long as all parties to the work intended to merge their contributions into a unitary whole. There-fore, they endorse a more rigorous test for determining joint authorship and de-emphasize collaboration in favor of independent copyrightability and mutual intent regarding joint authorship.

The focus of this discussion is on the mutual intent component of the judiciary's test for joint authorship, although the independently copy-rightable standard is certainly not problem-free.[102] Rochelle Dreyfuss has observed that by virtue of its inevitable operation, the risk exists that the mutual intent standard will result in privileging the narrative of the dominant author over the nondominant author.[103] Indeed, under a sub-jective standard focusing on what the parties said and thought, the domi-nant author or her representatives always will dispute the intent of coau-thorship as was the case in *Thomson*. It is reasonable to wonder why the dominant author's intent should be paramount if that person nonetheless is dependent upon the intellectual work product of others.[104]

Perhaps courts would be more sensitive to the nondominant author's narrative if they would be willing to depart from the notion that coau-thorship necessitates an equal sharing of the profits. This sense of man-dated equality of profit pervades these cases. In *Thomson v. Larson*, the court noted that "[j]oint authorship entitles the co-authors to equal undi-vided interests in the whole work—in other words, each joint author has the right to use or to license the work as he or she wishes, subject only to the obligation to account to the other joint owner for any profits that are made."[105] In *Community for Creative Non-Violence v. Reid*, the appel-late court stated that absent an agreement to the contrary, any profits earned by joint authors are to be evenly divided, even where their respec-tive contributions are not equal.[106]

The courts are misguided in their focus on the need to divide the prof-its of jointly authored works equally. The legislative history of the statu-tory provision provides that joint authors co-owning copyright in a work are deemed to be tenants in common.[107] According to property law, ten-ants in common own undivided interests in the property and no tenant can exclude the others from any portion of the property. Significantly, there is no requirement that this undivided interest be equal.[108] More-over, the language of the 1976 Copyright Act does not explicitly specify that the ownership shares must be equal.[109] If courts were to recognize the possibility that coauthors do not necessarily have to enjoy equal shares of the work, they would be in a position to consider the possibility that collaborative efforts should be rewarded under copyright law to the extent of the collaboration. Currently, however, in the area of joint authorship the law remains largely unresponsive to the increasingly large number of collaborative endeavors.[110]

With respect to moral rights, as opposed to copyright ownership, collaborative works present even greater challenges. Whereas the economic interests of copyright owners do not have to be equal, the notion of moral rights almost demands that each coauthor's contribution, meaning, and message be given its due. This may be problematic, however, if coauthors disagree on matters pertaining to the work's integrity. Aside from objectionable modifications, one joint author can use or license the work in a manner deemed objectionable by the other joint authors. For example, what should be the result if a joint author of a hymn intended to be used for services in connection with a particular religion licenses it for use in the liturgy of a different religion over the objection of her fellow coauthor?[111] Further, it is necessary to determine what level of contribution a putative coauthor must make to an otherwise covered work in order to exercise moral rights.

Under a model of coauthorship in which the participants either make relatively equal contributions, or otherwise are significantly invested in the final product, a system embodying moral rights for all joint authors is compelling. Indeed, preservation of authorship dignity and protection for the spiritual interests safeguarded by moral rights are important, regardless of whether the creative process is shared with respect to any particular work. The relationship between jointly authored works and moral rights has, however, become more complicated in recent years where the models of authorship often conflict with that of the solitary author, or even that of the joint author as that concept has been invoked traditionally. Consider the difficulties presented by tattoo art, which may be viewed as the ultimate "site-specific" art. Tattoo artist Matthew Reed sued professional basketball player Rasheed Wallace and Nike, Inc. for copyright infringement because the tattoo Reed created for Wallace was highlighted in an advertising campaign for Nike's products on television and on the Nike Web site during the Spring 2004 Detroit Pistons' championship run. The advertisement included a close-up of the tattoo and featured the tattoo being created by a computerized simulation with a voice-over from Wallace describing and explaining the meaning behind the tattoo.[112] Reed's claims against Wallace individually were for contributory infringement based on Wallace's representation to Nike that he was the exclusive owner of the tattoo, and for an accounting of any revenue Wallace might receive from the advertisement if Wallace were found to be a co-owner of the artwork.[113] The complaint suggested that Reed and Wallace collaborated on the idea and theme for the tattoo. Wallace never asked Reed to execute an agreement transferring to Wallace ownership or other rights with respect to the tattoo.[114]

When attempting to discern whose meaning and message a work conveys, tattoo art is particularly troublesome because both the artist and the person on whose body the tattoo resides can make credible claims as to being the source of the work's meaning and message. Industry norms are such that the artist expects the exposure that accompanies a celebrity's public display of a tattoo.[115] As Reed's lawsuit shows, however, these norms do not necessarily govern cases at the margin. The parties ultimately dismissed the case[116] but its aftermath reveals uncertainty as to how joint-authorship law should apply in this situation. A moral rights claim by the tattoo artist is more complicated in light of the tattoo being incorporated into the very being of another individual. What should be the result, then, when someone in Wallace's position advertises something to which the tattoo artist objects, and the tattoo is a prominent part of the advertisement? Perhaps this situation can be resolved by invoking a type of public display right pursuant to which the subject of the tattoo can display the tattoo publicly under the theory that once the tattoo artist puts her artwork into the public eye by placing it on another person, she arguably loses the ability to control subsequent displays of her work by the person bearing the tattoo.[117]

In the digital environment, the process of creation can be particularly interactive and dependent upon a multitude of voices, as works often are formulated in large part as a result of audience participation and reinterpretation.[118] Margaret Chon has studied one such effort, the Chain Art Project, a collaborationist category of visual digital art housed on a Web site whose design and execution "depended on the deliberate changing by many authors of a single author's original image."[119] The project was conceived by artist Bonnie Mitchell, who solicited participants to engage in an interactive artistic project designed to redefine "individual and self."[120] One of the project's participants wanted to commercialize the work by licensing it to an art gallery.[121] This decision prompted the emergence of emotions rooted in individual ownership and possessiveness on the part of the participants.[122] In this regard, Bonnie Mitchell has observed:

It was very interesting to watch the students' reactions as they received the new images each week. They felt very attached to the image that they had started and were very upset when someone changed the image in a way they were unhappy with. . . . They often referred to the image as belonging to them, but did it really?[123]

Although Professor Chon's article is concerned primarily with the copyright status of such works, she acknowledges that "even in the absence of a commercial incentive, there might be a moral-rights basis for ensuring the inviolability of a work through copyright."[124]

The challenge for our legal system is to devise a framework that allows the exercise of moral rights with respect to creations born in a collaborative context. Endeavors such as the Chain Art Project suggest that in certain contexts, the exercise of moral rights by a joint author might not be feasible, or even desirable. On the other hand, if the exercise of moral rights is significantly hampered in a joint-authorship context, the law is failing to recognize the joint author's dignity interests. An analogy to the parental metaphor of authorship suggests that joint authors can be analogized to co-parents: "[t]he collaboration process bears the artistic children of the joint author relationship."[125] This analogy underscores three critical points about the joint-authorship relationship. First, joint authors are heavily invested in their "progeny"; second, joint authors share a special and unique relationship between themselves;[126] and third, joint authors do not necessarily have equal say or bargaining power with respect to both their personal relationship and their relationships with their progeny.[127]

With respect to attribution, the principal issue is the extent of the contribution a coauthor must provide in order to receive attribution credit. This inquiry relates to the discussion regarding originality because its resolution lies in requiring, on the part of each coauthor, a contribution manifesting a heightened standard of originality with substantial creativity. Such a standard is compatible with requiring each collaborator to furnish material that independently meets this heightened standard. Moreover, a standard with criteria that are readily articulated and applied has the advantage of transparency, meaning that the criteria for awarding credit are publicly known and capable of providing adequate motivation.[128] In the collaborative context, this standard can be judged from both a qualitative and quantitative standpoint.[129] For example, recall that in *CCNV v. Reid*, although Reid sculpted the three human figures, CCNV made the steam grate and pedestal for the statute. The proposed standard suggests that in a situation such as this, where one party contributes material that is functional and lacking in artistic rank, attribution should be denied.

One issue deserving of considerable attention with respect to allocating attribution among collaborators is the appropriate relationship between legal standards and industry norms, particularly with respect to works that would be subject to moral rights protection. The standard proposed in this chapter for determining credit in particular collaborative enterprises must be adopted with an eye toward the continued existence and development of industry norms in areas characterized by a specialized history and mode of operation. For example, the movie and television industries are subject to legally enforceable rules governing credits that are entirely within the province of the Hollywood guilds with respect to negotiation and administration.[130] Other regimes function according to much less formalized, but no less pervasive, social norms. It is worth noting that the open-source software movement, although not strictly relevant to this discussion given my view that software should not be afforded moral rights,[131] nonetheless depends upon providing appropriate attribution to the movement's participants.[132] Moreover, some open-source licenses also require that those who modify a particular program place a notice in the source files regarding the modification so that others will be aware of these changes and will not attribute them to the original authors.[133]

As suggested by these open-source licensing agreements, another global problem concerning the interface between collaborative works and moral rights is how attribution should be addressed in conjunction with works that have been modified. This question involves both attribution and right of integrity issues.[134] In the context of collaborative works, there may also be disagreement among the joint authors as to what type of conduct is objectionable. Recall the earlier hypothetical situation of the joint author of a hymn who licenses its use against the will of her coauthor.[135] VARA provides that one joint author can waive the specified rights for all of the other joint authors pursuant to a written instrument.[136] The rationale supporting this provision of VARA derives from the economic focus of copyright law, and ignores the author's intrinsic motivations for creating. The legislative history contains the following explanation:

[This provision] is consistent with current practice under title 17, in which one joint author may exploit the economic rights in a work, subject only to a duty to account to other joint authors for any profits earned from that exploitation. Similarly, if a joint author waives the right of attribution or integrity in exchange for compensation, that joint author has a duty to account to the other joint authors.[137]

This feature of VARA has been criticized and has been the subject of a recommendation for amendment by the Register of Copyrights.[138] A strong argument can be made that allowing one joint author to waive the rights under VARA for all other joint authors significantly undermines the rationale for moral rights protection. According to one commentator, this provision "seems designed, unintentionally or not, to rob otherwise protected artists of the right to object to violations of their moral rights in a joint work."[139]

The case law involving non-VARA works reveals that joint authors of such works fare no better when one joint author attempts to alter or modify a work in a manner deemed objectionable by the other joint authors.[140] Simply stated, no adequate cause of action exists in this country to address a moral rights violation committed by one coauthor who, in the opinion of her coauthors, mutilates the work. For example, the relationship between joint authorship and moral rights arose in *Weinstein v. University of Illinois*.[141] In that case, the plaintiff was alleging that the publication of an article with the authors' names in the wrong order violated the due process clause of the Fourteenth Amendment. The Seventh Circuit observed that the coauthor of a copyrighted work can make a unilateral decision to license the work, subject to an accounting to the other coauthors.[142] The court also noted that coauthors can make changes in a work and publish the original or the revision.[143] In a footnote, the court observed that although the plaintiff attempts to avoid this result by relying on moral rights,[144] such an attempt must fail because no jurisdiction has created such a right in this context. Therefore, this federal court was "not about to foist so novel a principle on Illinois."[145]

Weinstein is a troublesome opinion not necessarily because of the ultimate result the court reached,[146] but because it underscores that no remedy exists for a joint author when her fellow joint authors publish the work in an altered or objectionable state.[147] In essence, the issue of one joint author taking measures that are viewed by the other collaborators as violative of the work's integrity is not all that different from integrity violations committed by independent third parties. These issues will be discussed more fully in Chapter 10.

CHAPTER 8

Personas

NO COUNTRY IN THE WORLD is so driven by personality as is the United States. According to media studies professor Jib Fowles, "[t]he prominence of the star role has been one of the most defining features of American culture as distinct from other cultures."[1] Fame is used to persuade, inspire, and inform Americans in nearly every aspect of their lives and our fascination with fame has reached epic proportions. The impact of the "fame phenomenon" on the legal system has spawned a legal doctrine, the right of publicity, whose primary function is to prevent the unauthorized commercial exploitation of celebrity and other personas. A right of publicity action can involve a claim that essentially is analogous to the moral right of integrity when an individual's persona is being appropriated in an objectionable context or for an objectionable purpose. In these instances, neither an award of injunctive relief nor monetary damages will erase the damage that the persona perceives as having already been inflicted by virtue of the user's prior unauthorized appropriation. No judicially mandated relief can eliminate the prior effects of the user's objectionable public exposure of the persona. These are situations involving morally based, as opposed to economically based, objections to the use.

Assuming a legal structure in which moral rights will apply only to a subset of copyrightable works, the issue regarding the application of moral rights to personas is not so much whether personas are sufficiently original but rather whether personas should be considered works of authorship within the meaning of copyright law. Recall that the Constitution's Copyright Clause specifically extends protection to "writings" but the original meaning of this term is not clear.[2] The constitutional grant of authority concerning copyrights does not require Congress to act with respect to all categories of materials that may meet the constitutional definitions.[3] Instead, "whether any specific category of 'Writings' is to be brought within the purview of the federal statutory scheme is left to the discretion of Congress."[4] In discussing the term *writings* in this context in 1879, the Supreme Court in the *Trademark Cases* stated that the writings that are to be protected are the "fruits of intellectual labor."[5] Moreover, in *Goldstein v. California*, the Supreme Court emphasized that the "history of federal copyright statutes indicates that the congressional determination to consider specific classes of writings is dependent, not only on the character of the writing, but also on the commercial importance of the product to the national economy."[6] Given the tremendous impact of commercial celebrity endorsements on our consumer culture, a topic that will be examined more fully below, the Supreme Court's rationale provides additional support for recognizing celebrity personas as within the scope of "writings" within the meaning of the Copyright Clause.

Celebrities, as active participants in the construction of their personas, arguably can be regarded as "authors" and their personas as "works of authorship" for purposes of copyright law. The constitutional grant of power is sufficiently broad to extend to any work that is the product of an "author." As early as 1884, the Supreme Court in *Burrow-Giles Lithographic Co. v. Sarony* defined "author" as "he to whom anything owes its origin; originator; maker."[7] Through labor and personal investment of "self," an individual creates a "persona-text"—a text where the subject matter is a persona—in much the same way that an author creates a work of literature or a painting. In fact, this personal investment can be even greater with respect to the creation of a persona-text since it invokes the creator's sense of self in a much more personalized way than virtually any other type of work. Although the initial part of this discussion highlights celebrity persona-texts, every individual, regardless of fame or renown, has the capacity to author her persona-text.

Despite the logic of this argument, most of the scant case law on this point takes the view that a persona does not come within the subject matter of copyright because it is not a writing of an author within the meaning of the Copyright Clause.[8] Nevertheless, the courts that have addressed this issue have done so within the context of determining that the Copyright Act should not preempt a state law right of publicity action in a given instance because the plaintiff's identity does not come within the "subject matter" of copyright protection.[9] According to these decisions, the publicity plaintiffs prevailed in their attempts to use state law to protect their identities.[10] In contrast, in an unreported appellate decision from California, the court implicitly acknowledged that a radio persona created by the plaintiff was, at least in theory, capable of being viewed as a work of authorship.[11]

If copyright law were to embrace attribution and integrity rights for a broader category of copyrightable works than the narrow designations of visual art currently covered under VARA, conceivably Congress might be inclined to define "personas" as writings within the scope of the statute's coverage.[12] Thus, the personal interests that plaintiffs sometimes attempt to protect through the right of publicity could be addressed directly by copyright law's moral rights provisions. This approach has several distinct advantages, both theoretically and practically, which will be explored below. Of course, a system of "persona" registration also would need to be established. In keeping with traditional copyright doctrine, an individual could be required to file an application to register her persona prior to initiating a lawsuit. Moreover, although the 1976 Copyright Act also requires that original works of authorship be "fixed in any tangible medium of expression, now known or later developed,"[13] this requirement should not provide a major obstacle given that fixations of an individual's persona can be effectuated through any number of means.[14]

A closer look at why we place such a premium on fame can help inform our understanding of the legal protection for personas in the United States. In this regard, it is important to understand our democratic tradition, the "American Dream," our capitalist culture, and celebrity role modeling as factors driving the fame phenomenon in the United States. The most obvious connection between our tradition of democracy and our conception of fame is that in America, "fame has been democratized."[15] The prospect of being famous is now open to everyone, rather than reserved for a select, elite few.[16] Historically, the American Dream, which is strongly tied to our democratic tradition, embodied a political element (e.g., anyone can grow up to be president),[17] but the development of motion pictures and other modern media provided another context for the American success story. By attributing ordinariness to media celebrities, people nurture the hope that someday they too will be visible to the world at large. Thus, the image of stardom and its emphasis on "consumption, success, and ordinariness" fits perfectly within the contours of the American Dream.[18]

The American public enjoys identifying with its celebrities. People like viewing celebrities as mirror images of themselves. Studies have shown that "people's favourite stars tend to be of the same sex as themselves."[19] One of the defining characteristics of the famous is their ability to consume, and Americans love to model celebrities' buying patterns.[20] Notwithstanding the economic crisis in recent years, our capitalist tradition and the notion of the American Dream have fostered the development of a vast American middle class possessing more economic resources and leisure time than was ever possible in past centuries.[21] In the words of Professor Fowles, "[t]he rapid rise of this consumer culture has created a need for prototypical consumers who can model appropriate purchasing decisions."[22] This modeling role is consistent with the American view of celebrities, who are the "acmes of consumerism."[23] Celebrities may spend more money than the average person, but they nonetheless can be imitated on a smaller scale. Moreover, Americans love to imitate their buying patterns to get a feeling of "what it would be like if money were no object."[24] Accordingly, it is not difficult for celebrities to influence buying decisions since the visibility of celebrities and the public's need to know about products lead consumers to listen closely to celebrity endorsements.[25] This pattern has further escalated in recent years with the advent of television and movie-themed Web sites offering fans the ability to buy clothing, accessories, and other items used by their favorite characters on the big and small screen. This shopping-enabled entertainment is fueled by consumerism and celebrity worship.[26] In a sense, then, celebrity endorsements function in much the same way as do trademarks—to communicate information about the product. Celebrity in America thus is proof of the American Dream of money and power, and our capitalist culture ensures that the benefits of this American Dream accrue not only to the celebrities themselves, but also to the businesses and causes the celebrities endorse.[27]

Thus, the influences of the American Dream, capitalism, and consumerism help to explain our gravitation toward the right of publicity. A legal framework that allows people to retain the economic rewards of fame makes sense in this country because our culture holds out the promise that anyone is capable of achieving greatness. Allowing people to own the economic benefits flowing from the cachet of fame thus serves as a measure of security and comfort for all Americans. Interestingly, the economic orientation of these influences probably also explains why a conception of the right of publicity that protects not only economic interests but also morally based interests has been slow to develop.[28]

Of course, all the cultural messages conveyed by celebrities would be impossible to communicate without the technological mediums of expression. Without doubt, the communication industries derive enormous economic benefits from the celebrity phenomenon in this country. Daniel Boorstin has observed that "[t]oday every American, child or adult, encounters a vastly larger number of names, faces, and voices than at any earlier period."[29] The means through which these encounters are accomplished are the various branches of the mass media, whose development is closely tied to the growth of the fame phenomenon in this country.[30] Our society's view of fame was most influenced at the outset by print, and then was completely revolutionized in the wake of the birth of film and broadcasting.[31] Today, the Internet accelerates this tendency in an unprecedented manner. Thus, the power of the media in our times cannot be overstated.

The media revolution has fostered the multifaceted process of packaging the celebrity persona, one of the most integral factors fueling our society's fascination with fame. The complex celebrity packaging is engaged in by virtually all branches of the modern mass media and its accumulative effect is what gives celebrity status its current impact.[32] Today, "visibility-building" not only is a process, but also a big business. The manner in which celebrities are packaged currently takes the form of a complete media construction package, in which their individual achievements are processed in the context of both their prior works as well as their media image. The "hype" surrounding their achievements essentially establishes a trademark of attributes by which the celebrity is known and recognized.

The strong emphasis on the packaging of the celebrity product may be of relatively recent origins, but the first well-known example of the deliberate manufacturing of a celebrity's image occurred in 1910. Movie producer Carl Laemmle, who later established Universal Pictures, hired Florence Lawrence, known by the American audience as the "Biograph Girl," and planted in a St. Louis newspaper a story about her tragic, premature death in a trolley car accident. Subsequently, Laemmle announced that the story was a lie and had her make a tremendously publicized appearance in St. Louis, all with the objective of giving his independent production company an edge over the Motion Picture Patents Company, the industry leader at that time.[33] Today, such efforts are far more abundant, although no less calculated.

The celebrity-packaging strategies established near the turn of the century remained widely in use until the early 1950s, and some of these techniques are used even today.[34] Still, the presentation to the public of celebrities and politicians such as Elvis, the Beatles, and John F. Kennedy had a much more innocent feel than the promotions of current celebrities. Moreover, the technologies have evolved considerably, and public perceptions and reactions have kept pace with these changes. The striking popularity of the Internet undoubtedly will continue to yield even more ways of packaging celebrities and exploiting the celebrity phenomenon.

The amount of work, thought, and planning that goes into controlling and planting star information is extremely surprising to those who have never given the matter much thought. One of the most interesting and comprehensive studies of this topic is the work of sociologist Joshua Gamson, *Claims to Fame*.[35] Gamson probes the fabric of the celebrity packaging process by exploring not only what the texts are saying about celebrities but also by researching the celebrity production process and studying audience reaction through focus groups and firsthand observations of celebrity events. Among other things, his work documents how celebrity stories typically are planted by publicists in accordance with certain patterns and themes and consist of semi-fictional events; how the management process frequently results in a tug-of-war between the celebrities, their publicists, and the media organizations, and how insignificant the consumer audience essentially is to the entire process.[36] The reader of Gamson's work will find herself pondering whether the media's celebrity packaging processes are simply a response to society's needs for celebrities or whether society's needs are in part being defined by the media's activities.

Viewed in this light, it is manifest that celebrities themselves laboriously construct their personas, and they enlist the cooperation of the media and other entities to package and promote their personas as images. In this construction process, the celebrity does not act alone, given the substantial assistance provided by publicists, fashion advisors, media consultants, fitness trainers, and the like. Scholars of the postmodern, such as Rosemary Coombe, emphasize that celebrities often invoke earlier celebrities as well as cultural reference points in constructing their personas.[37] Moreover, Susan Scafidi and Justin Hughes have focused specifically on the role of audience groups that have contributed to the creation of celebrity personas.[38] This collaborative process, however, also lies at the heart of the issue whether celebrity personas should enjoy exclusively the legal ability to maintain the integrity of their persona-texts.

In the context of personas, perhaps the most extreme example of the ability of an individual to claim ownership of a text to which others have contributed involves right of publicity protection for characters played by particular actors in movies or television. In these instances, a consideration of other people's efforts in constructing a celebrity's persona is perhaps the most compelling since it can be argued, quite persuasively, that the character is as much the creation of the individual playing the character as the author of the script and the show's producer. The Third Circuit considered this issue in a suit brought by George McFarland, who played the character "Spanky" in the original movie and television versions of *Our Gang and Little Rascals,* against a restaurant that had misappropriated his name and likeness.[39] Applying New Jersey law, the court viewed the concept of "associative value" as the heart of the issue.[40] Specifically, to the extent the character has become "so associated" with the actor "that it becomes inseparable from the actor's own public image, the actor obtains an interest in the image" that enables him to prevent misappropriation.[41] Other courts have followed a similar analysis in favoring the publicity plaintiff only "when it is shown that the two personalities are inseparable in the public's mind."[42] This view recognizes that the actor playing the character is the most direct link to the character in the public's mind in those instances where the "associative value" is high, even though others may be involved in the character's presentation to the public.

Of course, production companies still own the rights to make derivative works of their shows and invariably, they select other actors to play already developed characters in sequels and reunion shows when the original actors are not available. Occasionally, original actors must be replaced even during the original runs of television shows as was the case when Lecy Goranson, the actress who played daughter Becky in the long-running comedy *Roseanne*, went to college and was replaced for a period with Sarah Chalke. Ninth Circuit Judge Alex Kozinski has criticized the expansive scope of the right of publicity generally and particularly in connection with its application to television characters.[43] His concerns have merit to the extent the doctrine would prevent the use of a character developed by a particular actor in a derivative work to which the production company owns the copyright.[44] On the other hand, when an independent character virtually defines the public persona of a particular actor, the actor still has a direct interest in public presentations of the character embodying the actor's likeness.

Thus, despite the efforts of other parties, celebrities still maintain the most direct connection to their personas, even when these personas are intimately tied to an independent character. Those who assist the celebrity in creating a marketable image typically are paid handsomely for their time and efforts. Further, when a celebrity borrows from the cultural fabric in creating her persona, it is still the unique combination of the past and the celebrity's original contributions that give the persona its present appeal.

Other types of property are subject to individual ownership and control despite the existence of multiple influences in its creation.[45] For example, trademark law furnishes a strong analogy to the right of publicity because ownership of both publicity rights and trademarks constitutes a right to a signal, or control over an information-filled message that flows from the owner to the public. The content of a trademark's signal often is derived from advertising, and therefore, its meaning typically is a function of the efforts not only of the owner, but more importantly, of the advertising agencies that devise the clever advertising techniques that help to establish the meaning of a particular mark and the audiences who respond to this message. Yet, no question exists that the producer of the good or service to which the trademark is attached is the owner of the mark. Similarly, the extent to which works of art or literature are valued often derives from their popularity. The value of such copyrighted works may be viewed as a social construct, the product of forces operating independently of the author. Society does not deprive the owners of famous trademarks or the copyright owners of popular works of art or literature of their rights just because the public has played some role in placing a value on these works.

The reality that a particular individual's constructed image derives from the efforts of people in addition to that of the persona should not impact the ownership of the value flowing from the persona-text, or the level of control that may be exercised with respect to its use. The effort in constructing the celebrity persona-text represents an intellectual, emotional, and physical effort on the part of the celebrity similar to that engaged in by any author. This effort requires protection, not just from economic encroachment, but also from damage to the human spirit as a result of unauthorized uses of the persona the celebrity would find objectionable on moral grounds. The impact of decisions regarding the use of a celebrity's persona-text are felt more directly by the celebrity rather than by anyone else. As Mark McKenna observes, "because an individual bears uniquely any costs attendant to the meaning of her identity, she has an important interest in controlling uses of her identity that affect her ability to author that meaning."[46] Identity is a concept completely intrinsic to the individual to whom it is attached and therefore properly subject to that individual's control.[47]

Publicity actions typically are regarded as the means of achieving compensation for the loss of financial gain associated with a defendant's unauthorized appropriation. In contrast, the right of privacy continues to be regarded as the predicate for actions based on hurt feelings.[48] The reasons for this distinction are partially historical, and partially the result of the legal system's failure to embrace a cohesive legal doctrine that would afford both celebrities and noncelebrities the ability to redress unauthorized appropriations of their identities involving either economic or reputational damage, or both.

As early as the beginning of the twentieth century, some courts recognized the proprietary interest of an individual in her name and likeness when deciding invasion of privacy suits.[49] These courts were compelled to focus on the property right of an individual in her name and likeness to counter the defendants' argument that the law does not afford relief for invasion of privacy unless such an intrusion is accompanied by injury to, or interference with, a person's property.[50] Recognition of the property right of an individual in her name and likeness prompted these courts to recognize explicitly that any value inherent in an individual's likeness belongs exclusively to that individual. Although most of the plaintiffs in the early invasion-of-privacy decisions were private individuals seeking compensation for the injury to their feelings caused by the defendants' appropriation of their likenesses, these decisions nevertheless support the proposition that those wishing to capitalize upon another's name or likeness for advertising purposes should not be free to do so without compensating the principal. Had any of these pioneer plaintiffs instead sought compensation for the economic benefits received by the defendants from the unauthorized appropriation, the right of publicity might have taken an entirely different course.

As legal history stands, however, the right of publicity was not recognized officially as a legal theory distinct from the right of privacy until 1953, when the Second Circuit decided *Haelan Laboratories, Inc. v. Topps Chewing Gum, Inc.*, declaring that an individual has, independent of the right of privacy, a right in the publicity value of her photograph.[51] In *Haelan*, the photographs were of baseball players, individuals with obvious celebrity status. Writing back in 1954, Professor Melville Nimmer observed that the right of privacy is inadequate to meet the demands of the entertainment industry, in part because the celebrity status of an individual frequently is construed as a waiver of the right of privacy.[52] Nimmer's analysis seems directly responsive to the situation in *O'Brien v. Pabst Sales Co.*,[53] in which the Fifth Circuit denied recovery to a renowned football player for invasion of his privacy when the defendant company published his picture, without consent, in the 1939 Pabst Football Calendar. The court predicated its holding, in part, upon the plaintiff's status as a public personality who constantly sought publicity in other contexts. Absent from the court's rationale, however, was recognition of the possibility that perhaps the plaintiff might have experienced hurt feelings by virtue of the defendant's particular use of his identity.[54]

Thus, from the outset, confusion surrounded the application of the right of privacy and the right of publicity, particularly in instances in which celebrities were suing for invasion of privacy and noncelebrities were seeking compensation for the appropriation of their identities. At least one court observed explicitly that a private citizen can rely upon the right of privacy to prevent the appropriation of her photograph for commercial purposes, whereas a public figure or celebrity has a "similar" right of publicity.[55] This distinction, however, is not necessarily the norm because celebrities have been able to recover under the right of privacy for mental distress resulting from the unauthorized commercial use of their identities,[56] and private citizens have prevailed under the right of publicity for commercial misappropriations.[57] This confusion regarding the applicability of privacy and publicity is confounded by the reality that in several states such as Nebraska, New York, Virginia, and Wisconsin, privacy statutes make actionable the unauthorized appropriation of personas for all individuals. Moreover, state statutes typically are sufficiently broad to incorporate both commercial and personal interests.[58] A federal district court in New York, the home of many such lawsuits, specifically held that the right of publicity is subsumed in the state statutory right of privacy.[59]

The complexities surrounding the application of the right of publicity surfaced in September, 2006, when the father of Ron Goldman sued to gain control over O. J. Simpson's publicity rights with respect to the celebrity's name, likeness, and persona in order to satisfy the 1997 multimillion-dollar civil wrongful death action judgment. As soon as the lawsuit was announced, intellectual property law professors mused on their listserv for several days as to whether Fred Goldman would, and should, be allowed to control how Simpson's image is used, even if he has a right to receive licensing proceeds deriving from Simpson's right of publicity. The notion that someone other than the persona can control the more "personal" aspects of the right of publicity created a degree of discomfort for most of the participants in this discussion.

Therefore, notwithstanding the confusion between privacy and publicity, and between commercial and personal interests, the reality is that both celebrities and noncelebrities bring actions based on the unauthorized use of their persona-texts that involve morally as well as economically based harms. Although Shakespeare likened the world to a stage and its inhabitants to actors,[60] in the age of "reality television" the line between celebrity and noncelebrity is becoming especially fuzzy. Today, more so than ever before, an increasing number of ordinary people have the opportunity to garner their so-called "fifteen minutes" of fame.[61] Thus, with respect to both celebrities and noncelebrities, the integrity of persona-texts can be damaged by morally based harms in much the same way as other authored texts. Everyone has, to some degree, constructed her own persona-text that is projected to the public. Noncelebrity persona-texts have far less economic value and perhaps are not as deliberately or visibly constructed, but they nonetheless can be viewed as "works of authorship" in just the same way as the celebrity persona-texts. Private individuals, no less than celebrities, manifest associational choices reflecting their character and values, choices that can be viewed as "the text" of their identities.[62]

Morally based objections can take different forms, and the degree of the harm can differ accordingly. In a purely commercial context, for example, an individual can object to the use of her persona in connection with the advertisement of a product that she personally dislikes. In such cases, the individual's dignity is compromised even though the world at large may not realize that the individual feels the way she does about the product, and even though her unauthorized association with the product may not negatively affect her reputation. An even more problematic situation occurs when an individual's persona is used in connection with a product that the individual does not use and with which she would not want to be associated. An example of such a situation is a diet program's appropriation of the persona of an actress who is naturally slender and has never used the program. Such an appropriation not only compromises the actress's credibility but also gives her a reputation for having a tendency to be overweight, which may be both personally and professionally damaging. A more extreme example of this situation occurs when a company invokes an individual's persona in connection with a product that is either inherently or potentially dangerous. For example, in *Tin Pan Apple, Inc. v. Miller Brewing Co.*,[63] a rap group emphasizing avoidance of drugs and alcohol to its youthful listeners brought an action under the New York privacy statute against a beer company that used a look-alike/ sound-alike group in a beer commercial after the original group had declined to appear in the commercial.[64] Such unauthorized uses obviously can adversely affect an individual's personal and professional reputation.

In addition, situations can occur where the plaintiff is not objecting to the particular context or content of the use itself, but rather to the unauthorized use as a general matter. For example, some celebrities eschew all forms of endorsements and shy away from any type of publicity that would place them in the public eye. Litigation on this point has involved the deceased actor Cary Grant and the late former first lady Jacqueline Kennedy Onassis.[65] Another example of this situation is *Waits v. Frito-Lay, Inc.*,[66] discussed in Chapter 3, in which Tom Waits sued Frito-Lay for using a sound-alike in a commercial for chips, thus undermining the integrity of Waits' artistic image and persona.

Morally based objections also can occur in conjunction with less clear-cut commercial appropriations that often are the most difficult controversies to resolve due to the strong First Amendment interests at stake. Many of the same First Amendment considerations discussed in Chapter 5 apply both in the context of personas as well as more conventional works of authorship. In fact, because celebrities in particular "take on public meaning, the appropriation of their likenesses may have important uses in uninhibited debate on public issues, particularly debates about culture and values."[67] Thus, the First Amendment concerns must be taken seriously.

In general, informational uses are not likely to result in morally based objections, although in certain situations they can. Suppose an individual objects to the publication of an unauthorized biography that depicts her in an unflattering light. A useful example is furnished by *Loft v. Fuller*,[68] in which the wife and son of a pilot killed in a well-publicized plane crash brought an action based on a work of nonfiction that referred to the decedent as a "reappearing ghost."[69] The court denied their cause of action under the relevant state statute prohibiting the unauthorized publication of someone's name or likeness for commercial or advertising purposes because the language of the statute specifically provides that it shall not apply in the case of any book that is published "as part of a bona fide news report or presentation having a current and legitimate public interest."[70] From a First Amendment standpoint, it seems clear that society's interest in the dissemination of information should outweigh the plaintiff's interest in these circumstances.

More frequently, plaintiffs have raised morally based objections in the context of entertainment-oriented uses as opposed to informational uses, since creators in the entertainment arena generally can invoke an individual's persona in a greater variety of ways than is the case with informationally oriented works. For example, in *Valentine v. C.B.S., Inc.*,[71] the plaintiff sued the writers and distributors of a popular song about a murder trial in which the plaintiff was a witness. The plaintiff claimed that the song defamed her because it implied that she participated in the conspiracy of a crime and that the defendants failed to check the veracity of the lyrics. The court held, however, that the plaintiff's interpretation of the song was unreasonable.[72]

Where it is obvious that the defendant's work is fiction, the First Amendment argument generally should outweigh whatever contextual or morally based objections a plaintiff may raise. With respect to pure fictionalizations clearly marketed as such, there is virtually no chance of public deception or tarnishment of the persona's reputation. Thus, the basis for an individual's moral objection is diminished in these circumstances. With respect to fictionalized works, an argument also can be made that typically, they derive their appeal more from the independent contribution of the work's creator, as opposed to the persona-text. Moreover, there would be a tremendous chilling of incentives if writers were forced to compensate someone every time they created a character who resembled or was based upon a real individual. These points are illustrated in *Hicks v. Casablanca Records*,[73] in which the heirs and assignees of Agatha Christie sought to enjoin movie producers and a publisher from distributing a movie and book fictionalizing an actual eleven-day disappearance in the mystery writer's life. The works in question portrayed Christie "as an emotionally unstable woman, who, during her eleven-day disappearance, engages in a sinister plot to murder her husband's mistress, in an attempt to regain the alienated affections of her husband."[74] The court held that since "books and movies are vehicles through which ideas and opinions are disseminated," the free speech interests should prevail over those of the right of publicity.[75]

More recently, the Sixth Circuit reached the same conclusion in a case involving a miniseries depicting the story of the singing group *The Temptations* that was based on a novel written by Otis Williams, a founding member of the group. The plaintiffs in that right of publicity case included relatives of other members of the group as well as Williams's first wife and the group's first agent, all of whom were alleging that the miniseries contained false and unflattering depictions of either the plaintiffs themselves or their deceased relatives. The court concluded, however, that the right of publicity does not extend to "fictionalized likenesses in a work protected by the First Amendment and the advertising incidental to such uses."[76]

The analysis becomes far more complicated when the unauthorized use is a combination of fiction and fact. According to literary critic Michiko Kakutani, we are being besieged with "books, movies and television docudramas that hopscotch back and forth between the realms of history and fiction, reality and virtual reality, with impunity."[77] Kakutani is especially critical of such works because "they do not even announce themselves as works of fiction, but instead masquerade as the truth," and "unabashedly play both to people's hunger for information and relevance, and to their appetite for entertainment."[78]

Kakutani's concerns might be alleviated, at least in part, if the producers of fictionalized accounts resorted more frequently to using disclaimers. In 2000, Warner Brothers released the movie *The Perfect Storm*, which told the story of a fishing vessel that was lost at sea off the New England coast due to a powerful storm. The movie admittedly took liberties in conjunction with its negative depictions of several of the individual crew members and their families, including the main character, the ship's captain. The relatives of those depicted sued under a state statute for unauthorized commercial appropriation of the decedents' names and likenesses, but the court found that the defendants' use was an expressive use under the statute.[79] The court noted, although did not emphasize in its analysis, that the movie did not claim to be factually accurate and in fact included a fictionalization disclaimer as part of the closing credits.[80] Admittedly, the relatives of the deceased crew members still brought suit despite the disclaimer, but the case nonetheless suggests the potential of disclaimers to mitigate the negative impact of morally based harms in situations where enjoining a particular use might not otherwise be feasible given our First Amendment jurisprudence.

Other examples illustrate the difficulties of reconciling First Amendment concerns with morally based harms resulting from unauthorized uses in contexts other than pure fictionalizations. Consider comedian Jackie Mason's suit against Jews for Jesus, based on the group's use of his name, likeness, and act in a pamphlet featuring a caricature of Mason on the front and a riff on one of his routines inside. Mason is an ordained rabbi and the self-proclaimed founding member of "Jews for It's OK to Say Merry Christmas," but he is not a Jew for Jesus. He claimed that the group's use of his attributes and personality to attract attention and converts has damaged him to an "incalculable degree."[81] This situation is analogous to the examples discussed in Chapter 1 involving the objectionable contexts in which the works of Frederick Hart, Carl Perkins, and Connie Francis were used.[82] To the extent the facts of this case suggest a prominent use of Mason's persona with a high potential for unjust enrichment, Mason's claim is a sympathetic one. The facts of this case also suggest a highly coercive, prominent use of Mason's persona, especially with respect to the cover of the defendant's pamphlet which featured a caricature of Mason accompanied by the legend: "Jackie Mason . . . A Jew for Jesus!?"[83] Nonetheless, the court denied his motion for a preliminary injunction.[84]

In a similar vein are two cases from New York, *Nussenzweig v. DiCorcia*[85] and *Arrington v. New York Times Co.*[86] In *Nussenzweig*, the defendant, a professional and well-known photographer, took a series of candid photographs on the streets of New York, without the permission of his subjects, which he compiled into a particular collection. One of the photographs he used was of the plaintiff, a Hasidic Jew who believes that the defendant's use of his image violates the Second Commandment's prohibition against graven images. The suit was brought under New York's privacy statute that requires that the use be "for advertising or for trade" in order to be actionable.[87] The court accepted the defendant's argument that art is exempt from the privacy statute as protected speech, and concluded that a "profit motive in itself does not necessarily compel a conclusion that art has been used for trade purposes."[88]

In *Arrington,* upon which *Nussenzweig* relied, the plaintiff was an African-American man whose picture, but not name, appeared on the cover of the *New York Times Magazine* in connection with an article about the expanding black middle class in America. The plaintiff disagreed with the views in the article and alleged that he and readers who knew him found it "insulting, degrading, distorting and disparaging," thus subjecting him to public scorn and ridicule.[89] Here too, the suit was brought pursuant to New York's privacy statute and the court also held in favor of the defendant. Both *Nussenzweig* and *Arrington* upheld First Amendment protections in the face of "deeply and spiritually offensive" uses,[90] thus demonstrating that speech causing emotional harm to particular individuals cannot be regulated in all contexts. Yet, these cases have a different feel from the one involving Jackie Mason in that they involve a less visible or prominent focus on the persona. In *Nussenzweig,* the plaintiff's picture appeared as part of a collection; in *Arrington,* the reference was much less direct in that the plaintiff was not a celebrity and his name was not used. If personas are considered within the scope of eligible "works of authorship" for purposes of moral rights protection, the First Amendment can accommodate a modest disclaimer remedy especially in instances such as the Jackie Mason situation in which the unauthorized use of the persona plays a significant role in the appropriator's work and entails a significant moral harm to the persona.

The technology that makes virtual actors, or synthespians, a present-day reality presents additional difficulties with respect to preserving the authorship dignity of persona-texts. Modern performance capture technology allows for the production of a "digital blueprint" of a source actor that can be stored, modified, and eventually used in ways that could be offensive to the actor upon whose image the synthespian is based. In 2006, the late actor Paul Newman testified before the Connecticut legislature in support of stronger publicity laws given the potential negative impact of technology on an individual's image.[91] If a producer owns the copyright in the virtual clone rather than the source actor, the latter may not be in a position to prevent these objectionable uses of her digital persona.[92] Although a contract provision might be sufficient to protect the interests of more established source actors, such protection may be beyond the reach of less well-known personalities. One commentator has observed that the potential for such exploitation of source actors "borders on de facto virtual economic and dignitary slavery."[93] The rights of source actors in these situations are not clear under the current law.

The foregoing discussion of situations involving unauthorized uses of persona-texts deemed objectionable by either the persona or a relative of the deceased persona illustrates that when noncommercial, unauthorized uses are at issue, First Amendment concerns will be a particular focus. First Amendment considerations also permeate the analysis with respect to other difficult right of publicity issues such as the right's scope and its application to deceased personas. For example, one important area of litigation concerns which attributes of an individual's identity should be protected by the right of publicity. Some courts have approved expansive applications of the right of publicity by holding that the doctrine protects aspects of an individual's identity such as a nickname,[94] and a distinctive racing car.[95] In an opinion that proved to be controversial, the Ninth Circuit held that Vanna White could maintain a common law right of publicity action against a company that used in an advertisement, without her consent, a robot attired to resemble White and posted next to a game board recognizable as the *Wheel of Fortune* game show set.[96] With respect to noncelebrities, and more regionally known personas, the issue of which attributes should be protected is even more complex because public recognition of their identities is community based, as opposed to determined on a national scale. Still, if public recognition were to be the touchstone for determining which attributes should be covered by the right of publicity, at a minimum the names and likenesses of every individual would be within the scope of protection because every persona is identified by at least these two attributes.[97]

In many of the cases discussed in this chapter, the individual whose identity has been appropriated is no longer alive. Many of the state statutes governing the right of publicity recognize that the right is descendible, meaning that it can be exercised by the heirs and assignees of the person to whom the right originally attached. The statutes vary in terms of how many years after a person's death his or her right of publicity is protected, and the range is as wide as an initial ten-year period in Tennessee[98] to 100 years in Indiana and Oklahoma.[99] In the state of Washington, an individual's persona is protected against unauthorized exploitation for ten years after death, whereas a "personality," defined as someone whose publicity has commercial value, enjoys protection for seventy-five years after death.[100] In California, legislation was recently passed extending the seventy-year postmortem protection to celebrities who died prior to the enactment of the 1984 California statute providing for a descendible right of publicity.[101] In other jurisdictions, the right of publicity is descendible as a matter of common law rather than by statute.[102] In those jurisdictions that allow the unauthorized appropriation of protected attributes to be actionable under the state's privacy law,[103] there is disagreement regarding whether relatives of a deceased persona are precluded from suing since the right of privacy is held to be personal in nature.[104]

Although protection for an individual's right of publicity following death is justified to some degree when the right of publicity is conceived solely as a property right steeped in economic benefits,[105] the argument for extending such protection is less compelling when a relative of a deceased persona is attempting to protect the integrity of a persona-text. Granted, often the relatives of a deceased persona will want to protect the reputational interests of the persona-text. On the other hand, if the reasons for protecting the integrity of an individual's text—be it a work of authorship or a persona—center on the personal nature of the text and its relationship to the author, allowing others the ability to sue for such violations seems to embody a misinterpretation of the theoretical predicate for protection.[106] Moreover, limiting protection for the integrity interests of a persona-text to living individuals would promote a more uniform application of the law in this particular context. Under this standard, advertisers who use a persona-text of someone who has died in a way that arguably undermines its integrity would no longer face liability in certain jurisdictions but not others. Even if state publicity law continued to govern the economic interests of deceased personas, uniformity could be achieved with respect to unauthorized uses that implicate integrity concerns.

Thus, if copyright law were to be reformulated to incorporate enhanced moral rights protections, it is important to contemplate the extension of such protection to persona-texts. Indeed, the dignity interests at stake in moral rights claims often are operative in right of publicity disputes focusing on the reputational and personality interests of personas. From a conceptual standpoint, it makes sense to address these dignity interests through moral rights law. The type of federal protection I propose, for both personas and conventional works or authorship, concerns misappropriations or mutilations in situations where damage to the human spirit, rather than economic harm, is the focus. In contrast, protection for the more economic aspects of publicity rights still can be achieved pursuant to state right of publicity statutes, most of which cover only commercial uses.[107]

Another advantage to considering persona-texts within the scope of moral rights protection is that courts could avoid becoming enmeshed in the commercial/noncommercial distinction that has plagued the right of publicity case law.[108] Critics of the right of publicity argue that the doctrine lacks a principled mechanism for limiting the scope of the right.[109] If, however, the dignity interests of personas were treated as part of federal copyright law's moral rights doctrine, not only would there be a uniform application but also the limiting doctrines that would be applicable to moral rights generally could be applied to personas. As discussed more fully in Chapter 10, invoking these limiting doctrines would be especially helpful in facilitating a resolution of those situations involving noncommercial appropriations presenting conflicts between the rights of persona-texts and free speech or societal access issues.

CHAPTER 9

Human Rights Laws and Authorship Norms

AS LAURENCE HELFER NOTES, "[h]uman rights and intellectual property, two bodies of law that were once strangers, are now becoming increasingly intimate bedfellows."[1] Given this intimacy, can we justify enhanced protection for moral rights on the ground that they are human rights? The basis for situating moral rights within a human rights discourse lies in the dignity interest with which both areas are concerned.

Three documents compose the core legal framework for the "International Bill of Human Rights." The first of these key instruments, the Universal Declaration of Human Rights (UDHR), was adopted in 1948.[2] As a declaration rather than a covenant, the UDHR does not represent binding international law. However, according to many authorities, the UDHR has the force of "customary" international law and is considered an authentic interpretation of the United Nations Charter.[3] The other two instruments composing the International Bill of Human Rights are covenants and were passed decades later.[4]

Mary Ann Glendon skillfully documents the story of how the UDHR came about in *A World Made New*. Although she does not specifically address moral rights in her book, her treatment underscores that World War II and the Holocaust were the events motivating the framers of the UDHR.[5] During the drafting process, the UDHR delegates repeatedly condemned the numerous atrocities committed by the Nazis during the war, including forced intellectual labor such as that suffered by Dina Babbitt, the artist whose plight was discussed in Chapter 7.[6]

The key UDHR provision dealing with human rights in relation to moral rights is Article 27, Paragraph 2, which provides that "[e]veryone has the right to the protection of the moral and material interests resulting from any scientific, literary or artistic production of which he is the author."[7] It is interesting to note that the UDHR language does not require an author to create a copyrightable work to secure protection. This provision was extremely controversial because there was no international consensus on how interests in intellectual creations should be protected. The protection of authors' moral interests was added by the French delegate who was prompted by the lack of protection for this interest in the Anglo-American copyright regimes.[8] Despite the objection by American and British delegates to the "moral and material interests" inclusion on the ground that this type of right should more properly be considered within the domain of copyrights, the provision ultimately was included after considerable discussion.[9] Still, there was disagreement with respect to whether the protection of interests in intellectual property should be seen as a basic human right.[10] Even with respect to those who voted favorably for the provision, there were mixed and varied motives. Specifically, not all of the delegates who cast a favorable vote necessarily agreed with the French delegate's concern for moral rights.[11] Nonetheless, according to Paul Torremans, the UDHR embodies "the single most authoritative source of human rights norms," and has served as a basis for validating authors' moral rights in several cases.[12]

The second instrument providing additional authoritative support for a human rights framework in intellectual property is the International Convention on Economic, Social and Cultural Rights of 1966 (ICESCR).[13] As a covenant, ICESCR represents binding international law for over 190 member nations.[14] Although the United States signed the Covenant in 1979, to date it has not been ratified in this country.[15] Therefore, ICESCR is not binding here, unlike the Berne Convention or TRIPS. Article 15(1)(c) of the ICESCR essentially borrowed language from Article 27 of the UDHR by recognizing the right of everyone "[t]o benefit from the protection of the moral and material interests resulting from any scientific, literary or artistic production of which he is the author."[16] This language also is similar to that of Article 27(2) of the UDHR in that authors of works that are not copyrightable can be protected. The material interests referred to in the ICESCR were based on the right to just remuneration for intellectual labor, while the moral interests were based on the French *droit moral*. Significantly, the legislative history of the ICESCR also illustrates an ongoing debate over intellectual property's worthiness as a human right.[17] Finally, the third instrument, the International Covenant on Civil and Political Rights (ICCPR) was passed in 1966, and became effective on March 23, 1976.[18] The United States fully ratified the ICCPR in 1992. Although the ICCPR does not specifically address intellectual property rights, it does provide protection for the freedom of expression.[19]

Since the beginning of the twenty-first century, the United Nation's Committee on Economic, Social and Cultural Rights (CESCR) has increased its support for a human rights framework for intellectual property rights by focusing on the connection between the protection for intellectual creations and human dignity.[20] The CESCR published a 2001 Statement on Article 15(1)(c)[21] and a 2005 General Comment interpreting this provision.[22] In its 2001 Statement, the CESCR recommended that states take a balancing approach between protecting the intellectual property rights contained in Article 15(1)(c) and "the right to take part in cultural life and to enjoy the benefits of scientific progress" as specified in the balancing provisions of the ICESCR Articles 15(1)(a) & (b).[23] This Statement underscores that the key tension in a human rights framework is the protection of an author's moral and material interests versus the right of the public to enjoy and share in the benefits of works. The Statement provides that "[t]he end which intellectual property protections should serve is the objective of human well-being, to which international human rights instruments give legal expression."[24] Thus, it "encourages the development of intellectual property systems and the use of intellectual property rights in a balanced manner that meets the objective of providing protection for the moral and material interests of authors," while simultaneously promoting "the enjoyment of these and other human rights."[25]

The 2005 General Comment picks up where the 2001 Statement leaves off, lending additional support for a human rights framework for moral interests.[26] It begins by stating that the right to the protection of interests in intellectual creations "derives from the inherent dignity and worth of all persons" and that these rights should be contrasted with "most legal entitlements recognized in intellectual property systems."[27] The Committee considered moral and material interests to be of primary importance to the dignity of the author because they safeguard "the personal link between authors and their creations."[28] In speaking of "moral interests," the General Comment referred to the intention of article 27(2) of the UDHR as recognizing the "intrinsically personal character of every creation of the human mind and the ensuing durable link between creators and their creations."[29] According to the Comment, the moral rights within the scope of the ICESCR include the rights of attribution and integrity.[30] Thus, individual authors' moral interests are indeed conceived of as human rights.[31]

In the end, the drafting processes of these documents are characterized more by the similarity among the participants than by their differences. Peter Yu notes that notwithstanding their differences, the human rights instruments discussed above do not dictate a particular level of protection with respect to the right to the protection of intellectual creations. Thus, "the drafting history strongly suggests that the drafters were determined to create a universal document."[32] Yet, there remain differing opinions concerning whether intellectual property rights such as copyright can properly be considered within the scope of human rights. It is fair to say that although some types of intellectual property rights legitimately can be seen as having a strong human rights basis, this is not necessarily the case with all intellectual property rights.[33]

Despite the conceptual and practical difficulties of viewing all intellectual property rights as human rights, moral rights present a special situation. Although moral rights may not rise to the level of other rights we think of as human rights, arguably they present a more compelling case for human rights based on their concern with the dignity of human beings.[34] Laurence Helfer, pointing to the CESCR's 2005 General Comment, emphasizes a core moral type of right embracing a "zone of personal autonomy in which authors can achieve their creative potential, control their productive output, and lead independent, intellectual lives."[35] Paul Torremans suggests that "the higher the level of creativity and the more important the input of the creator is, the stronger the Human Rights claim."[36] This observation would appear to underscore the human rights significance for works meeting the standard of heightened originality with substantial creativity. Peter Drahos also hesitatingly posits that a personality-based theory might justify at least some intellectual property rights as human rights.[37]

Still, the issue of moral rights being accepted as a human right is far from an easy call. In the first place, to the extent something is categorized as a human right, it is beyond the power of individual states to adjust for their convenience or preference.[38] As the late Professor H. G. Schemers concluded, "human rights are of such importance that their international protection includes the right, perhaps even the obligation, of international enforcement."[39] Moreover, even if one were to accept the premise that, notwithstanding the above concern, universal recognition equates to a universal, human rights norm as a general matter,[40] with respect to moral rights there is the additional complication that they are not universally recognized, or at least not recognized in a universal manner. In discussing the historical compliance with Article 6bis of Berne, Justin Hughes has observed that "state practice has been so varied that heightened deference to national autonomy should pervade any analysis of the 6bis provisions."[41] Specifically, he demonstrates that in the period following 1928, several Berne members complied with their 6bis obligations in a weak manner that was very similar to current compliance by the United States.[42] Presently, universal recognition presents an especially high hurdle in light of the United States' failure to embrace its moral rights obligation under Berne. Recall from Chapter 4 that the United States was particularly instrumental in the elimination of article 6bis from the TRIPs agreement, and thus successfully avoided being subjected to the mandatory dispute resolution process on moral rights despite our obligation to enforce moral rights pursuant to Berne.[43]

At best, then, we can say that moral rights enjoy widespread recognition. For example, the history of the drafting of the UDHR and ICESCR shows that although there may not have been a universal consensus as to whether moral rights are human rights, there was a significant recognition that these interests are deemed worthy of protection in a human rights framework. I suggest that rather than asking whether moral rights are within the scope of human rights, it is more appropriate to focus on moral rights as "authorship norms," or common rules of engagement shared among the majority of interested citizens. Although traditionally norms are developed and enforced outside the legal system,[44] they also can influence the development of the law by creating de facto standards that can either substitute for the law or encourage legal compliance.[45] Thus, if attribution and integrity interests are understood as widespread authorship norms, the question is whether and how these norms ought to be translated into our legal system.

In bolstering the claim that attribution and integrity interests constitute authorship norms, it is instructive to consider legal traditions in addition to those of the common and civil law. Jewish law presents a distinct legal tradition that can be mined for its treatment of these interests. Although most intellectual property laws are derived from the system of royal privilege-giving prevalent in medieval Europe,[46] the origins of intellectual property law under the Jewish legal system are unique. Jewish copyright law originated with a dispute in the sixteenth century involving the unauthorized copying of a new edition of Moses Maimonides's code of Jewish law along with original commentaries.[47]

With respect to attribution and integrity interests, however, the origins of Jewish law are far more ancient. In fact, according to Jewish tradition, a lack of regard for these interests was the cause of the first sin and thus responsible for the downfall of humanity. In chapter 2, verse 17 of Genesis, God commanded Adam not to *eat* from the Tree of Knowledge.[48] In chapter 3, verse 3 of Genesis, Eve tells the serpent that she may not eat the fruit or *touch* it, or she will die.[49] The tradition of the Oral Law, used by Rabbinic authorities to understand Biblical passages, reveals that the serpent shoved Eve against the fruit and then said to her, "See, you did not die." As she saw that she did not die from touching the fruit, the serpent convinced her that there would be no negative consequences from eating the fruit. The tradition then explains how this happened. Adam wanted to add a safeguard on the commandment of not eating the fruit, so he said not to even *touch* it. Nonetheless, Adam did not tell Eve that the commandment not to touch the fruit was his own innovation. He let her think that is was God's commandment. Thus, according to Jewish tradition, by modifying God's original statement and by not correctly identifying what was God's command and what was his own addition, Adam triggered the expulsion from Eden.[50] In this narrative, Adam's incorporation of the safeguard regarding not touching the fruit and his failure to properly attribute this safeguard violated the meaning and message of God's original words. Recall from Chapter 2 that the parallel between human and Divine creativity is emphasized in the Rabbinic tradition that understands human "creativity" as rooted in the inspirational element of mirroring God's creative capacities.[51]

Jewish law regarding attribution and integrity flows from the concept of *duty* as opposed to *right*. Although the moral lesson regarding the rights of attribution and integrity derives from this Creation narrative in Genesis, all relevant works of Jewish law on these points cite as the direct legal source a statement from the Ethics of the Fathers, a tractate embodying the accumulated ethical and moral wisdom of the Jewish Sages dating back to between 200 and 500 CE.[52] The importance of having one's words properly attributed to the original source is emphasized in the Ethics of the Fathers in the following verse: "Whoever repeats a thing in the name of the one who said it brings redemption to the world."[53] The commentary emphasizes that "[o]ne must display indebtedness to a source and mention him by name," thus proscribing taking false credit for someone else's statement.[54] This verse also implicitly embodies a responsibility to quote the source accurately. Based on the language of this tractate, the responsibility for accurate quotation and attribution is viewed as a duty of the second speaker rather than a right of the first speaker. A duty, indeed, is perpetual; a right lasts only so long as the first speaker or her representative has the ability to enforce it.

The Ethics of the Fathers is contained in the Talmud, the central book of Jewish law encompassing over forty tractates of materials with a multitude of commentary.[55] Significantly, the Talmud as a whole underscores the importance of attribution by establishing attribution through several generations of students and teachers.[56] For example, from an attribution standpoint, the phrase "Rabbi X said" as used in the Talmud does not necessarily mean "Rabbi X himself" but rather Rabbi X's later disciples.[57] In the case of a disciple quoting his master, the omission of the true author or source was "probably a matter of convenience."[58] Authorship of the material in the Talmud thus cannot be regarded the same as authorship in Western terms.[59] In contrast, as Jewish Studies scholar Sacha Stern notes, "if the true author of a saying is not obvious or known to all, failure to attribute is considered plagiaristic and condemned."[60] Therefore, because the idea of misattribution in the Talmud must be accessed within its tradition of flexible, collection authorship,[61] "only *deceptive* plagiarism would have constituted a breach of the practice of attribution."[62]

In contrast to Jewish law's morally based concern with attribution and integrity interests, the censorship and licensing regimes in seventeenth-century England with respect to literary works represent some of the earliest *de facto* attribution and integrity protections. In order to earn the exclusive copyright protection of the Stationers' Company charter, a publisher needed to obtain the author's written permission.[63] Specifically, once the censors operating in connection with the Stationers' Company in London approved a particular version of a book, a bookseller had an exclusive license to print that would be jeopardized by making modifications. Moreover, licensing protected against an author being designated as the author of a work she did not create. In addition, as Susan Liemer has observed, "misattribution or modification of a work would thwart the registration system upon which the monopoly relied, because then something other than the registered work would be competing in the marketplace."[64] Thus, this intricate dynamic protected aspects of authors' rights in a limited way, although the impetus was economic concern with works registered to guild members rather than a focus on authorship dignity. Still, there was general displeasure by authors with respect to their overall lack of control regarding their creations.

As discussed in Chapter 4, moral rights developed in the civil law tradition in the nineteenth century, and it is in this milieu that we see most clearly the author's personal interest in her creations as a justification for embracing moral rights as authorship norms.[65] The French choice of the term *moral* for the designation of this personality interest underscores the idea of moral rights encompassing authorship norms given that the French definition of "moral" has a broad meaning that pertains to principles or rules of appropriate conduct in a particular society.[66] Moreover, the civil law tradition supports both attribution and integrity interests equally as authorship norms. In contrast, the United States copyright discourse always has been very rights centered. Recall that utilitarianism is the predominant copyright justification in the United States, as evidenced by the Copyright Clause's affording protection for a limited time as an incentive to create.[67] Although the history of the Copyright Clause specifically contains evidence of a focus on utilitarian concerns, this perspective does not have to represent the entire story. Assuming the ongoing relevance of the utilitarian conception that has shaped our thinking about copyrights, the question is whether we are free at this point in time to incorporate additional narratives into the discourse-shaping copyright law. I suggest that we are free to do so[68] and that pursuant to this perspective, copyright law should be assessed in the context of a more fluid, multidimensional approach.

In recent years scholars and even the judiciary are beginning to call for a more nuanced approach to intellectual property law generally. For example, both Madhavi Sunder and Peter Yu have argued that the utilitarian economically oriented justifications for intellectual property are insufficient and therefore, a broader spectrum of justifications is needed. Specifically, Yu maintains that there is a need for the development of a holistic perspective on intellectual property so that the interface between intellectual property and human rights can be more fully mined.[69] Sunder contends that "intellectual property is about social relations and should serve human values."[70] Thus, whereas the traditional narrative of economic incentive is concerned with fostering creativity, a narrative steeped in social and cultural theory offers a "broader normative purpose for intellectual property."[71] Peter Drahos posits an instrumentalist view of intellectual property that echoes similar themes. He believes that the rights created through intellectual property laws should serve fundamental human needs and values.[72] In his view, therefore, "[v]iewing intellectual property through the prism of human rights discourse will encourage us to think about ways in which the property mechanism might be reshaped to include interests and needs that it currently does not."[73]

This theoretical approach suggests that we should be considering copyright law's underlying theoretical framework as encompassing more than just the conventional utilitarian justification. In *MGM v. Grokster*,[74] the Supreme Court implicitly endorsed this very approach by holding that a defendant can be liable for inducing copyright infringement, even absent specific statutory authority in the copyright statute.[75] In *Grokster*, the defendants distributed software that enabled users to exchange digital media through a peer-to-peer transfer network entirely outside of the defendants' control.[76] The Court invoked the doctrine of inducement familiar under patent law as the basis for the defendants' liability.[77] According to the majority opinion, "the record was replete with evidence that from the moment [the defendants] began to distribute their free software, each one clearly voiced the objective that recipients use it to download copyrighted works, and each took active steps to encourage infringement."[78] This result has been applauded on moral and ethical grounds.[79] In commenting on this decision, Madavi Sunder notes that "the Supreme Court chose to impose liability for what it saw as moral wrongdoing" rather than sanctify the economic argument as "supreme over all other arguments."[80]

A more fluid view of copyright generally would allow us to make room for the inclusion of the right of attribution and even a cabined right of integrity in our legal system. These rights are not concerned with economic reward but instead support a different agenda. A broader view of copyright would allow the United States to recognize explicitly the existence of authorship norms that support moral rights protection. John Merryman perceived these shared authorship norms years ago when he wrote that "the moral right is the product of legal development in western, bourgeois, capitalist nations with whom we have deep cultural affinity."[81] He further remarked that "even though our legal traditions often seem quite different from theirs, the differences are superimposed on a common, shared cultural base."[82] Indeed, the Final Report of the Ad Hoc Working Group on the United States' Adherence to the Berne Convention similarly recognizes attribution and integrity as part of the authorship norms of "fair dealing." The Report states that "[f]ailure to identify the author on the work defeats the statutory purpose; and is 'unfair dealing' with respect to the author and public."[83] It also recognized the norms of integrity protections by noting that courts could protect against integrity violations by invoking implied covenants of fair dealing and good faith, as well as resorting to industry practice to close contractual loopholes.[84]

Moreover, even within our current framework, attribution in particular exists as an authorship norm even if it is not explicitly codified in the copyright statute. Attribution violations in general and plagiarism in particular are viewed as moral wrongs in our society among both authors and audiences.[85] Writing from a criminal law perspective with respect to plagiarism, Stuart Green calls the "norm of attribution" as one grounded in the desire for esteem.[86] He sees plagiarism as a corollary to the rule of attribution and argues that they constitute a "powerful pair of social norms."[87] Although attribution and plagiarism share a somewhat similar theoretical basis, they do differ in important respects insofar as a moral rights framework is concerned. First, whereas someone commits plagiarism by copying from deceased authors, the theory underlying the moral right of attribution really applies with the most force during the author's lifetime.[88] Also, the norms of plagiarism are such that the conduct is adjudicated and punished largely within the confines of academic or other such particularized professional spheres.[89] Lastly, plagiarism can occur even if the offender takes a relatively small amount of material or work that is otherwise unprotected by copyright law.[90] In contrast, as Chapter 6 argues, an attribution violation should only be triggered when the offender takes something from a work protected by copyright law (indeed the argument was made that moral rights should apply only to a subset of copyrightable works).

Notwithstanding these distinctions, however, both attribution and plagiarism share a concern for giving credit where credit is due. With respect to both attribution and plagiarism violations, the offender "steals" the credit to which the true author is entitled.[91] The notion that such "theft" is simply wrong represents a powerful authorship norm. Attribution is garnering increased attention by scholars working in law, the sciences, and the humanities.[92] Interestingly, in the intellectual property academy, both low protectionists as well as high protectionists have proposed enhanced protections for attribution. Although it is not surprising that the high protectionists who otherwise favor increased moral rights protections would urge stronger attribution interests,[93] Rebecca Tushnet notes that even low protectionists who place the public interest over that of authors are advancing attribution concerns as "a matter of fairness to authors."[94] Jennifer Rothman argues that attribution customs deserve more consideration because they are motivated by aspirational objectives rather than goals such as avoiding litigation.[95] Greg Lastowka notes that providing attribution protection "would acknowledge the fundamentally different dynamics of open copyright practices and promote the smooth functioning of reputation economies."[96] Scholars also have demonstrated that attribution is important in a wide variety of creative enterprises including cuisine and even scholarship by law professors.[97]

In the United States, the right of integrity is viewed with far more suspicion and resistance than the right of attribution, largely as a result of a culture emphasizing strong First Amendment and public access values. As a result of these concerns, theorists question why the voice of the author of the original text should be privileged above subsequent creators.[98] Charles Beitz indicates that, with respect to the issue of privileging, moral rights laws should somehow take into account the degree to which a work is well-known and widely recognized.[99] Although Beitz does not specifically say why this should be the case, I suggest that the reason has to do with the underlying theory of moral rights as a legal measure designed to safeguard the dignity interests of authors. Recall from Chapter 1 the discussion regarding dignity being realized in the external embodiments of the author's inner creative process.[100] Underlying the importance of the external is, I believe, the idea of the author's esteem that derives from a public acknowledgment of her creative efforts. Authorship dignity is facilitated by an appropriate regard for a work's meaning and for the external embodiment of an author's work as the means through which her message is communicated to the public. As seen through this lens, the damage resulting from a right of integrity violation is particularly problematic when the modified work is linked to the author through specific attribution or widespread public recognition.

Thus, although attribution may present a more clear-cut, and easier to administer area than the right of integrity, both are deeply concerned with the author's dignity and esteem. In order for a right of integrity to be viable in the United States, it will need to balance carefully competing interests and incorporate a large degree of cabining measures. Interestingly, such balancing is characteristic of the human rights instruments discussed at the beginning of this chapter. Both the UDHR and ICESCR contain, in addition to the provisions calling for the author's right to be protected with respect to her moral and material interests,[101] separate provisions emphasizing the public's right to enjoy and benefit from works.[102] In light of the challenge ahead for the right of integrity specifically, and moral rights as a whole, a new paradigm beyond VARA is needed for these interests. Until now, this text has focused on developing a multidimensional theoretical groundwork for moral rights. The final chapter develops the contours of a moral rights framework specific to the interests and needs of the United States.

CHAPTER 10

Looking Forward to Legal Reform

VARA IS THE LOGICAL STARTING POINT for designing stronger moral rights protections. Although VARA has been criticized on the ground that its scope is far too narrow, the real problem is that its confined scope was not the result of thoughtful deliberations regarding the appropriate content of moral rights protection for our particular legal system. The resulting legislation not only is poorly drafted, but also reflects questionable and seemingly inexplicable choices. Any proposal for enhanced moral rights protection will need to grapple with three intersecting considerations: the existing provisions in VARA, the constitutional issues concerning enhanced protection, and the practicalities of successfully implementing stronger protection. This chapter focuses on the first two considerations. Regarding the third consideration pertaining to practical implementation, it is reasonable to assume that a cabined framework for moral rights likely would enjoy a greater degree of acceptance and eventual legislative success. With this observation, I invite others to examine more thoroughly this important area of inquiry.

The proposal I develop in this chapter does not attempt to address every possible issue in connection with enhanced moral rights legislation. On the contrary, it explores some general themes and offers guidance with respect to how these themes can impact the mechanics of a new statute. There are, however, many issues that I either consciously or unconsciously ignore. Among the areas in the "conscious" category are whether to retain VARA's treatment of works of visual art that have become part of buildings,[1] coverage of site specific art,[2] a statute of limitations,[3] and governmental immunity.[4] Certainly these areas are deserving of attention and they would have to be addressed in any proposed legislation. My interest, however, lies in exploring the parameters of the broader picture as it has been developed in the foregoing chapters. Therefore, I confine the elements of my proposal to matters such as scope of coverage, works written by authors in disguise, remedies and other public access issues, duration, preemption, and safeguarding the integrity of personas.

Chapter 6 develops the argument that moral rights should be applicable to works manifesting heightened originality with substantial creativity. If Congress were to follow this approach, it would be appropriate to exclude completely works from coverage that are largely functional and therefore lacking in significant artistic characteristics. A proposed statute can also address works straddling the boundary between the functional and the artistic by instructing courts to perform individualized assessments based upon two criteria: first, whether the author's narrative of decision making during the design process demonstrates design choices reflecting heightened originality with substantial creativity;[5] and second, whether reasonable observers perceive the work in question as creative.[6]

Chapter 6 also discusses how VARA, by legislating a circumscribed definition of "visual art," provides a model for how Congress can, in more general terms, delineate a limited scope of coverage for moral rights. Still, my proposal would necessitate a substantial departure from even the current categories of covered works. For example, VARA covers certain categories of works but only in limited editions, and photographs are covered only to the extent they are produced for exhibition purposes.[7] I am skeptical of these restrictions because they are irrelevant to what I see as the operative issue concerning the scope of moral rights— namely, the level of originality of the work in question. Therefore, to the extent Congress were to consider moral rights from a fresh perspective, I advocate eliminating the current scope of coverage for works of visual art and replacing it with a definition of coverage according to the parameters I have outlined.

My recommendations regarding what conduct should be actionable also would require a substantial overhaul of VARA's current terms of protection for moral rights. Some authors' rights advocates may be disturbed that my proposal cuts back on certain existing protections, particularly with respect to the right of integrity, for works of visual art that qualify for protection under VARA. Nonetheless, as will be explored more fully below, in other respects such as coverage for reproductions and objectionable contextual uses, my proposal affords enhanced protection for visual artists. Moreover, although an amended statute could retain the current statutory measures for visual artists but confine the scope of protection for other authors, uniformity among authors is the preferable goal. There is no theoretical basis upon which to differentiate visual artists from other types of authors whose works manifest heightened originality with substantial creativity.

With respect to actionable conduct, I advocate following the approach of both Berne and VARA that only the rights of attribution and integrity be legislated. This proposal does not incorporate an explicit right of disclosure for two reasons. First, the Berne Union does not require any such provision.[8] Second, since the copyright in a work typically "vests initially in the author or authors of the work,"[9] in the vast majority of instances the right of first publication will be within the control of the author.[10]

In crafting appropriate attribution and integrity rights, the underlying objectives of moral rights protections must be carefully assessed and measured against critical limitations inherent in the existing legal structure. Such an analysis compels the conclusion that attribution rights should be defined far more broadly than integrity rights. With respect to attribution, I believe a viable statute in the United States should make actionable the following conduct: (1) actual uses that are more than *de minimis* of an author's original work without attribution, or with false attribution; (2) reproductions of an author's work that are more than *de minimis* without attribution, or with false attribution; (3) modifications of an author's original work, or modifications of an exact reproduction or close copy of the author's work, resulting in a substantially similar version to the original, without attribution, or with false attribution; and (4) false attribution of authorship of a work to an author. The first three elements of this standard safeguard the right of attribution when an author's work is used directly, or reproduced or modified, and the original author is not given credit for the work. These elements also proscribe reverse passing off, which occurs when someone else takes credit for an author's work. The fourth element prohibits designating someone as the author of a work she did not create.[11] In addition, the author should have the right to publish a work anonymously or pseudonymously, and to claim authorship at a later point in time should she so desire.

The proposed standard for attribution admittedly is broader than VARA in several respects. Initially, VARA excludes protection for reproductions of covered works, and therefore does not encompass the second or third elements of the attribution standards I propose.[12] In this respect, VARA is far too narrow because textual integrity violations often occur in connection with reproductions or close copies of works.

Moreover, VARA does not include the negative rights of anonymity or pseudonymity.[13] Nor does it specifically prohibit reverse passing off, although such conduct arguably could be construed as interfering with the author's right to "claim authorship" of a work covered under VARA.[14] These components should be included in a revised federal moral rights statute. With respect to the author's right to publish anonymously or pseudonymously, these rights are important because, from a theoretical perspective, such authorship decisions represent branding choices that can be a fundamental part of the author's meaning and message.[15] Moreover, these rights comport with the intent of the Berne Convention.[16] As for providing authors with the ability to redress reverse passing off claims in the context of works of authorship, this explicit protection is necessary in light of the uncertainties created by the case law, both prior and especially subsequent to *Dastar*.[17] It is also consistent with interpretations of the First Amendment that do not extend protection to "knowing falsehoods."[18] Moreover, the codification of these measures recognizes authorship norms vital to a complete conception of creativity.

Despite the breadth of this proposed attribution standard, the public should not be harmed by a requirement of accurate authorship designation, especially in light of the proposed law's application only to works that manifest heightened originality in the form of substantial creativity.[19] Such pure attribution violations should be enforceable by declaratory relief governing future distributions. In light of the predominant noneconomic nature of the injury, a damage remedy should be eschewed except in the following instances: where a clear showing of economic harm exists as a result of the attribution violation; where the violation is entirely in the past and future injunctive relief therefore is meaningless; or where exceptionally willful violations are involved.[20] Some might argue that such an attribution standard is nonetheless worrisome given the prevalent use of cease and desist letters threatening economic sanctions in connection with alleged attribution violations.[21] Even if cease and desist letters do have a chilling impact with respect to some legitimate behavior, economic penalties can only be enforced through judicial involvement. Moreover, if Congress were to adopt standards for both attribution violations and the imposition of damages, in this area as in so many others, the existence of the law will eventually have an impact on the relevant behavioral norms of both authors and users.

In contrast to a broadly defined right of attribution, I recommend a narrowly tailored right of integrity designed to vindicate the author's right to *inform the public* about the original nature of her artistic message and the meaning of her work.[22] Specifically, this standard encompasses damage to the integrity of texts in the following two circumstances—(1) when objectionable modifications are made to the work or a reproduction of the work or close copy, or (2) when the original work, or a reproduction or close copy, is publicly displayed, distributed, or transmitted in a context deemed objectionable by the author—and the work is either expressly attributed to the original author, or absent attribution, still likely to be recognized as the original author's work. When such conduct occurs, the actor should be required to provide a disclaimer adequate to inform the public of the author's objection to the modification or contextual usage. This standard assumes that, absent the proposed right of integrity, the actor would otherwise have the unencumbered right to use the author's work pursuant to copyright law.[23]

As with the attribution right, an author should be entitled to enforce the right of integrity prospectively through declaratory relief mandating a disclaimer. Further, an author should be unable to enjoin a proposed use accompanied by an appropriate disclaimer. For prior objectionable uses lacking a disclaimer, an author should be able to obtain damages in cases involving clear economic harm, willfulness, or where the conduct is entirely past and the possibility of a prospective disclaimer is unrealistic. Moreover, as an additional safeguard, the statute should incorporate a requirement that the author's objections to the use of her work be reasonably "credible."

My proposal is narrower than VARA in certain respects, while in other areas, it is significantly broader. One way in which it is more narrow concerns the linkage it requires between attribution and integrity violations. In contrast, VARA prohibits integrity violations, even absent attribution violations, in situations involving intentional distortions, mutilations, or other modifications that are prejudicial to the author's honor or reputation.[24] Thus, my proposal differs from VARA to the extent it makes actionable only integrity violations in conjunction with recognition, either express or implicit, of the original author. This standard, however, advances the objectives of the Copyright Clause to the extent it seeks to ensure that the public is informed of the existence of the original author's meaning and message in situations where the original author would be associated with the covered work. Moreover, requiring a connection between attribution and integrity also is supported by the analysis of authorship norms developed earlier.[25] If a work is modified in a manner the author deems objectionable, her artistic dignity theoretically can be violated regardless of whether the public is aware of the damage. On the other hand, recall that authorship dignity demands an external embodiment allowing the inner personality to commodify and explain itself to the outside world.[26] This conception of authorship dignity requires a public linkage between the author's inner labor and its external embodiment, and absent a setting in which this linkage is made the dignity violation is diminished.[27]

The remedial nature of my proposal for integrity violations also is more narrowly crafted than VARA in that it requires a disclaimer remedy and disallows prospective injunctive relief for works displaying an appropriate disclaimer. In this regard, my proposal recognizes the duality of the First Amendment interests at stake[28] and thus forges a compromise between respecting the author's intrinsic dimension of creativity and the user's freedom to create and build upon prior works. This remedy comports with First Amendment theory to the extent it adopts a balancing mechanism to address both users' interests and the original author's autonomy interests in not being subjected to coercive uses of her expression that diminish the integrity of her message.[29] The disclaimer component also aims to reinforce the objectives of the Copyright Clause by promoting and disseminating accurate knowledge about the storehouse of our creative surroundings. Further, requiring a disclaimer when integrity and attribution interests are violated simultaneously facilitates congruence between the purported harm and its remedy. When authorship dignity is compromised, the communication of information designed to educate the public about the nature of the authentic external embodiment of the author's message is vital. The content of the required disclaimer inevitably will vary. At a minimum, however, disclaimers can inform the public that the material in question was used without the author's permission. Depending on the circumstances of the use and subject to the dictates of the First Amendment, a disclaimer also can provide more substantive information regarding the inconsistency of the use and the author's original message.[30]

Some may take issue with my proposal regarding the disclaimer remedy on the grounds that it does not go far enough in protecting authors' integrity interests.[31] After all, disclaimers can be small and barely noticeable. This is a fair criticism from a practical standpoint, but my position is that a legal requirement mandating disclaimers in instances of integrity violations provides an important indication—even if somewhat symbolic in certain instances—that the United States is sensitive to integrity interests. The development and reaffirmation of this sensitivity is vital for authors whose integrity interests are jeopardized by the creative liberties of others. Greg Lastowka makes a similar point in the context of attribution credit when he observes that even the most obscure film credits are not "simply superfluous nonsense" because they can serve as motivational vehicles and important informational tools for those in the industry.[32] Although Lastowka also notes that a long list of film credits may not provide much practical benefit in the context of average consumers,[33] their very existence reaffirms important industry norms and provides a psychological comfort for those who participate in the enterprise of film authorship.

Therefore, as a general matter, even if a given disclaimer may not be noticed, its very existence is reaffirming at a psychological level for authors whose works have been distorted without their permission. For example, Samuel Beckett once tried to enjoin the American Repertory

Theater's production of his play *Endgame*, which he saw as offensive. He did not seek monetary damages but instead sought an injunction as his first choice, and a notification to audiences informing them of the production's deviations from the original as his second choice. Ultimately, the case settled allowing the production to go forward with a notice in the program indicating that Beckett denounced the production.[34] As this example demonstrates, in their ideal world, authors such as Samuel Beckett, Frederick Hart, Carl Perkins, Connie Francis, and Monty Python would prefer to preclude certain creative actions involving their works, even if those actions do not otherwise violate copyright law. Realistically, however, the legal system in the United States may not be ready at this point, or possibly ever, to adopt a system of moral rights that would effectively preclude uses that otherwise are allowed by copyright law. Therefore, creative remedial approaches are necessary to effectuate authorship norms.

The history of VARA and of moral rights generally in this country suggests that a system of moral rights will be adopted here only if it is viewed as practically feasible, constitutionally sound, and not otherwise out of step with much of the copyright system already in place. These realities indicate that a compelling argument can be made for the adoption of a cabined system of moral rights under which integrity violations are addressed through required disclaimers. This remedy may not be viewed as ideal by everyone, but it is practical, constitutionally sound, and better than the current system under which only a small minority of works are offered somewhat broader protection from a remedial context. In essence, the remedial structure I advocate for combined attribution and integrity violations is similar to a liability rule approach in which the user's conduct is allowed as long as the appropriate remedial measures are implemented.[35] This approach avoids the concern that stronger protections for the integrity interests of today's authors will privatize more than is necessary to provide an incentive for tomorrow's creators. Moreover, in many instances digital technology and the Internet offer efficient and inexpensive means of complying with these suggested reforms.

As a practical matter, there is precedent for the type of disclaimer remedy I am suggesting. For example, recall that in the United Kingdom the right of integrity can be limited to a disclaimer dissociating the author from the modified work.[36] With respect to the moral rights of performers in the United Kingdom, the right of integrity can be similarly limited.[37] In the United States, several of the state moral rights statutes embrace an analogous idea to the extent they prohibit the display or publication of a work, or the reproduction of a work, in an altered or mutilated condition if it is labeled as that of the author or would be reasonably understood as the work of the author.[38]

Despite the more narrow aspects of my proposal concerning the right of integrity as compared to VARA, it is important to emphasize that it is broader than VARA in several significant ways. For example, VARA affords a covered author the "right to prevent the use of his or her name as the author of the work . . . in the event of a distortion, mutilation, or other modification of the work which would be prejudicial to . . . [the author's] honor or reputation."[39] I do not believe this language is sufficient because it does not cover instances in which the public is exposed to a work that has been the subject of an integrity violation and the original author is well-known as the creator among a segment of the public but not specifically attributed in connection with the modified work. Under my proposal, a disclaimer regarding lack of permission would be mandated in these instances.

There are three other ways in which my proposal enhances VARA's protections. First, under VARA, stand-alone integrity violations are actionable only to the extent they are intentional. Second, VARA's integrity protections are triggered only when the actions in question are prejudicial to the author's honor or reputation. Third, VARA does not cover objectionable contextual modifications or any reproductions of covered works.[40] My proposal eliminates these caveats, thus broadening the protection afforded authors.

VARA's limitation of integrity violations to those that are intentional and prejudicial to the author's honor or reputation mistakenly puts the focus of the standard for violation on the motives of the user and the public's perception of the author and her work rather than where it belongs—on the author's intrinsic motivations in creating. The primary reason to redress integrity violations is to recognize the authorship dignity deriving from the intrinsic dimension of the creative process and its embodiment in an external medium. The proposed standard, when applied in conjunction with a heightened originality requirement calling for substantial creativity, is designed to facilitate public knowledge of the original author's message regarding works possessing these qualities. Whether the violation was intentional or prejudicial to the author's honor or reputation is irrelevant.[41] Moreover, the proposed protection extends not only to actual modifications but also to objectionable contextual displays, performances, and transmissions. As discussed earlier in connection with modifications and the attribution requirement, my proposal also covers modifications made to exact reproductions and close copies of the original. These additional protections address situations such as Warner Brothers' objectionable reproduction of Frederick Hart's sculpture *Ex Nihilo* in the movie *The Devil's Advocate,* discussed in Chapter 1.[42]

Interestingly, VARA actually provides greater protection than the civil law jurisdictions to the extent it prohibits destruction of works of "recognized stature."[43] Although it may be argued that a work that is destroyed completely cannot reflect adversely upon the creator's honor or reputation,[44] this is not necessarily true in situations where works are destroyed in a manner that subjects the creator to public shame or embarrassment.[45] Again, a public linkage between the author's inner labor and its external embodiment is necessary to realize authorship dignity. If the author's external embodiment is destroyed, it stands to reason that her authorship dignity is compromised.[46] For this reason, the right to prevent destruction of *original* versions of works of visual art should be retained.[47] If the United States were to continue to protect against destruction, the additional "recognized stature" limitation should be eliminated given the new heightened originality standard.[48] However, the right against destruction should be cabined by protecting only the originals created by the author because the harm to authorship dignity is greatest when the original version of a work has been destroyed.[49] In this one respect, then, reproductions would be treated differently from the originals.

In light of this proposal's circumscribed protections for moral rights, formal waivers should be inoperative as a general matter. Given that moral rights are designed to recognize inspirational motivations for creativity, any system sanctioning waiver is inconsistent from a theoretical standpoint with the justifications for adopting these protections. In other words, if moral rights protections are intended to redress violations of authorship dignity, they should not be capable of being waived.[50] An author always should be in a position to inform the public that a publicly displayed or distributed version of her work does not comport with her artistic vision, absent situations involving colloquial authors as discussed below, or parody in which it is otherwise obvious to the public that the modified use has not been authorized. In addition, an author whose message and meaning is embodied in a work should not have to forfeit claiming attribution, subject to the norms governing the particular type of work at issue. Moreover, allowing waiver exacerbates the disparity of bargaining power between authors and those with whom they contract.[51] Finally, given the limited nature of protection for authors' integrity interests I am proposing, the typical reasons supporting a waiver provision are absent.

By mandating appropriate attribution and public acknowledgment of variations inconsistent with the author's original meaning and message, this proposal affords authors a viable remedial structure tailored to recognizing the intrinsic dimension of innovation. These limited measures supporting authors' dignity interests should not be compromised by affording the possibility of their elimination through a formal waiver mechanism.[52] For these reasons, our system of moral rights should afford authors in disguise, such as ghostwriters and employees for hire, the opportunity to exercise the right of attribution and a narrowly crafted right of integrity as defined in this proposal where the works in question manifest the colloquial author's meaning and message, and otherwise meet the heightened originality standard for protection. Therefore, this proposal rejects the notion that ghostwriting and work for hire agreements operate as *de facto* waivers of moral rights. In circumstances involving these types of works by authors in disguise, the operative inquiries should be whether the work in question conveys the colloquial author's meaning and message (as opposed to that of the named author or hiring party), and whether a misattribution or presentation of the work distorts these communicative qualities. Such a standard can be stated in general terms in the statute itself, but of course the application of this standard would be made on a case-by-case basis.

My proposal, therefore, necessitates a repeal of VARA's exclusion of works for hire from coverage. Instead, I propose that the statute adopt a presumption that colloquial authors of works meeting the heightened originality standard retain their moral rights, absent compelling reasons for divestment. This presumption can be overcome by a showing that the work in question was created under someone else's direction or control to a point where it no longer represents the colloquial author's meaning or message. In addition, the statute can incorporate a general "public policy" caveat that can militate against a colloquial author's exercise of moral rights in a particular instance. Although the language of Article *6bis* in Berne may suggest that protection survives alienation,[53] Chapter 4 demonstrates that even countries with strong moral rights protection have adopted certain limitations with respect to the exercise of the right of attribution in connection with works by ghostwriters,[54] and the right of integrity in connection with film and other types of works.[55]

Chapter 7 also demonstrates why collaborative works present a particular challenge for moral rights, and how this challenge is exacerbated by VARA's especially indefensible position that one joint author should be allowed to waive the moral rights of her collaborators.[56] I suggested that the attribution issues regarding collaborative works can be handled by requiring that each collaborator furnish material that meets, on an independent basis, the heightened originality requirement.[57] Moreover, this proposed standard must be applied with sensitivity to established industry norms. In other words, the determination of credit in particular collaborative enterprises should continue to be influenced by existing industry norms in specialized areas such as the television and movie industries.[58] In short, a proposed statute can simply provide that attribution should be determined in accordance with the particular medium of expression and the nature and extent of the author's contribution.[59] The right of integrity probably presents a greater challenge for collaborative works, especially if coauthors have different conceptions of what conduct constitutes a violation. The proposed disclaimer remedy is particularly suitable to resolving such disputes because the dignity concerns of coauthors can be individualized in the event there is disagreement. Thus, the proposed disclaimer remedy can facilitate a way to address different sets of objections by coauthors to unauthorized uses.

The issues of whether, and under what circumstances, moral rights can be circumvented in particular situations also relates to the question of whether moral rights should be subject to fair use. The copyright statute currently provides that VARA is subject to fair use.[60] As a theoretical matter, fair use is concerned with determining the circumstances under which uncompensated copying should be allowed. The right of attribution and integrity, on the other hand, are about the extent to which an author can safeguard the textual integrity of her work. There may be instances in which the author should be able to exercise control over textual integrity that may also qualify as fair uses, but the two doctrines are conceptually distinct.[61] In the context of attribution, my proposal makes actionable attribution violations when the uses are more than *de minimis*. Therefore, parties who use insignificant amounts of someone's work without attribution would be excluded from liability. With respect to the right of integrity, the remedial framework of fair use is irrelevant under my proposal because uses that are otherwise allowed pursuant to copyright law are not prohibited. Moreover, uses that may qualify as fair but are still objectionable to an author from a moral rights standpoint can go forward as long as an appropriate disclaimer is furnished. There may also be instances in which a disclaimer will not be required. For reasons discussed shortly in connection with personas, parody presents one such example because when works are parodied, an implicit disclaimer essentially exists.[62] One significant benefit of this proposal is that it allows the determination of when disclaimers should be required to be conducted within the context of considerations pertaining to noneconomic motivations for human enterprise that are relevant to moral rights discourse rather than to copyright's economically based framework.[63]

In Chapter 5, I suggest that from a theoretical standpoint, moral rights protection should exist for the author's lifetime, but not beyond.[64]

For joint works, protection should end at the death of the last surviving joint author.[65] An author's external work embodies her personal meaning and intended message and thus is reflective of her individual, intrinsic creative process. No one, not even the author's spouse and children, can substitute a personal judgment regarding the substance of the author's meaning and message of her work. Therefore, the author functions as the guardian of her work's original meaning and message during her lifetime. Moreover, a duration equivalent to the author's life reinforces a vibrant public domain. A more limited duration also is consistent with the confined approach to moral rights I advocate in general terms. For these reasons, moral rights protection should expire upon the author's death.

One possible difficulty with this position, however, is that my recommended period of protection is not consistent with the Berne Convention's recommendation, the norms in the international community, or with the entirety of VARA. Therefore, despite the theoretical advantages of this approach, its wisdom merits further discussion. Berne provides that the covered rights are to be maintained after an author's death "at least until the expiry of the economic rights."[66] This provision regarding duration derives from the 1971 Conference amendment to Article 6*bis*.[67] Berne also states that if a given country, at the time it ratifies Berne, does not provide for postmortem moral rights, "some of these rights may" end with the author's death.[68] Of course, there is a lack of clarity concerning the meaning of "some of these rights." Nonetheless, a duration for moral rights limited to the author's lifetime would seem to be legally appropriate pursuant to Berne given the absence of postmortem moral rights in the United States at the time we ratified Berne. Berne's clear directive is that the specific legislation of the respective Union members will govern substantive applications of the right.[69] The WIPO Guide provides that Berne "allows the Union countries to permit one of the rights comprising the moral right to lapse, after [the author's death]."[70] On its face, this Guide would appear to allow either the attribution or integrity right pertaining to any newly enacted moral rights provisions to be confined to a duration of the author's lifetime. The Final Report on the Ad Hoc Working Group on U.S. Adherence to the Berne Convention appears to support an even broader degree of latitude since it concluded that in light of the protections for moral rights available at the time of our adherence to the Berne Convention, there were sufficient patchwork protections for an author's moral rights extending beyond an author's death to comply with Berne.[71]

The duration of moral rights specified in VARA is particularly odd in that it varies, depending on when the work was created with respect to VARA's effective date. Section 106A(d)(1) provides that the moral rights safeguarded by the statute expire with the death of the author for works created on or after VARA's effective date. For works created before the effective date of VARA, but to which title has not been transferred as of the effective date, the duration of rights under § 106A is coextensive with those under copyright law.[72] Neither the statute nor the legislative history offers any explanation for this strange dichotomy, but in its original form VARA provided a duration of protection equal to that of copyright law for all covered works.[73] The more limited duration for works created on or after the effective date of VARA was a result of a last-minute amendment by the Senate. In addition, VARA provides that the rights in joint works last until the death of the last surviving author.[74] Interestingly, several of the state moral rights statutes provide authors with a longer period of protection than does VARA,[75] creating the irony that authors of works created post-VARA obtain more protection for their works after their deaths than during their lifetimes given that many of these same state statutes offer broader coverage than does VARA.[76] Thus, my proposal to limit the term of protection to the author's lifetime, or in the case of joint works, to the last surviving joint author's death, is essentially consistent with the current provisions of VARA, but for a seemingly inconsistent provision regarding works created prior to VARA's enactment.

If the United States were to enact a moral rights statute along the lines I am proposing, the question of whether such a statute should explicitly preempt the existing state moral rights statutes requires serious attention. VARA currently provides that subsequent to its effective date, "all legal or equitable rights that are equivalent to any of the rights conferred by § 106A" are governed by VARA.[77] The statute continues with several exceptions to preemption that include activities that began before

VARA's effective date, activities violating nonequivalent rights, and activities violating "rights which extend beyond the life of the author."[78] For several reasons, I am inclined to favor a provision providing explicit and comprehensive preemption of the state moral rights statutes in contrast to VARA's complex preemption provisions. First, given that my proposal for a federal moral rights statute embraces protections that are in compliance with Berne and are far more complete than VARA, there would not be a need for individual states to protect authors' moral rights. Second, the application of the current preemption provisions in VARA requires a difficult and often tortured analysis that is best eliminated if possible. For example, the equivalent rights preemption provision requires that the elements of the state moral rights laws be measured against the elements and objectives of VARA. This can be an extraordinarily complex analysis given that the specific content of the state statutes varies considerably from one another, and from VARA.

Moreover, it has been argued that those state law provisions providing more comprehensive protection to authors are preempted on the ground that their broader protections do not qualify as different rights.[79] Another complexity is posed by those state statutes providing posthumous protection for moral rights. As noted above, VARA expressly exempts from preemption state statutes offering longer periods of protection. Given my position that moral rights protection should expire with the death of the author,[80] there would seem to be no reason to allow states to provide for a longer duration. A final reason supporting an express, comprehensive provision preempting all state moral rights statutes is that uniformity in this area is highly desirable.

Chapter 8 demonstrates how a right of publicity action can involve a claim that essentially is analogous to the moral right of integrity when a persona is appropriated in a context or for a purpose deemed objectionable by the persona. These are instances of morally based harms to the persona, and in this context, mandatory disclaimers can also provide a viable remedy for integrity violations. For example, the case involving the movie *The Perfect Storm* suggests the potential of disclaimers to mitigate the negative impact of morally based harms in situations such as entertainment-oriented uses combining fact and fiction. That case involved a negative depiction of characters in a movie based on a real event, but where creative liberties were taken in conjunction with the characters. In such situations, enjoining a particular use might otherwise not be feasible given our First Amendment jurisprudence, but the morally based harm can be mitigated to a degree with appropriate disclaimers. A disclaimer was, in fact, contained in the film credits stating: "This film is based on actual historical events contained in *The Perfect Storm* by Sebastian Junger. Dialogue and certain events and characters in the film were created for the purpose of fictionalization."[81]

Parodies create their own unique set of circumstances in connection with personas, just as they do with respect to conventional copyrighted texts. One well-known publicity case illustrating this point is *Cardtoons, L.C. v. Major League Baseball Players Association*,[82] in which Cardtoons sought declaratory relief that its parody trading cards featuring current baseball players do not infringe the players' publicity rights. The court held in favor of Cardtoons, emphasizing that parody merits complete protection under the First Amendment.[83] In its balancing analysis of the players' property rights against Cardtoons' free speech rights, the court emphasized the reality that parody typically does not entail a high degree of likelihood of confusion and presents a particularly compelling form of self-expression.[84] Moreover, the court noted that "parodies of celebrities are an especially valuable means of expression because of the role celebrities play in modern society."[85] Of course, typically parodies involve uses that are not flattering. The director of licensing for the Major League Baseball Players Association testified that his organization would not license a parody poking fun at the players.[86] Similarly, Carol Burnett would not have authorized the television show *Family Guy* to depict her character Charwoman mopping the floor in a porn shop.[87] It is precisely because the public understands that such parodies are not authorized that the public is not deceived as to the persona's involvement in parody.[88] Moreover, parody lacks the necessary public linkage between the author and the externalized commodity[89] because it is apparent that the author has not authorized the use.

On the other hand, some types of textual integrity violations involving personas arguably may call for the imposition of injunctive relief. For example, should a persona be able to bar the use by a political candidate of a song recorded by, and publicly associated with, the persona?[90] Similarly, should Jackie Mason be allowed to enjoin the Jews for Jesus from using his persona in connection with its literature? These cases present situations that are somewhat analogous to the examples discussed in Chapter 1 involving the objectionable contexts in which the works of Frederick Hart, Carl Perkins, and Connie Francis were used.[91] Such cases can involve a high potential for unjust enrichment by the unauthorized user, a likelihood of consumer confusion, and the existence of forcing the persona to say something she does not believe. In these instances, injunctive relief may be appropriate although this position is likely to be controversial. Personas are not regarded as "works of authorship" currently and the introduction of this concept breaks new ground in and of itself. Moreover, the conflict between the First Amendment and the right of publicity is complex in situations involving pronounced free speech concerns. For these reasons, if Congress were to consider designating personas as capable of receiving moral rights protection, it might be more prudent to limit the remedies for violation to those specified for conventional works of authorship.

My overall objective in writing this book has been to offer a theoretical grounding for moral rights and to propose a viable means for implementing such legislation in the United States based on the conceptual underpinnings of the doctrine. My proposal achieves a balance between stronger protections for authors' rights and the public's interest in maintaining access to protected works. Its operative provisions are not only sensitive to the objectives of the Copyright Clause as they have been understood historically, but also provide important safeguards for authorship norms.

I seek not only to advance the discourse but also to invite others to participate. A close friend of mine who is both a law professor and an amateur actor once told me that the basis of improvisation is the concept of "yes . . . and." I like the idea of "yes . . . and." Life is filled with far more optimism and inspiration when we live by "yes . . . and" rather than "no . . . but." At a minimum, I challenge lawmakers and those who are actively engaged in thinking about intellectual property policy to rethink the basis of and justifications for the United States' "no . . . but" policy regarding moral rights. This challenge is important on both a practical and legal level given our duty to comply with the Berne Convention and our relative individualistic stance regarding moral rights in an era of globalization. In short, my mission here is to show why and how a "yes . . . and" approach to moral rights can accommodate our legal system, history, and culture. Time will tell whether inertia will give way to action.

Notes

1. The parental metaphor of authorship is explored more fully in Chapters 2 and 7. Robert Fuller has emphasized the distinction between "spiritual" and "religious": "A large number of Americans identify themselves as 'spiritual, but not religious.' . . . The word *spiritual* gradually came to be associated with the private realm of thought and experience while the word *religious* came to be connected with the public realm of membership in religious institutions, participation in formal rituals, and adherence to official denominational doctrines." ROBERT FULLER, SPIRITUAL BUT NOT RELIGIOUS: UNDERSTANDING UNCHURCHED AMERICA 5 (2001) (citations omitted). This observation is consistent with the contemplative, inwardly-focused quality characteristic of inspiration or spirituality as these terms are used in this book. *See* Lucia Ann Silecchia, *Integrating Spiritual Perspectives with the Law School Experience: An Essay and an Invitation*, 37 SAN DIEGO L. REV. 167, 179 (2000) (defining spirituality broadly as "entail[ing] a way of defining and pursuing truth beyond oneself that is more important than the individual, giving the individual's actions meaning and purpose in a larger context").

2. JOHN S. DACEY & KATHLEEN H. LENNON, UNDERSTANDING CREATIVITY 226 (1998).

3. *Cf.* Alfred Yen, *The Interdisciplinary Future of Copyright Theory*, in THE CONSTRUCTION OF AUTHORSHIP: TEXTUAL APPROPRIATION IN LAW AND LITERATURE 159, 170–71 (Martha Woodmansee & Peter Jaszi eds., 1994) (arguing that sole reliance on economic theory to determine copyright law is misguided and favoring the introduction of a natural law model to supplement the theoretical analysis).

4. The enactment of the Digital Millennium Copyright Act in 1998 continues to spawn a host of litigation.

5. *See Eldred v. Ashcroft*, 537 U.S. 186 (2003) (upholding the Copyright Term Extension Act, which provides copyright protection for most works for the life of the author plus seventy years).

6. *See Metro-Goldwyn-Mayer Studios, Inc. v. Grokster*, 545 U.S. 913 (2005) (holding that a party who distributes a device with the objective of promoting its use to infringe copyrights is liable for the resulting acts of third-party infringement).

1. Justin Hughes, *The Personality Interest of Artists and Inventors in Intellectual Property*, 16 CARDOZO ARTS & ENT. L.J. 81, 84–85 (1998) (citing ROBERT NOZICK, ANARCHY, STATE AND UTOPIA 174–75 [1974]).

2. *See, e.g.*, Peter Jaszi, *On the Author Effect: Contemporary Copyright and Collective Creativity*, in THE CONSTRUCTION OF AUTHORSHIP: TEXTUAL APPROPRIATION IN LAW AND LITERATURE 29 (Martha Woodmansee & Peter Jaszi eds., 1994) [hereinafter THE CONSTRUCTION OF AUTHORSHIP]. *See* LIOR ZEMER, THE IDEA OF AUTHORSHIP IN COPYRIGHT

(2007) (suggesting that "the public" should be regarded as a joint author of all copyright-able works).

3. *See* Martha Woodmansee, *The Genius and the Copyright: Economic and Legal Conditions of the Emergence of the "Author,"* 17 EIGHTEENTH-CENTURY STUD. 425, 441 (1984) (observing that when a book is viewed as a truth-conveying vehicle, there is no reason to privilege any of the numerous craftsmen involved in its production). A similar view was exemplified in China during the Cultural Revolution in the 1960s, during which time the Communist government instituted radical policies undermining property rights and material incentives. The prevailing view was that "if a steel worker need not put his name on an ingot he had produced, why should a writer enjoy the privilege of putting his name on the article he produced?" As a result of this position, all works of creativity were unprotected. *See* Shin-yi-Peng, *The WTO Legalistic Approach and East Asia: From the Legal Culture Perspective*, 1 ASIAN-PAC. L. & POL'Y 13, 17 n.88 (2000); David B. Dreyfus, *Confucianism and Compact Discs: Alternative Dispute Resolution and Its Role in the Protection of United States Intellectual Property Rights in China*, 13 OHIO ST. J. ON DISP. RESOL. 947 (1998).

4. ROLAND BARTHES, *The Death of the Author*, in IMAGE, MUSIC, TEXT (Stephen Heath trans., 1977); *see also* Michel Foucault, *What Is an Author?* in TEXTUAL STRATEGIES: PERSPECTIVES IN POST-STRUCTURALIST CRITICISM 141 (Josue V. Harari ed., 1979); Woodmansee, supra note 3.

5. Woodmansee, supra note 3, at 425–26.

6. Id.; *see also* Jaszi, supra note 2, at 33 (discussing the work of scholars who document the influences that contributed to the current construction of "authorship").

7. Alfred Yen, *The Interdisciplinary Future of Copyright Theory*, in THE CONSTRUCTION OF AUTHORSHIP, supra note 2, at 166.

8. *See* Jaszi, supra note 2, at 29 (discussing the work of Michel Foucault).

9. *See, e.g., Campbell v. Acuff-Rose Music, Inc.,* 510 U.S. 569, 579 (1994) (invoking "meaning" and "message" in a discussion of the concept of "transformative" in the context of the first fair use factor).

10. I am indebted to Wendy Gordon for her insights with respect to framing this distinction. Charles Beitz recognizes a similar distinction when he speaks of a creator's interest in preserving a work's communicative content (an idea comparable to the term *message*) and the creator's "desire to transfigure a world experience as lacking in meaning or value" (embodying the notion of "meaning" as used in this text). Charles R. Beitz, *The Moral Rights of Creators of Artistic and Literary Works*, 13 J. POL. PHIL. 330, 340–42 (2005).

11. *See* The Art of Leon Azoulay, About Leon's Gallery, www.leon-gallery.co.il/about.asp (last visited Sept. 1, 2008).

12. Beitz, supra note 10, at 341.

13. Edward J. Bloustein, *Privacy as an Aspect of Human Dignity: An Answer to Dean Prosser*, 39 N.Y.U. L. REV. 962, 971 (1964).

14. Id. (quoting Samuel D. Warren & Louis D. Brandeis, *The Right to Privacy*, 4 HARV. L. REV. 193, 198 [1890]).

15. JOSEPH B. SOLOVEITCHIK, THE LONELY MAN OF FAITH 26 (1965).

16. Id. ("There is no dignity in anonymity. If one succeeds in putting his message across he may lay claim to dignity. The silent person, whose message remains hidden and suppressed in the in-depth personality, cannot be considered dignified.")

17. *See* Ilhyung Lee, *Toward an American Moral Rights in Copyright*, 58 WASH. & LEE L. REV. 795, 837 (2001) (noting that authorship dignity encompasses respect for an author's choice to be an author and to create one work over another).

18. Tom R. Tyler, *Compliance with Intellectual Property Laws: A Psychological Perspective*, 29 N.Y.U. J. INT'L L. & POL. 219, 225–26 (1997). Although the focus of Tyler's research is on criminal justice, he notes that research in intellectual property reveals similar conclusions.

19. Id. at 227.

20. Id. at 232.

21. Id. at 233.

22. *See* Creative Commons, http://creativecommons.org/license (last visited Sept. 1, 2008).

23. Anupam Chander & Madhavi Sunder, *The Romance of the Public Domain*, 92 CAL. L. REV. 1331, 1361 (2004). Conceivably, a guarantee of desired attribution can be analogized to economic reward, and therefore also can be regarded as an external motivation. The fact that attribution possesses this dual quality, however, does not detract from its importance as an appropriate mechanism to recognize the intrinsic dimension of creativity.

24. Catherine L. Fisk, *Credit Where It's Due: The Law and Norms of Attribution*, 95 GEO. L.J. 49, 91 (2006).

25. Susan P. Liemer, *Understanding Artists' Moral Rights: A Primer*, 7 B.U. PUB. INT. L.J. 41, 49 (1998).

26. 179 F.3d 217 (5th Cir. 1999).

27. Id. at 220.

28. Id.

29. Lawrence Siskind, *When the Profane Contends with the Sacred, Law Protects the Rights of . . . the Devil's Advocate*, LEGAL TIMES, Mar. 23, 1998, at A2. Hart also created the bronze statue, "Three Soldiers," at the Vietnam Veterans Memorial.

30. Joseph Curl, *Sculptor Says He Found His Faith While Carving Masterpiece*, WASH. TIMES, Dec. 14, 1997 [hereinafter Curl I].

31. *See* Curl I, supra note 30; Christopher Stern, *Sculptor Casts Doubt on "Devil,"* DAILY VARIETY, Feb. 11, 1998.

32. William Neuman, *Hell to Pay Over Film's "Devil" Art*, N.Y. POST, Dec. 8, 1997, at 007 (quoting Hart).

33. *See* Joseph Curl, *Warner Settles Lawsuit in Film; Will Alter Scene in "Devil's Advocate,"* WASH. TIMES, Feb. 14, 1998, at A1.

34. Patrick G. Zabatta, *Moral Rights and Musical Works: Are Composers Getting Burned?* 43 SYRACUSE L. REV. 1095, 1125 (1992) (quoting Perkins); *see also* Morgan Black, *After Years of Fighting Child Abuse . . . Carl Perkins Fumes as Barbra Streisand Uses One of His Songs in Movie Rape Scene*, STAR, Mar. 10, 1992, at 17.

35. In this lawsuit, Francis was alleging that her "moral rights" were violated under unidentified foreign laws and the court observed that it is unclear how the defendant "is liable under foreign law for licensing songs to films distributors—not parties to this action—who in turn distributed the films into foreign markets." *Franconero v. Universal Music Corp.*, 70 U.S.P.Q.2d 1398 (S.D.N.Y. 2003). In addition to the moral rights claim, Francis alleged that UMG took advantage of her mental impairment and ceased paying royalties. The court dismissed this claim as time-barred.

36. *See* infra notes 67–71 and accompanying text in Chapter 3.

37. *See* Richard Masur, *Right of Publicity from the Performer's Point of View*, 10 DePaul-LCA J. Art & Ent. L. & Pol'y 253, 258 (2000). Mr. Masur's comments focused specifically on unauthorized uses of an individual's persona in circumstances that "would either invade personal privacy or tend to damage, destroy, diminish or dilute the property value of that persona." Id. at 257. He presented these remarks to the Intellectual Property Section of the American Association of Law Schools' annual meeting in 2000, when he was the immediate past president of the Screen Actors Guild.

38. Id. at 258; *see also* Alice Haemmerli, *Whose Who? The Case for a Kantian Right of Publicity*, 49 Duke L.J. 383, 389 n.21 (1999) (discussing examples of technology's ability to "kidnap" an individual's likeness and position that likeness in fictitious, lewd, or violent acts).

CHAPTER 2

1. *See* Julia Cameron, The Artist's Way: A Spiritual Path to Higher Creativity 19 (1992) (quoting Carl Jung). For an early study of the characteristics of play, see John Huizinga, Homo Ludens: A Study of the Play Element in Culture 8–11 (1938). *See also* Julie Cohen, *Creativity and Culture in Copyright Theory*, 40 U.C. Davis L. Rev. 1151, 1190–92 (2007) (discussing the relevance of both creative play by humans and the "play of culture" to human creativity); Linda Lacey, *Of Bread and Roses and Copyrights*, 1989 Duke L. Rev. 1532, 1568–84 (exploring human creativity from a multifaceted perspective).

2. Teresa M. Amabile, Creativity in Context 115 (1996).

3. Id.

4. Id. at 127.

5. *See* Jennifer T. Olsson, Note, *Rights in Fine Art Photography: Through a Lens Darkly*, 70 Tex. L. Rev. 1489, 1501 n.78 (1992) (citing Sam Hamill, A Poet's Work: The Other Side of Poetry 35–43 [1990]) (discussing "shadow work" done without expectation of payment); *see also* Lacey, supra note 1, at 1571–80 (discussing artists' numerous reasons for creating beyond monetary gain).

6. Susan Scafidi, Who Owns Culture? Appropriation and Authenticity in American law 117 (2005) (citing Karim R. Lakhani & Robert G. Wolf, *Why Hackers Do What They Do: Understanding Motivation Effort in Free/Open Source Software Projects* [MIT Sloan Sch. of Mgmt., Working Paper 4425-03, Sept. 2003], available at: http://papers .ssrn.com/id=443040). Other important factors for creativity in this context found by the survey included "user need, a desire to improve programming skills, belief in the principle of open source, and a sense of obligation to give back to the open-source community." Id.

7. *See generally* Cohen, supra note 1, at 1151.

8. For an interesting account of why these influences should render the public a joint author of any copyrighted work, see Lior Zemer, The Idea of Authorship in Copyright (2007).

9. Henry Miller, *Why Don't You Try to Write?* in Creators on Creating 27–28 (Frank Barron et al. eds., 1997).

10. Henri Poincaré, *Mathematical Creation*, in The Creative Process: Reflections on the Invention in the Arts and Sciences 33 (Brewster Ghiselin ed., 1952) [hereinafter The Creative Process].

11. Amy Lowell, *The Making of Poetry*, in THE CREATIVE PROCESS, supra note 10, at 109–10.

12. Brewster Ghiselin, *Introduction*, in THE CREATIVE PROCESS, supra note 10, at 11, 26.

13. Id.

14. A nuanced examination of the Creation texts in Genesis discloses two distinct Creation stories, each depicting a different image of Adam. *See generally* JOSEPH B. SOLOVEITCHIK, THE LONELY MAN OF FAITH (1965). Differences exist within the Rabbinic and Biblical scholarly communities as to whether these two accounts derive from two different traditions or sources. The Orthodox view is that the Scriptures were written in their entirety by God. Id. at 9–10. Other movements of Judaism are inclined toward the view that the Scriptures, though perhaps divinely inspired, were composed by man. For an excellent introductory study of the human authorship theory, see RICHARD ELLIOT FRIEDMAN, WHO WROTE THE BIBLE? (1987).

15. *See* Karen L. Mulder, *He Made Stone Talk*, CHRISTIANITY TODAY, Mar. 6, 2000, available at: www.christianitytoday.com/ct/2000/003/7.80.html (last visited Sept. 6, 2008) (discussing Thomas Wolfe's account of Hart's creation of *Ex Nihilo*); *see also* supra notes 29–33 and accompanying text in Chapter 1.

16. ETZ HAYIM: TORAH AND COMMENTARY 10 (David L. Leiber et al. eds., Rabbinical Assembly 2001) (1985) [hereinafter ETZ HAYIM] (corresponds to *Genesis* 1:27).

17. DANIEL J. BOORSTIN, THE CREATORS: A HISTORY OF HEROES OF THE IMAGINATION 41 (1992).

18. SOLOVEITCHIK, supra note 14, at 12.

19. Russ VerSteeg, *Rethinking Originality*, 34 WM. & MARY L. REV. 801, 826 (1993) (quoting OXFORD LATIN DICTIONARY 456 [P. G. W. Glare ed., 1982]).

20. Howard A. Addison, *The God of Israel*, in ETZ HAYIM, supra note 16, at 1392.

21. ABRAHAM R. BESDIN, REFLECTIONS OF THE RAV 27–28 (Ktav Publ'g House, rev. ed. 1993) (1979) (quoting a lecture by Rabbi Joseph Soloveitchik and referring specifically to the first Creation narrative).

22. Rabbi Karyn D. Kedar, *The Many Names of God*, in THE WOMEN'S TORAH COMMENTARY 129 (Rabbi Elyse Goldstein ed., 2000).

23. *Legal Issues That Arise When Color Is Added to Films Originally Produced, Sold, and Distributed in Black and White: Hearings on Legal Issues That Arise When Color Is Added to Black-and-White Movies, Before the Subcomm. on Technology and the Law, of the S. Comm. on the Judiciary*, 100th Cong., 1st Sess. 7–12 (1987) (emphasis added) (statement of Elliot Silverstein, Directors Guild of America). Mr. Silverstein's remarks have been edited, where indicated, for a more global applicability beyond the colorization issue.

24. MADELEINE L'ENGLE, WALKING ON WATER: REFLECTIONS ON FAITH AND ART 18 (1980). L'Engle also authored the popular children's book, A WRINKLE IN TIME (1962).

25. KEMBREW MCLEOD, FREEDOM OF EXPRESSION®: OVERZEALOUS COPYRIGHT BOZOS AND OTHER ENEMIES OF CREATIVITY 166 (2005).

26. Id.

27. Roger Sessions, *The Composer and His Message*, in THE CREATIVE PROCESS, supra note 10, at 45, 49.

28. Id.

29. LEWIS HYDE, THE GIFT: IMAGINATION AND THE EROTIC LIFE OF PROPERTY xii (1983).

30. Id. at 279.

31. Thomas Wolfe, *The Story of a Novel*, in THE CREATIVE PROCESS, supra note 10, at 186–87.

32. HYDE, supra note 29, at 279.

33. ETZ HAYIM, supra note 16, at 13 (corresponds to *Genesis* 2:7).

34. *See* RASHI, THE TORAH WITH RASHI'S COMMENTARY 23 (Rabbi Yisrael Herczeg trans., 1995). According to classical Jewish belief, although man was created alive, his true form was not attained until God took the further step of infusing him with the soul. A. J. ROSENBERG, THE BOOK OF GENESIS 37–39 (1993).

35. RASHI, supra note 34, at 23–24.

36. Initially, research on creative thinking was "deterred not so much by ignorance as by the conviction that the nature of innovative thinking was already understood as a gift from above." JOHN S. DACEY & KATHLEEN H. LENNON, UNDERSTANDING CREATIVITY: THE INTERPLAY OF BIOLOGICAL, PSYCHOLOGICAL, AND SOCIAL FACTORS 15 (1998) (noting that the "first effective scholarly inquiry [on creative thinking] was undertaken only a little more than a century ago").

37. Id. at 130.

38. Id. at 42–43.

39. HYDE, supra note 29, at 53.

40. Ghiselin, supra note 12, at 11, 13 (quoting Carl Jung).

41. Id. at 15; *see also* AMABILE, supra note 2, at 10 (citation omitted) (quoting Anne Sexton for the proposition that the gift has more rights than the ego that wants approval).

42. Pamela Travers, *The Interviewer*, in CREATORS ON CREATING, supra note 9, at 36, 42–43.

43. Alan L. Durham, *The Random Muse: Authorship and Indeterminacy*, 44 WM. & MARY L. REV. 569, 597 (2002).

44. Id. at 598 (quoting Arp from HARRIET ANN WATTS, CHANCE: A PERSPECTIVE ON DADA 51 [1980]).

45. Anna Halprin, *The Process is the Purpose*, in CREATORS ON CREATING, supra note 9, at 44, 46.

46. Max Ernst, *Inspiration to Order*, in THE CREATIVE PROCESS, supra note 10, at 64–65.

47. HYDE, supra note 29, at 148.

48. L'ENGLE, supra note 24, at 23–24.

49. Id. at 24.

50. Id. at 55.

51. Id. at 148.

52. Renowned Old Testament scholar Avivah Zornberg has applied the connection between creativity and the creator's cession of control to God's creation of man. AVIVAH GOTTLIEB ZORNBERG, GENESIS: THE BEGINNING OF DESIRE 19, 35–36 (1995).

53. "When we speak, we emulate God speaking the world into being. We, too, create." WEEK IN REVIEW, Vol. IX, No. 8, Chayei Sarah 5758 (Vaad Hanochos Hatmimim Nov. 22, 1997).

54. ETZ HAYIM, supra note 16, at 4–5 (corresponds to *Genesis* 1:3). These "speakings" are referred to as the "Ten Utterances" with which, according to the text, God created the world. *See* RABBI BEREL WEIN, PIRKEI AVOS—TEACHINGS FOR OUR TIMES 184–85 (Shaar Press 2003); BABYLONIAN TALMUD, Rosh Hashanah 32a, Megillah 21b (Talman Inc., 1981).

55. WEEK IN REVIEW, supra note 53, at 5758.

56. ETZ HAYIM, supra note 16, at 22 (corresponds to *Genesis* 1:3); *see also* id. at 13 (corresponds to *Genesis* 1:3). ("[T]he Lord God formed man from the dust of the earth.")

57. Rainer Maria Rilke, *Letters to Merline*, in CREATORS ON CREATING, supra note 9, at 53 (emphasis added).

58. HYDE, supra note 29, at 146.

59. Id. at 147.

60. Id.

61. Id.

62. Id. at 4.

63. Id. at 273.

64. The concept of stewardship was present to an extent in the Jewish tradition as the Old Testament contemplates that the Israelites are to be God's tenants on the land, and only if they live up to the terms of their Covenant with God will they remain there. *See* ETZ HAYIM, supra note 16, at 741 (corresponds to *Leviticus* 25:23). ("But the land must not be sold beyond reclaim, for the land is Mine; you are but strangers resident with me.")

65. Sibyl Schwarzenbach, *Locke's Two Conceptions of Property*, 14 SOC. THEORY & PRAC. 145 (1988).

66. Roger Syn, *Copyright God: Enforcement of Copyright in the Bible and Religious Works*, 14 REGENT U. L. REV. 1, 23 (2002).

67. Schwarzenbach, supra note 65, at 146. Syn notes, however, that the Christian publishing industry follows the view of modern courts regarding copyright ownership, opting to view copyrights as capable of human ownership. Syn, supra note 66, at 24. This view, however, is not inconsistent with the stewardship concept to the extent that humans are regarded as holding the intellectual property in trust.

68. *See* Mulder, supra note 15, at 3.

69. *See* supra Chapter 1 for a further discussion of Frederick Hart's saga.

70. *See* Roberta M. Harding, *Gallery of the Doomed: An Exploration of Creative Endeavors by the Condemned*, 28 NEW ENG. J. ON CRIM. & CIV. CONFINEMENT 195 (2002).

71. The Diary of Anne Frank is one of the greatest classics of Holocaust literature. ANNE FRANK, ANNE FRANK: THE DIARY OF A YOUNG GIRL (B. M. Mooyaart trans., Doubleday 1952).

72. Judith Graham, *Pioneer Who Taught World to Live with Death, Dying*, CHI. TRIB., Aug. 26, 2004, at 1–2.

73. SUSAN GOLDMAN RUBIN, ART AGAINST THE ODDS: FROM SLAVE QUILTS TO PRISON PAINTINGS (2004).

74. Justin Hughes, *The Personality Interest of Artists and Inventors in Intellectual Property*, 16 CARDOZO ARTS & ENT. L.J. 81, 83 (1998).

75. Durham, supra note 43, at 623–42.

76. Poincaré, supra note 10, at 33, 38.

77. *See* supra text accompanying note 10.

78. HYDE, supra note 29, at xiii.

79. *See* AMABILE, supra note 2, at 8–13.

80. Mark Rose, *Copyright and Its Metaphors*, 50 UCLA L. REV. 1, 9 (2002).

81. *See* Wendy Gordon, *Render Copyright unto Caesar: On Taking Incentives Seriously*, 71 U. CHI. L. REV. 75, 76 n.5 (2004) (arguing that "we need to identify the optimal

mix of monetary and non-monetary incentives for various contexts within the cultural industries").

CHAPTER 3

1. 17 U.S.C. § 106 (2000). This provision also affords the copyright owner of a sound recording the right "to perform the copyrighted work publicly by means of a digital audio transmission."

2. *See* 17 U.S.C. § 201(a) (providing that copyright in a work vests initially in the author) and § 201(d) (providing that the ownership of a copyright, or any of the exclusive rights comprised in a copyright, may be transferred in whole or in part).

3. The Statute of Anne was the first statute to protect the literary work of creators and it was followed by the Engravers' Act of 1735, the first statute to afford protection to works of visual art. The Engravers' Act manifested a much greater understanding of the creative process than the Statute of Anne, and it furnished a precursor to the modern right of integrity. *See* Susan P. Liemer, *How We Lost Our Moral Rights and the Door Closed on Non-Economic Values in Copyright*, 5 J. MARSHALL REV. INTELL. PROP. L. 1, 19 (2005) (observing that "economic and non-economic concerns swam in the same primordial soup of intellectual property law ideas").

4. *See* Jane Ginsburg, *A Tale of Two Copyrights: Literary Property in Revolutionary France and America*, 64 TUL. L. REV. 991, 995, 999–1001 & n.44 (1990).

5. U.S. CONST. art. I, § 8, cl. 8.

6. L. Ray Patterson & Craig Joyce, *Copyright in 1791: An Essay Concerning the Founders' View of the Copyright Power Granted to Congress in Article I, Section 8, Clause 8 of the U.S. Constitution*, 52 EMORY L.J. 910, 938, 945 (2003) (providing a succinct analysis of the history of the Copyright Clause).

7. *See* Paul J. Heald & Suzanna Sherry, *Implied Limits on the Legislative Power: The Intellectual Property Clause as an Absolute Constraint on Congress*, 2000 UNIV. ILL. L. REV. 1119, 1148.

8. Edward C. Walterscheid, *To Promote the Progress of Science and Useful Arts: The Anatomy of a Congressional Power*, 43 IDEA 1, 9 (2002).

9. Id. at 37.

10. Irah Donner, *The Copyright Clause of the U.S. Constitution: Why Did the Framers Include It with Unanimous Approval?* 36 AM. J. LEGAL HIST. 361, 372–74 (1992).

11. Id. at 374–75.

12. *See* Alred Yen, *Restoring the Natural Law: Copyright as Labor and Possession*, 51 OHIO ST. L.J. 517 (1990).

13. John Locke, *Two Treatises on Government*, Book II, ch. V (1690).

14. Neil Netanel, *Copyright Alienability Restrictions and the Enhancement of Author Autonomy: A Normative Evaluation*, 24 RUTGERS L.J. 347, 357 (1992). *But see* Seana Valentine Shiffrin, *Lockean Arguments for Private Intellectual Property*, in NEW ESSAYS IN THE LEGAL AND POLITICAL THEORY OF PROPERTY 138, 143, 149, 154–57 (Stephen R. Munzer ed., 2001) (questioning whether Lockean theory supports privatization of intellectual property since such ownership is not necessary to make effective use of the resources).

15. Sibyl Schwarzenbach, *Locke's Two Conceptions of Property*, 14 SOC. THEORY & PRAC. 141, 146–47 (1988) (noting that the " 'spoilage clause' [that we appropriate only so much as we can use before it spoils], as well as the 'sharing clause' [that there be 'enough

and as good' left in common for others]" represent the "most visible expression in Locke of such inherent limitations imposed by our guardian roles").

16. Id. at 146, 148–49.

17. Netanel, supra note 14, at 366–67.

18. Schwarzenbach, supra note 15, at 154–55.

19. Id. at 157.

20. Id. at 151. ("My act of labor grants a right to its products in Locke, not because the latter is some sort of physical . . . extension of 'me,' but only because my producing, or causing such things to be, furthers God's underlying intentions for the preservation of mankind.")

21. 17 U.S.C. § 115(a)(2) (2000).

22. *See* 70 NEWS no. 1726 at 232 (2005).

23. 17 U.S.C. § 1202(a).

24. 17 U.S.C. § 1202(b).

25. *See* 17 U.S.C. § 1202; S. REP. NO. 105-190 (1998). ("CMI need not be in digital form."); *McClatchey v. Associated Press*, 2007 WL 776103 (W.D. Pa. Mar. 9, 2007) (holding that the statute also protects nondigital information). *But see IQ Group v. Wiesner Publ'g*, 409 F. Supp. 2d 587, 597 (D.N.J. 2006) (suggesting that CMI only applies to "copyright management performed by the technological measures of automated systems"). To date, there have been relatively few decisions involving this provision.

26. Greg Lastowka, *Digital Attribution: Copyright and the Right to Credit*, 87 B.U. L. REV. 41, 78 (2003).

27. Justin Hughes, *American Moral Rights and Fixing the Dastar "Gap,"* 2007 UTAH L. REV. 659, 674.

28. 17 U.S.C. § 106(2).

29. 17 U.S.C. § 101 (definition of a "derivative work").

30. In *Gilliam v. American Broadcasting Companies, Inc.*, 538 F.2d 14, 21 (2d Cir. 1976), the court applied the 1909 Copyright Act in a novel fashion to grant relief to the plaintiffs, a group of British writers and performers whose scripts had been edited extensively after they were produced into British television programs but prior to their broadcast on the defendant's American television network. The court ultimately concluded that the defendant, a remote sublicensee of the British Broadcasting Corporation (BBC), committed copyright infringement as a result of the extensive editing because the contract between the plaintiffs and BBC did not grant specifically to BBC the right to edit the programs once they had been recorded. BBC, therefore, could not grant rights that it did not possess to benefit its sublicensee. Critical to the court's ruling was its finding that the group had retained a common law copyright in its original, unpublished scripts upon which BBC based the recorded television programs. Id. at 19 n.3. Analogizing the situation to one in which a user licensed to create certain derivative works from a copyrighted script exceeds the media or time restrictions of her license in the production of a derivative work, the court held that the extensive editing exceeded the scope of any license that BBC was entitled to grant. Thus, the rationale of *Gilliam* supports an inferred condition that the right to make a derivative work cannot be exercised if the changes that are made constitute mutilation and the derivative work is billed as "based upon" the creator's underlying work. In such instances, the performance of alterations and resulting false attribution constitute an infringement under § 106(2), just as the performance of the unauthorized editing in *Gilliam* violated the rights granted to the defendants in that case.

31. Visual Artists Rights Act of 1990, Pub. L. No. 101-650 (tit. VI), 104 Stat. 5128 (codified in scattered sections of 17 U.S.C.).

32. Berne Convention for the Protection of Literary and Artistic Works, Sept. 9, 1886, 828 U.N.T.S. 221 (as last revised in Paris on July 24, 1971 and amended Sept. 28, 1979).

33. Adherence to the Berne Convention is not self-executing, which means that copyright protection still is achieved by bringing suit under the 1976 Copyright Act and not directly under the Berne Convention. *See* infra Chapter 4.

34. *See* infra Chapter 4 note 5 and accompanying text for the text of Article 6*bis*(1).

35. *See* Geri J. Yonover, *The "Dissing" of DaVinci: The Imaginary Case of Leonardo v. Duchamp: Moral Rights, Parody, and Fair Use*, 29 VAL. U. L. REV. 935, 965–66 (1995).

36. 17 U.S.C. § 106A(a)(3)(A) (2000).

37. 17 U.S.C. § 106A(a)(1) & (2).

38. 17 U.S.C. § 106A(a)(3)(B).

39. 17 U.S.C. § 113(d).

40. *See* § 101 (definition of a "work of visual art").

41. Courts have, however, invoked definitions for these terms. *See Carter v. Helmsley-Spear, Inc.*, 861 F. Supp. 303, 323, 325 (S.D.N.Y. 1994), *rev'd on other grounds*, 71 F.3d 77 (2d Cir. 1995), *cert. denied*, 517 U.S. 1208 (1996) (defining terms such as *honor, reputation*, and *prejudicial* in light of their "readily understood meanings"; and interpreting "recognized stature" as "a gate-keeping mechanism" affording protection only to art work "that art experts, the art community, or society in general views as possessing stature").

42. 17 U.S.C. § 106A(e)(1) (2000).

43. *See* H.R. REP. NO. 101-514, at 22 (1990), *reprinted in* 1990 U.S.C.C.A.N. 6915, 6932.

44. FINAL REPORT OF THE REGISTER OF COPYRIGHTS, WAIVER OF MORAL RIGHTS IN VISUAL ART WORKS 123, 124, 126, 131 (Mar. 1, 1996).

45. Id. at 132–33.

46. *See* RayMing Chang, *Revisiting the Visual Artists Rights Act of 1990: A Follow-Up Survey about Awareness and Waiver*, 13 TEX. INTELL. PROP. L.J. 144 (2005) (discussing results of a 2003 survey of 379 respondents, 308 of whom identified themselves as visual artists).

47. *Martin v. City of Indianapolis*, 982 F. Supp. 625 (S.D. Ind. 1997), 4 F. Supp. 2d 808 (S.D. Ind. 1998), 28 F. Supp. 2d 1098 (S.D. Ind. 1998), *aff'd*, 192 F.3d 608 (7th Cir. 1999). Damages in VARA suits are the same as those applicable in copyright infringement actions. *See* 17 U.S.C. §§ 504(c) & 505. A court may increase damages to a maximum of $100,000 for "willful" violations. 17 U.S.C. § 504(c)(2). *See* Liemer, supra note 3, at 1–2.

48. 17 U.S.C. § 301(f)(2)(b) (2000).

49. *See, e.g.*, LA. REV. STAT. ANN. § 51:2152(7) (2008) (visual or graphic works of recognized quality in any medium, excluding motion pictures); ME. REV. STAT. ANN. tit. 27, § 303(1)(D) (2008) (visual or graphic works without restriction regarding the quality of the work, excluding motion pictures); MASS. ANN. LAWS ch. 231, § 85S(b) (LexisNexis 2008) (visual or graphic works of recognized quality in any medium, including motion pictures); N.J. STAT. ANN. § 2A:24A-3(e) (West 2008) (visual or graphic works without restriction regarding the quality of the work, excluding motion pictures); N.M. STAT. ANN. § 13-4B-2(B) (LexisNexis 2008) (visual or graphic works of recognized quality in any medium, including motion pictures).

50. H.R. Rep. No. 101-514, at 21 (1990), *reprinted in* 1990 U.S.C.C.A.N. 6915, 6931.

51. For example, courts have held that additional elements such as awareness, intent, and commercial immorality or competitive use are insufficient to show a different right. *See, e.g.*, Briarpatch Ltd., *L.P. v. Phoenix Pictures, Inc.*, 373 F.3d 296, 306 (2d Cir. 2004); *Old South Home Co. v. Keystone Reality Group, Inc.*, 233 F. Supp. 2d 734, 737 (M.D.N.C. 2002). *See* infra Chapter 10 note 80 and accompanying text.

52. *Bd. of Managers of Soho Int'l Arts Condo. v. City of New York*, 2003 WL 21403333, at *12 (S.D.N.Y. June 17, 2003).

53. *See Final Report of the Ad Hoc Working Group on U.S. Adherence to the Berne Convention*, 10 Colum.-VLA J.L. & Arts 513, 555 (1986). Common-law principles such as unfair competition, breach of contract, defamation, and invasion of privacy also were discussed as possible substitutions for moral rights.

54. 15 U.S.C. § 1125(a) (2000).

55. 538 F.2d 14 (2d Cir. 1976).

56. Id. at 23–28.

57. *Film Disclosure Act of 1991: Hearing on S. 2256 before the Senate Committee on Patents, Trademarks, and Copyrights of the Committee on the Judiciary*, 102d Congress (Sept. 22, 1992) (statement of Nicholas Counter, President, Alliance of Motion Picture & Television Producers) 21, (statement of Roger L. Rayer, representing Turner Broadcasting) 43.

58. Reverse passing off also can be implicit in operation, such as when a defendant removes the name of the plaintiff and sells the product in an unbranded state. *See Smith v. Montoro*, 648 F.2d 602, 604–5 (9th Cir. 1981).

59. 539 U.S. 23 (2003).

60. *Dastar*, 539 U.S. at 35. Subsequently, the district court held a bench trial on the issue whether Dastar infringed the copyright in General Eisenhower's book, *Crusade in Europe*, by virtue of the defendants' unauthorized use of the book's text as part of the video's narration. The Ninth Circuit affirmed the lower court's holding that Dastar committed copyright infringement because the book was created as a work for hire and therefore, the publisher validly renewed the copyright in accordance with the statutory procedures in effect under the governing 1909 Copyright Act. *Twentieth Century Fox Film Corp. v. Entm't Distrib.*, 429 F.3d 869 (9th Cir. 2005), *cert. denied* 126 S. Ct. 2932 (June 26, 2006).

61. *Dastar*, 539 U.S. at 31–32.

62. Id. at 35.

63. *See, e.g., Zyla v. Wadsworth*, 360 F.3d 243 (1st Cir. 2004) (barring a § 43(a) claim by a former coauthor based on a new edition failing to give her credit); *Smith v. New Line Cinema*, No. 03 Civ. 5274 (DC), 2004 WL 2049232 (S.D.N.Y. Sept. 13, 2004) (dismissing § 43(a) claim arising from a screenplay allegedly lacking attribution); *Carroll v. Kahn*, No. 03-CV-0656, 2003 WL 22327299 (N.D.N.Y. Oct. 9, 2003) (dismissing § 43(a) claim based on failure to give plaintiff proper credit in film); *Williams v. UMG Recordings, Inc.*, 281 F. Supp. 2d 1177 (C.D. Cal. 2003) (foreclosing § 43(a) claim based on defendant's failure to credit film narrator and director). The Court in *Dastar* granted certiorari on the legal issue of "whether 43(a) of the Lanham Act . . . prevents the unaccredited copying of a work. . . ." *Dastar*, 539 U.S. at 25. Thus, since the issue certified for resolution was not limited expressly to works in the public domain, commentators have argued that the holding in the case applies to both works in the public domain as well as those protected by copyright.

See, e.g., Michael Landau, *Dastar v. Twentieth Century Fox: The Need for Stronger Protection of Attribution Rights in the United States,* 61 N.Y.U. ANN. SURV. AM. L. 273, 289 n.70 (2005); David Nimmer, *The Moral Imperative Against Academic Plagiarism (Without a Moral Right Against Reverse Passing Off),* 54 DEPAUL L. REV. 1 (2004). *But see* Jane Ginsburg, *The Right to Claim Authorship in U.S. Copyright and Trademark Law,* 41 HOUS. L. REV. 269 (2004) (noting that there is no reason why a court could not consider the application of § 43(a) in the context of reverse passing off claims for works still protected by copyright law).

64. *See Dastar,* 539 U.S. at 30.

65. Id. at 36. Section 43(a) creates two distinct types of violations. Section 43(a)(1)(A) addresses uses that are "likely to cause confusion . . . as to the origin" of goods or services. Section 43(a)(1)(B) governs uses that misrepresent the nature of goods or services. See Ginsburg, supra note 63, at 271–79 for a comprehensive treatment of these two possible exceptions to *Dastar*'s global holding.

66. Ginsburg, supra note 63, at 279.

67. 538 F.2d 14 (2d Cir. 1976).

68. *See, e.g., Holland v. Psychological Assessment Res., Inc.,* 2004 U.S. Dist. LEXIS 11006 (D. Md. June 16, 2004) (supporting author's contract claim in case involving publisher's objectionable Internet version of author's personality assessment guide). *See generally* Sidney Diamond, *Legal Protection for the "Moral Rights" of Authors and Other Creators,* 68 TRADEMARK REP. 244, 258 (1978). Moreover, some courts have concluded that actions under § 43(a) cannot be brought when a contractual provision authorizes the defendant's conduct. *See, e.g., Yarway Corp. v. Eur-Control USA Inc.,* 225 U.S.P.Q. 45, 47–48 (N.D. Ga. 1984) (refusing to allow suit under § 43(a) because the license contained express provisions regarding the placement of trademarks); *Wallace Computer Servs. Inc. v. Sun Microsystems Inc.,* 13 U.S.P.Q.2d 1324, 1328 (N.D. Ill. 1989) (denying summary judgment on reverse passing off claim because there was an issue of fact as to whether a license existed).

69. *See* Diamond, supra note 68, at 257, 261. The famous case involving the French artist Bernard Buffet illustrates this very point. Buffet decorated a refrigerator by painting a composition consisting of six panels covering the front, top, and sides of the refrigerator. Buffet considered the six panels to be one painting, and thus signed only one of the panels before auctioning the refrigerator. Subsequently, the catalogue of another auction featured a painting described as a Buffet painting on metal. An investigation revealed that this painting was one of the panels of the auctioned refrigerator. The French court entered an order preventing the separate sale of the panel. *Buffet v. Fersing,* 1962 Cours d'appel, Paris, Dalloz, *Jurisprudence* [D. Jur.] 570. *See generally* John Henry Merryman, *The Refrigerator of Bernard Buffet,* 27 HASTINGS L.J. 1023 (1976).

70. Yochai Benkler, *Free as the Air to Common Use: First Amendment Constraints on Enclosure of the Public Domain,* 74 N.Y.U. L. REV. 354, 432 (1999).

71. Adolf Dietz, *ALAI Congress: ANTWERP 1993, The Moral Right of the Author: Moral Rights and the Civil Law Countries,* 19 COLUM.-VLA J.L. & ARTS 199, 212 (1995).

72. *See, e.g., Edison v. Viva Int'l, Ltd.,* 70 A.D.2d 379 (N.Y. App. Div. 1979) (concluding that action for libel may be sustained by virtue of publication of author's article in substantially different form and content).

73. *See, e.g., Clevenger v. Baker, Voorhis & Co.,* 168 N.E.2d 643 (1960) (involving editorship of compilation with numerous inaccuracies falsely attributed to plaintiff).

74. *Cf. Muzikowski v. Paramount Pictures Corp.*, 477 F.3d 899, 903 (7th Cir. 2007) (affirming summary judgment for defendant based on plaintiff's defamation claim arising from film's unflattering depiction of character plaintiff alleged was a "thinly disguised" version of himself); *Geisel v. Poynter Prods., Inc.*, 295 F. Supp. 331, 357 (S.D.N.Y. 1968) (concluding that defamation claim not established when defendants exercised great care, skill, and judgment in manufacturing dolls based on plaintiff's drawings, thereby causing no injury to plaintiff's professional reputation).

75. Diamond, supra note 68, at 265.

76. *See, e.g., Zim v. West Publ'g Co.*, 573 F.2d 1318 (5th Cir. 1978) (holding that author stated cause of action for invasion of privacy by alleging that defendant published unauthorized revisions of his works); *Gieseking v. Urania Records*, 155 N.Y.S.2d 171 (1956) (concluding that plaintiff stated a cause of action under New York's statutory right of privacy by alleging that defendant record company made reproductions of plaintiff's piano performance and sold them as plaintiff's original recordings without his consent).

77. N.Y. CIV. RIGHTS LAW § 51 (McKinney 2005).

78. 978 F.2d 1093 (9th Cir. 1992), *cert. denied*, 506 U.S. 1080 (1993).

79. Id. at 1104.

80. *See* Cass R. Sunstein, *On Property and Constitutionalism*, 14 CARDOZO L. REV. 907, 912 (1993).

81. INTERNATIONAL INTELLECTUAL PROPERTY ANTHOLOGY 70 (Anthony D'Amato & Doris Estelle Long eds., 1996).

CHAPTER 4

1. *Cf.* David Nimmer, *The Moral Imperative Against Academic Plagiarism (Without a Moral Right Against Reverse Passing Off)*, 54 DEPAUL L. REV. 1, 19–20 (2004) (raising the question whether countries like England "have augmented their moral rights protection" since the United States joined the Berne Convention in 1988 "in a way that leaves the United States isolated").

2. According to Cyrill Rigamonti, "the adoption of civil-law style moral rights legislation is a major shift in terms of copyright theory, because it eliminates the key feature that distinguished common law from civil law copyright systems." Cyrill Rigamonti, *Deconstructing Moral Rights*, 47 HARV. INT'L. L.J. 353, 354 (2006).

3. *See* infra notes 40–42 & 58–50 and accompanying text.

4. Jane Ginsburg has called labeled U.S. compliance with Berne that of a "fig leaf" and she claims that after the Supreme Court's decision in *Dastar Corp. v. Twentieth Century Fox Film Corp.*, 539 U.S. 23 (2003), see supra Chapter 3, the state of the attribution right in this country "has been rendered the more precarious." Jane Ginsburg, *The Right to Claim Authorship in U.S. Copyright and Trademarks Law*, 41 HOUS. L. REV. 263, 307 (2004).

5. Berne Convention for the Protection of Literary and Artistic Works art. *6bis*(1), Sept. 9, 1886, 123 L.N.T.S. 233 [hereinafter Rome Revision] (as revised in Rome on June 2, 1928). The Berne Convention originally was signed in 1886, but Section *6bis* was added in 1928 during the Berne Convention's third revision. The current language is slightly modified from the 1928 provision, insofar as it speaks of "economic rights" rather than "copyright." *See* Berne Convention for the Protection of Literary and Artistic Works art. *6bis*(1), Sept. 9, 1886, 828 U.N.T.S. 221 [hereinafter Berne Convention] (as last revised in Paris on July 24, 1971 and amended Sept. 28, 1979).

6. Berne Convention, supra note 5, art. *6bis*(2); *see* infra Chapter 10 at notes 66–71 and accompanying text.

7. Berne Convention, supra note 5, art. *6bis*(3).

8. *See* Ginsburg, supra note 4, at 281; Agreement on Trade-Related Aspects of Intellectual Property Rights (TRIPs) art. 9, Apr. 15, 1994, 1869 U.N.T.S. 299.

9. Graeme W. Austin, *The Berne Convention as a Canon of Construction: Moral Rights After Dastar*, 61 N.Y.U. ANN. SURV. AM. L. 111, 116 (2005).

10. Rigamonti, supra note 2, at 357–58 (also noting that "the European Commission currently does not see any need for harmonization in this field").

11. WIPO Performances and Phonograms Treaty art. 5, Dec. 20, 1996, 36 I.L.M. 76.

12. *See* id. art. 23.

13. Emily Grant, *The Right of Publicity: Recovering Stolen Identities Under International Law*, 7 SAN DIEGO INT'L L.J. 559, 596–97 (2006) (noting that the treaty does not explicitly recognize the right of publicity, define "performance," or address the persona underlying the performance).

14. ELIZABETH ADENEY, THE MORAL RIGHTS OF AUTHORS AND PERFORMERS 211–12 (2006) (noting that although France is not yet a party to the WPPT, the law has afforded performers moral rights since 1985); id. at 260–66 (discussing Germany's system of neighboring rights for performers). In fact, in France and Germany, performers enjoy greater protection than is indicated by the WPPT in the sense that the visual aspects of performances are protected. *See* id. at 212, 260.

15. *See* Rigamonti, supra note 2, at 358. For a discussion of the performance regulations that became effective in the United Kingdom in 2006, see Robert C. Bird & Lucille M. Ponte, *Protecting Moral Rights in the United States and the United Kingdom: Challenges and Opportunities Under the U.K.'s New Performances Regulations*, 24 B.U. INT'L L.J. 213, 262 (2006).

16. *See* Rigamonti, supra note 2, at 358.

17. Id. at 356.

18. *See generally* id. Some common law jurisdictions have moral rights only for authors. *Cf.* the United Kingdom, which has also afforded performers moral rights. *See* supra note 15.

19. MARK ROSE, AUTHORS AND OWNERS: THE INVENTION OF COPYRIGHT 18 n.3 (1993).

20. Id. at 48, 81.

21. Jane Ginsburg, *A Tale of Two Copyrights: Literary Property in Revolutionary France and America*, 64 TUL. L. REV. 991, 994–95 (1990).

22. For a provocative history of moral rights in France, see Calvin D. Peeler, *From the Providence of Kings to Copyrighted Things (and French Moral Rights)*, 9 IND. INT'L & COMP. L. REV. 423 (1999). French copyright law in the nineteenth and early twentieth centuries was based on the law of July 19, 1793, which "gave authors generally a broad-based right against unauthorized reproduction of their works" but did not explicitly contain a moral rights provision. PAUL GOLDSTEIN, INTERNATIONAL COPYRIGHT: PRINCIPLES, LAW, AND PRACTICE 8 (2001); *see* Peeler, supra, at 426. With only minor amendments these laws remained in effect until the passage of the 1957 Copyright Act, which contained the first official codification of moral rights in France. GOLDSTEIN, supra, at 8–9; Peeler, supra, at 426. Thus, between 1793 and 1957, the development of authors' rights occurred primarily through judge-made law. GOLDSTEIN, supra, at 9.

23. Peeler, supra note 22, at 450.

24. Id. at 451.

25. Neil Netanel, *Copyright Alienability Restrictions and the Enhancement of Author Autonomy: A Normative Evaluation*, 24 RUTGERS L.J. 347, 377 (1993).

26. GEORG W. HEGEL, PHILOSOPHY OF RIGHT § 69 (T.M. Knox trans., Oxford Univ. Press 7th ed. 1969) (1821).

27. Id. § 43.

28. *See* Alan L. Durham, *The Random Use: Authorship and Indeterminacy*, 44 WM. & MARY L. REV. 569, 611 (2002); Alice Haemmerli, *Whose Who? The Case for a Kantian Right of Publicity*, 49 DUKE L.J. 383, 423 (1999); Netanel, supra note 25, at 380.

29. *See* Netanel, supra note 25, at 381.

30. IMMANUEL KANT, THE PHILOSOPHY OF LAW 64 (W. Hastie trans., T. & T. Clark 1887) (1797).

31. *See* Netanel, supra note 25, at 376.

32. *See* ADENEY, supra note 14, at 28–29.

33. Netanel, supra note 25, at 378.

34. *See* id.

35. Rigamonti, supra note 2, at 360. In an interesting historical analysis, Rigamonti demonstrates how the understanding of moral rights as part of copyright law was only one of several ways moral rights were originally conceptualized. *See* Cyrill Rigamonti, *The Conceptual Transformation of Moral Rights*, 55 AM. J. COMP. L. 67, 67–76 (2006). I wish to thank Elizabeth Adeney for clarifying that in Australia and the United Kingdom, moral rights are not conceptually part of copyright law because they are not considered property, although they are nonetheless contained in the copyright statutes of these countries.

36. Henry Hansmann & Marina Santilli, *Authors' and Artists' Moral Rights: A Comparative Legal and Economic Analysis*, 26 J. LEGAL STUD. 95, 134 (1997); *see* infra Chapter 7 at note 28 and accompanying text.

37. Hansmann & Santilli, supra note 36, at 134.

38. Id. at 134–35.

39. For example, in Germany, authors of cinematographic works and works used in their production can assert their right of integrity only where the works or contributions have been grossly distorted or mutilated. *See* Adolf Dietz, *Germany*, in 2 INTERNATIONAL COPYRIGHT LAW AND PRACTICE § 7[1][c] (Paul Edward Geller ed., 2007) (discussing § 93 of the Copyright Act). Thus, with respect to the exercise of moral rights for cinematographic works, "each author must take into account the other authors' and the producer's legitimate interests." Id. § 4[3][b][ii]; *see also* Hansmann & Santilli, supra note 36, at 135 n.106 (noting that in civil law countries, there are special rules governing film that "limit the director's power to assert" moral rights). *See* infra notes 54 & 65 and accompanying text.

40. Hansmann & Santilli, supra note 36, at 135 n.106.

41. *See Turner Entm't Co. v. Huston*, Cour d'appel [CA][regional court of appeal] Versailles, civ., ch., Dec. 19, 1994, No. 68, Roll 615/92, translated in 16 No. 10 Ent. L. Rep. 3 (1995).

42. *See Zinnemann Ruling a Victory for Artists Rights*, PRIMEZONE NEWSWIRE & MULTIMEDIA DISTRIBUTION, Oct. 27, 2005, www.primezone.com/newsroom/news.html ?d=88628. I thank Arnold Lutzker, who was a legal advisor for the plaintiff, for the following

citation information: Tribunale Roma, ruling no. 17260/2005, published on July 26, 2005; Appello Roma, ruling no. 2147/2007, published on May 14, 2007.

43. *See* Hansmann & Santilli, supra note 36, at 132. Interestingly, in this tradition, when someone attributes A's work to B, the right of attribution theoretically does not provide B with a right to object because B is not considered to be an "author" covered by moral rights. *See* Rigamonti, supra note 2, at 361; ADENEY, supra note 14, at 238 (noting that German moral rights law does not "give the author a right to object if his name is used in relation to a work that is not his own"). *Cf.* notes 120–22 and accompanying text.

44. *Eisenman v. Qimron*, 54(3) P.D. 817 (1993) CA 2790, 2811/93. The case has been translated unofficially by Dr. Michael Birnhack. *See* Unofficial Translation of the Dead Sea Scrolls Case, www.tau.ac.il/law/members/birnhack/DSStranslation.pdf (last visited Sept. 23, 2008) [hereinafter Dead Sea Scrolls Case].

45. *See, e.g.*, Copyright Ordinance of 1924, 1 Hukey Eretz Israel, 364 (Hebrew), 369 (English), as amended in 1981, 4A(1)(attribution) & 4A(2)(integrity), Copyright Ordinance (Amendment no. 4), 5741-1981, published at LSI 1029, May 28, 1981, p. 300. The new Israeli Copyright Act of 2007 went into effect on May 25, 2008. *See* Copyright Act of 2007, 5768-2007, 2007 LSI 34 (Isr.) (an unofficial translation is available online at: www .tau.ac.il/law/members/birnhack/IsraeliCopyrightAct2007.pdf [last visited Sept. 23, 2008] [Israeli Ministry of Justice trans., 2007]).

46. Dead Sea Scrolls Case, supra note 44, at 4.

47. *See* David Nimmer, *Copyright in the Dead Sea Scrolls: Authorship and Originality*, 38 HOUS. L. REV. 1, 66 (2001).

48. The case also involved the issue whether the deciphered text manifested sufficient originality to qualify for copyright protection. In addressing the copyright infringement issue, the court concluded that, when viewed in the aggregate, Qimron's work revealed originality and creativity, so that "the additional soul" Qimron poured into the fragments converted them into a living text capable of copyright protection. Dead Sea Scrolls Case, supra note 44, at 12–13. David Nimmer and Israeli copyright professor Niva Elkin-Koren have disputed this conclusion. Nimmer argues that if all Professor Qimron did in reconstructing the text was to decipher and track with precision a preexisting document, he should not enjoy copyright protection for his final product, because that work would not constitute an original work of authorship. The only originality would be in the mistakes. *See* Nimmer, supra note 47, at 211. Elkin-Koren claims that Qimron's work was scientific and therefore incapable of copyright protection. Niva Elkin-Koren, *Of Scientific Claims and Proprietary Rights: Lessons from the Dead Sea Scrolls Case*, 38 HOUS. L. REV. 445, 449 (2001).

49. Dead Sea Scrolls Case, supra note 44, at 21.

50. Id. at 20.

51. Id. at 21.

52. For a comprehensive discussion of the history and application of the "honor and reputation" requirements, see Elizabeth Adeney, *The Moral Right of Integrity: The Past and Future of "Honour,"* 2005 INTELL. PROP. Q. 111. *See* Berne Convention, supra note 5, art. 6bis(1); Copyright Act of 2007, 5768-2007, 2007 LSI 34, § 46(2) (Isr.); Copyright Act of 1941, Law No. 633, art. 20 (Italy).

53. Rigamonti, supra note 2, at 364. Instead of requiring distortions of works to be prejudicial to the author's honor or reputation in order to trigger protection, the German statute requires that the distortion or other impairment to the work endanger the author's

"legitimate intellectual or personal interests in the work." Urheberrechtsgesetz [Copyright Law], Sept. 9, 1965, BGBl. I at 1273, § 14 (F.R.G.). Personal interests, which include prestige and reputation, are those interests "that the author has in his own standing and well-being," whereas intellectual interests are those "that the author has in what happens to his work, without regard for himself as a person." ADENEY, supra note 14, at 246–47. The legitimacy of these interests is determined objectively "through a balancing of the interests of the plaintiff against the justified or legitimate interests of the defendant." Id. at 247.

54. Urheberrechtsgesetz [Copyright Law], Sept. 9, 1965, BGBl. I at 1273, § 93 (F.R.G.); see supra note 39.

55. Rigamonti, supra note 2, at 364–65. In France, an author is precluded from preventing any "adaptation of a computer program" that complies with rights transferred and from "exercising his right to retract or correct." See Andre Lucas & Pascal Kamina Robert Plaisant, France, in 1 INTERNATIONAL COPYRIGHT LAW AND PRACTICE § 7[2][a] (Paul Edward Geller ed., 2007) (quoting Article L. 121-7 of the I.P. Code). French law also precludes authors of computer programs from opposing modifications unless they are prejudicial to their honor or reputation. See Law No. 92-597 of July 1, 1992, art. L. 121-7 ¶ 1, Journal Officiel de la République Française [J.O.] [Official Gazette of France], July 3, 1992, p. 8801. In addition, French courts have given priority to urban planning demands over authors' moral rights claims respecting architectural works. Lucas & Plaisant, supra, § 7[2][b]; see also Jean-Luc Piotraut, An Authors' Rights-Based Copyright Law: The Fairness and Morality of French and American Copyright Law Compared, 24 CARDOZO ARTS & ENT. L.J. 549, 605 (2006) (noting that in France, an architect cannot "forbid the owner of the building to make required alterations in order to adjust it to the owner's new needs, unless those alterations happen to be seriously prejudicial to the architectural work").

56. Rigamonti, supra note 2, at 365; see also Marina Santilli, United States' Moral Rights Developments in European Perspective, 1 MARQ. INTELL. PROP. L. REV. 89, 101 (1997) (noting that courts in the civil law tradition address contextual modifications by balancing the benefits to the current owner of the work of art against the damage inuring to the artist and others).

57. Hansmann & Santilli, supra note 36, at 114 (citing Pretore of Rome, Nov. 15, 1986, Diritto di Autore 155 [1987]).

58. See Shostakovich v. Twentieth Century Fox Film Corp., 80 N.Y.S.2d 575 (1948), aff'd, 87 N.Y.S.2d 430 (1949).

59. Soc. Le Chant de Monde v. Soc. Fox Europe et Soc. Fox Americane Twentieth Century, 1 Gazette du Palais, 191 (Jan. 13, 1953), aff'd, D.A. Jur. 16, 80, Cour d'Appel Paris.

60. See infra note 89 and accompanying text; see also infra notes 66–76 and accompanying text in Chapter 10.

61. See Alan Riding, Victor Hugo Can't Rest in Peace, As a Sequel Makes Trouble, N.Y. TIMES, May 29, 2001, at E1.

62. See European Convention for the Protection of Human Rights and Fundamental Freedoms, opened for signature Nov. 4, 1950, 213 U.N.T.S. 222.

63. Cass. 1e Civ., January 30, 2007, J.C.P. édition générale February 2007, II 10024-10025; D. 2007, at 922. ("Qu'en statuant ainsi, [. . .], et sans avoir examiné les œuvres litigieuses ni constaté que celles-ci auraient altéré l'œuvre de Victor Hugo ou qu'un confusion serait née sur leur paternité, la cour d'appel, qui n'a pas ainsi caractérisé l'atteinte au

droit moral et s'est ainsi déterminée en méconnaissance de la liberté de création." [Emilie Potonet-Stec trans., 2007].)

64. *See Pierro Hugo v. Société Plon, S.A. Cass. 1e Civ.*, Jan. 30, 2007, D. 20007, 497 obs. J. Daleau (analysis by Jeanne Daleau, editor for Dalloz publisher). In December, 2008, the Paris Court of Appeal issued a decision holding that authors' moral rights are not absolute and cannot constitute a basis for preventing the creation of derivative works, particularly sequels. *See* CA Paris, 4e ch., sect. B, Dec. 19, 2008, J.C.P. 2009, II 10038, note Christophe Caron.

65. Hansmann & Santilli, supra note 36, at 139 (discussing Italian law providing that although screenwriters and directors are "authors" for purposes of moral rights, they do not have the unconditional ability to block distributions of a film).

66. *See* Rigamonti, supra note 2, at 362.

67. Id.

68. Id. at 363.

69. *See* Hansmann & Santilli, supra note 36, at 139.

70. Id.

71. Id. at 110.

72. *See* Santilli, supra note 56, at 100 (discussing the Swiss Federal Act on Copyright and Neighboring Rights of October 9, 1992 (RS 231.1), sec. 15 (1)).

73. *See* Sidney A. Diamond, *Legal Protection for the "Moral Rights" of Authors and Other Creators*, 68 TRADEMARK REP. 244, 257–58 (1978).

74. *See* id. at 258.

75. Rigamonti, supra note 2, at 361.

76. *See* Herman Cohen Jehoram, *Netherlands*, in 2 INTERNATIONAL COPYRIGHT LAW AND PRACTICE § 7[4] (Paul Edward Geller ed., 2007); ADENEY, supra note 14, at 381. *See also* Copyright Act of 1912, Stb. 1972 No. 579, art. 25(1)(d) (Neth.) (an unofficial translation is available online at: www.ivir.nl/legislation/nl/copyrightact1912_unofficial.pdf [last visited Sept. 23, 2008] [Ministry of Justice trans., 2008]).

77. Hansmann & Santilli, supra note 36, at 126.

78. *See* Phyllis Amarnick, *American Recognition of the Moral Right: Issues and Options*, 29 COPYRIGHT L. SYMP. (ASCAP) 31, 47–48 (1983); John Henry Merryman, *The Refrigerator of Bernard Buffet*, 27 HASTINGS L.J. 1023, 1044–45 (1976); Raymond Sarraute, *Current Theory on the Moral Right of Authors and Artists Under French Law*, 16 AM. J. COMP. L. 465, 481–82 (1968). *See also* Rigamonti, supra note 2, at 377 (noting, based on the case law of France and Germany, that "narrowly tailored waivers that involve reasonably foreseeable encroachments on the author's moral rights are generally valid"). With respect to the exercise of an author's right of integrity in the face of conflicts with the rights of a third party, particularly in cases involving modifications to architectural works by building owners, courts in civil law countries such as France and Germany tend to balance pragmatically the interests at stake rather than apply the prohibitions against modification mechanically. Id. at 366. Moreover, Rigamonti notes that as a general matter, "the precise scope of the moral right of integrity cannot be determined in the abstract, despite the fact that the inalienable rights rhetoric suggests otherwise." Id. at 367.

79. Hansmann & Santilli, supra note 36, at 129.

80. *See* Mike Holderness, *Moral Rights and Authors' Rights: The Keys to the Information Age*, J. INFO. L. & TECH., Feb. 27, 1998, § 3.3, available at: www2.warwick.ac.uk/fac/soc/law/elj/jilt/1998_1/Holderness (last visited Sept. 23, 2008).

81. Id. Interestingly, in 2006, Beckett's estate lost another case in Italy involving the same play, although the production in question featured two women in the lead roles who were nonetheless dressed and depicted as men. The court failed to find a violation to the integrity of Beckett's work under the circumstances. *See* Barbara McMahon, *Beckett Estate Fails to Stop Women Waiting for Godot*, GUARDIAN, Feb. 4, 2006, at 19, available at: www .guardian.co.uk/world/2006/feb/04/arts.italy/print (last visited Sept. 23, 2008).

82. Rigamonti, supra note 2, at 378. For a discussion of a German case finding in favor of a film producer whose film ending was alleged to have grossly distorted the author's novel, see Dietz, supra note 39, § 7[4][b]. The decision was in part based on the author's prior consent to a similar ending.

83. Rigamonti, supra note 2, at 377 (discussing the French *Fantômas* case at CA Paris, 1e ch., Nov. 23, 1970, 69 RIDA 1971, 74–76).

84. Id. at 378.

85. *See* Lucas & Plaisant, supra note 55, § 7[4][b][i]; *see also* Hansmann & Santilli, supra note 36, at 135.

86. Hansmann & Santilli, supra note 36, at 135 n.8.

87. *See* Dietz, supra note 39, § 7[4]; *see also* Adolf Dietz, *Urheberpersöhnlichkeitsrecht*, in URHEBERRECHT: KOMMENTAR § 13[28] (Gerhard Schricker ed., 2d ed. 1999) (F.R.G.) (noting that even though there are limited conditions where a ghostwriter's waiver is admissible, a binding renunciation for the entire duration of the copyright cannot be accepted for either the general recognition right or for the right to determine whether a work is to bear an author's designation and what form that designation should take, both of which are set out in § 13 of the German Copyright Act, Urheberrechtsgesetz, Sept. 9, 1965, BGBl. I at 1273, § 13 [Aaron White trans., 2008]).

88. *See* supra note 6 and accompanying text. For example, Germany and the Netherlands provide that moral rights expire with the copyright. *See* Urheberrechtsgesetz [Copyright Law], Sept. 9, 1965, BGBl. I at 1273, § 64 (F.R.G.); Dietz, supra note 39, § 7[3] (protection for moral rights lasts seventy years after an author's death, or seventy years after the death of the last surviving coauthor); Copyright Act of 1912, Stb. 1972 No. 579, art. 25 (Neth.); Jehoram, supra note 76, § 7[3].

89. Law No. 92-597 of July 1, 1992, art. L. 121-1, Journal Officiel de la République Française [J.O.] [Official Gazette of France], July 3, 1992, p. 8801, reprinted in WORLD INTELLECTUAL PROP. ORG, INTELLECTUAL PROPERTY LAWS AND TREATIES: COPYRIGHT AND RELATED RIGHTS LAWS AND TREATIES (2000). Other countries that have adopted this approach include: Ecuador, Law on Intellectual Property, *Registro Oficial*, Year II, No. 320 of May 19, 1998, art. 18; Guinea, Law No. 043/APN/CP Adopting Provisions on Copyright, Aug. 9, 1980, art. 3(a); Ivory Coast, Law No. 96-564 on the Protection of Intellectual Works and the Rights of Authors, Performers, and Phonogram and Videogram Producers, July 25, 1996, art. 23, Journal Officiel de la République de Côte d'Ivoire ; and Senegal, Law No. 73-52 on the Protection of Copyright, No. 4333 of Dec. 4, 1973, art. 3(a), Journal Officiel de la Republique du Senegal; collectively reprinted in WORLD INTELLECTUAL PROP. ORG., INTELLECTUAL PROPERTY LAWS AND TREATIES: COPYRIGHT AND RELATED RIGHTS LAWS AND TREATIES (2000). In addition, China has adopted this approach with regard to certain moral rights. Zhonghua Renmin Gongheguo Zhuzuoquanfa [Copyright Law of the People's Republic of China] (promulgated by the Standing Comm. Nat'l People's Cong., Sept. 7, 1990, effective June 1, 1991), Fagui Huibian 1990, art. 20 (providing that "[t]he rights of authorship, alteration and integrity of an author shall be unlimited in time"). The

duration of the right to publication in China is limited to the lifetime of the author plus fifty years. Id. art. 21.

90. *See* Diamond, supra note 73, at 247; *see also* supra notes 25–29 and accompanying text.

91. *See* Hansmann & Santilli, supra note 36, at 122–23 (discussing the right of integrity specifically).

92. Id. at 123; *see* Copyright Act of 1941, Law No. 633, art. 23 (Italy) (providing that "[i]f the public interest should so require . . . action may also be taken by the President of the Council of Ministers after hearing the competent professional association").

93. Hansmann & Santilli, supra note 36, at 123.

94. Some scholars, however, are not persuaded that at this point a significant practical difference exists between the civil and common law traditions. *See* Rigamonti, supra note 2, at 367 (noting that relying on the standard "moral rights orthodoxy" in the civil law countries "instead of focusing on the concrete rules that courts apply in practice creates the triple risk of overestimating the actual scope of moral rights in civil law countries, underestimating the contractual implications of moral rights, and generating an unreliable basis for the comparison of civil law moral rights with the law of legal systems that do not fully endorse the dominant concept of moral rights").

95. Copyright Amendment Act, R.S.C., ch. 8, § 12(7) (1931). The Canadian statute was updated in 1985. *See* Copyright Act, R.S.C., ch. C-42 (1985) (Can.).

96. Copyright, Designs & Patents Act, 1988, ch. 48, § 77 (U.K.) [hereinafter CDPA].

97. Copyright Act 1994, 1994 S.N.Z. No. 143, §§ 94–97; *see* Austin, supra note 9, at 137.

98. Copyright Amendment (Moral Rights) Act 2000 (Austrl.).

99. *See, e.g.*, Anna Kingsbury, *Protecting Indigenous Knowledge and Culture Through Indigenous Communal Moral Rights in Copyright Law: Is Australia Leading the Way?* 12 N.Z. BUS. L. Q. 162 (2006) (arguing that although the details of the model proposed in Australia are problematic, the concept should be seriously considered in New Zealand).

100. Copyright and Related Rights Act, 2000 (Act No. 28/2000) § 109(1) (Ir.), available at: www.irlgov.ie/bills28/acts/2000/a2800.pdf (last visited Sept. 23, 2008).

101. *See* Austin, supra note 9, at 137.

102. *See* Copyright Act, R.S.C., ch. C-42, art. 2 (1985) (Can.); Ysolde Gendreau & David Vaver, *Canada*, in 1 INTERNATIONAL COPYRIGHT LAW AND PRACTICE § 7(1) (Paul Edward Geller ed., 2007) (noting that moral rights do not apply to performances, sound recordings, and broadcasts "because they are not 'works' and do not have 'authors' ").

103. CDPA § 9(2)(a).

104. *See* id. § 77(1) (providing that the director of a copyright film "has the right to be identified as the author or director of the work"); id. § 80 (providing that the director of a copyright film "has the right . . . not to have his work subjected to derogatory treatment"). Under § 10, the director could potentially qualify as a joint author of the film if the film is a "collaboration of two or more authors in which the contribution of each author is not distinct from that of the other author or authors." Id. § 10.

105. Id. §§ 79(2), 81(2). See infra note 28 in Chapter 7 for a discussion of how employees are treated under the CDPA. Note that under the new copyright law in Israel, see supra note 45, the authors of computer programs are also excluded from moral rights protection. *See* Copyright Act of 2007, 5768-2007, 2007 LSI 34, ch. 7, § 45 (Isr.).

106. CDPA §§ 79(3), 82. See generally ADENEY, supra note 14, at 392–93.

107. Copyright Act, 1968, No. 63, § 127(1) (Austl.).

108. Copyright Amendment (Moral Rights) Act, 2000, § 189 (Austl.).

109. Id. § 189.

110. Copyright Act, R.S.C., ch. C-42, § 14.1(1) (1985) (Can.); *see also* ADENEY, supra note 14, at 325 (noting uncertainty whether the reasonableness standard is a defense or part of the plaintiff's burden of proof).

111. Copyright Act, R.S.C., ch. C-42, § 14.1(1) (1985) (Can.); *see also* ADENEY, supra note 14, at 322–23.

112. ADENEY, supra note 14, at 395.

113. *See* Rigamonti, supra note 2, at 402; ADENEY, supra note 14, at 397–98 (noting that in this respect, the statute in the United Kingdom "does not go so far as its Canadian counterpart in its protection of purely personal interests").

114. CDPA § 77(8); *see also* ADENEY, supra note 14, at 397.

115. Jane Ginsburg has noted that in the United Kingdom, attribution rights "are grudgingly given and easily lost." Ginsburg, supra note 4, at 288 (noting the same with respect to New Zealand).

116. ADENEY, supra note 14, at 398.

117. Ginsburg, supra note 4, at 291; *see* CDPA § 78(2). Irini Stamatoudi suggests that the assertion requirement may be satisfied more easily for artistic works than for literary works because the CDPA provides that the signature of the artist on the original, an authorized copy, or on the frame of the work while the work is exhibited in public, qualifies as an assertion. In contrast, the prominent display of an author's name on the cover of her book may not qualify as an assertion sufficient to trigger the right of attribution. Irini A. Stamatoudi, *Moral Rights of Authors in England: The Missing Emphasis on the Role of Creators*, 1997 INTELL. PROP. Q. 478, 489; *see also* CDPA § 78(2)–(3).

118. Ginsburg, supra note 4, at 291; *see* supra note 5 and accompanying text.

119. Ginsburg, supra note 4, at 291 (quoting Berne Convention art. 5(2)). Ginsburg is critical of this assertion requirement and also ponders its effect on third parties. Id. at 291–92. The language of New Zealand's assertion requirement is identical to that in the CDPA. *See* Copyright Act 1994, 1994 S.N.Z. No. 143, § 96; CDPA § 78.

120. CDPA § 84(1).

121. ADENEY, supra note 14, at 402.

122. CDPA §§ 84(2), (3), (4), (6). Some do not consider this right to be a "moral right" because it is not concerned with an *author's* relationship to her work. *Cf.* supra note 43.

123. Unlike the false attribution provision in the United Kingdom, which protects a person's right not to have the work of another falsely attributed to her, the false attribution provision in Australia protects an author from having the name of another wrongly placed on her work. *See* Copyright Act, 1968, No. 63, § 195AC(1) (Austl.); CDPA § 84(1). *See also* ADENEY, supra note 14, at 402, 577. As noted in the text, this right is not covered explicitly in the United Kingdom. *See* supra note 112 and accompanying text. According to Elizabeth Adeney:

> The right [in Australia] has two limbs: the author's right: (1) not to have another's name (a pseudonym, initials, or monogram) wrongly appear on or with the work in such a way as to denote authorship, and (2) not to have the work, as altered by another, dealt with in such a way as to indicate that the alterations are the work of the author.
>
> Conceptually, the two limbs are very different. The first protects the author's connection with the work and wish to be associated with it. The second protects the author

from being associated with a work that is no longer entirely his own. (Both have a secondary effect of protecting the consumer against false information about the authorship of the work.) The first differs dramatically from its namesake in the United Kingdom, since it is not aimed at the protection of a person's name against misuse on a work created by another. ADENEY, supra note 14, at 577; *see* Copyright Act, 1968, No. 63, § 195AC(1)–(2) (Austl.).

124. *See* ADENEY, supra note 14, at 576; *see also* Copyright Act, 1968, No. 63, § 193 (Austl.).

125. Copyright Act, 1968, No. 63, § 195AR(2) (Austl.). The "reasonableness" defense is not available for false attribution, however, since a false attribution is, by nature, unreasonable. *See* ADENEY, supra note 14, at 589.

126. *See* Copyright Act, 1968, No. 63, § 195AR(1) (Austl.); ADENEY, supra note 14, at 589; Ginsburg, supra note 4, at 299.

127. CDPA § 80(2)(b) (emphasis added). Interestingly, Ireland's moral rights law mirrors that of the United Kingdom in many respects, but the Irish statute's standard for integrity violations eliminated "honor" from the requirement, making actionable violations that are prejudicial to the author's "reputation." Copyright and Related Rights Act, 2000 (Act No. 28/2000), § 109(1) (Ir.), available at: www.irlgov.ie/bills28/acts/2000/a2800.pdf (last visited Sept. 23, 2008); *see also* Adeney, supra note 52, at 111.

128. For a further discussion of this point and conflicting case authority, see Bird & Ponte, supra note 15, at 240–46; ADENEY, supra note 14, at 407–9. In 2003, the Chancery Division of the High Court held that unless a work has been distorted or mutilated so as to prejudice the author's honor or reputation, there is no claim. *Confetti Records v. Warner Music UK Ltd.*, [2003] E.M.L.R. 35. Adeney notes that although the New Zealand statute essentially comports with the United Kingdom model, it avoids this ambiguity by clarifying that prejudicial treatment is an element. ADENEY, supra note 14, at 408 n.139. However, "treatment" under the New Zealand statute is a narrower concept than Berne contemplates. *See* Kingsbury, supra note 99, at 167. In addition, the CDPA is unclear as to whether the determination of whether a distortion or mutilation has occurred should be governed by the view of the author, the court, or an independent third party. *See* Bird & Ponte, supra note 15, at 245–46.

129. Rigamonti, supra note 2, at 402; Leslie Kim Treiger-Bar-Am, *The Moral Right of Integrity: A Freedom of Expression*, in 2 NEW DIRECTIONS IN COPYRIGHT 152 (Fiona Macmillan ed., 2006).

130. CDPA § 103(2); *see also* Rigamonti, supra note 2, at 402 n.284.

131. *See* Copyright Act, R.S.C., ch. C-42, § 28.2(1)–(2) (1985) (Can.).

132. Id. § 28.2(1)(b) (emphasis added).

133. *See* id. § 14.1(1) (emphasis added); *see also* supra note 110 and accompanying text.

134. Copyright Act, 1968, No. 63, § 195AJ (Austl.).

135. Id.

136. Id. §§ 195AS(2)(h), (3)(i).

137. Hansmann & Santilli, supra note 36, at 125.

138. Copyright Act, R.S.C., ch. C-42, § 14.1(1) (1985) (Can.).

139. Ginsburg, supra note 4, at 293.

140. CDPA § 87(2) (providing that any of the moral rights "may be waived by instrument in writing signed by the person giving up the right"); *see also* ADENEY, supra note 14, at 422–23 (noting that waiver may relate to any work and may be conditional or unconditional). For a discussion of the distinction between waiver and consent in the CDPA, see ADENEY, supra note 14, at 423–24.

141. CDPA § 87(2).

142. CDPA § 87(3).

143. Rigamonti, supra note 2, at 403.

144. Ginsburg, supra note 4, at 292.

145. ADENEY, supra note 14, at 598.

146. Copyright Act, 1968, No. 63, § 195AWA(2) (Austl.).

147. Ginsburg, supra note 4, at 298; *see* Copyright Act, 1968, No. 63, § 195AWA(4) (Austl.). With respect to films, the statute omits the word "genuinely."

148. Elizabeth Adeney suggests that this blanket waiver is also applicable to the right of false attribution, despite the lack of availability of the reasonableness defense to this right. ADENEY, supra note 14, at 600; *see also* supra note 123.

149. Ginsburg, supra note 4, at 298.

CHAPTER 5

1. Diane Leenheer Zimmerman, *Is There a Right to Have Something to Say? One View of the Public Domain*, 73 FORDHAM L. REV. 297, 308–9 (2004) (discussing both the views of those who favor a strong public domain and their opponents).

2. Pamela Samuelson, *Enriching Discourse on Public Domains*, 55 DUKE L.J. 783 (2006).

3. Id. at 826–27 (footnotes omitted).

4. THE FUTURE OF THE PUBLIC DOMAIN—IDENTIFYING THE COMMONS IN INFORMATION LAW (Lucie Guibault & P. Bernt Hugenholtz eds., Kluwer Law International, 2006) [hereinafter THE FUTURE OF THE PUBLIC DOMAIN]; *Collected Papers, Duke Conference on the Public Domain*, 66 LAW & CONTEMP. PROBS. 1 (2003).

5. *See* Niva Elkin-Koren, *Exploring Creative Commons: A Skeptical View of a Worthy Pursuit*, in THE FUTURE OF THE PUBLIC DOMAIN, supra note 4, at 325, 326.

6. Tyler T. Ochoa, *Origins and Meanings of the Public Domain*, 28 DAYTON L. REV. 215, 261–62 (2003).

7. *See, e.g.*, Samuelson, supra note 2, at 801, 815–16 (discussing scholars who maintain an interchangeable understanding of these terms and comparing specialized uses of "commons" within scientific communities); Edward Lee, *The Public's Domain: The Evolution of Legal Restraints on the Government's Power to Control Public Access Through Secrecy or Intellectual Property*, 55 HASTINGS L.J. 91, 100 (2003) (briefly discussing distinctions between these terms despite their interchangeable use).

8. Samuelson, supra note 2, at 816.

9. Id. at 817–18.

10. Id. at 818–19.

11. Id. at 819–20.

12. Id. at 824.

13. See generally Justin Hughes, *"Recoding" Intellectual Property and Overlooked Audience Interests*, 77 TEX. L. REV. 923 (1999) for a detailed treatment of this topic.

14. *See* Lee, supra note 7, at 99.

15. Neil Netanel, *Locating Copyright within the First Amendment Skein*, 54 STAN. L. REV. 1, 65 (2001) [hereinafter *First Amendment Skein*]. Jessica Litman has carefully documented this aspect of copyright law history in JESSICA LITMAN, DIGITAL COPYRIGHT 35–63 (2001). *See also* Jessica Litman, *Copyright, Compromise and Legislative History*, 72 CORNELL L. REV. 857 (1987); C. Edwin Baker, *First Amendment Limits on Copyright*, 55 VAND. L. REV. 891, 950 (2002) ("The losing side in the legislative decision to approve copyright 'enclosures' often is not represented by well-organized, financially and politically powerful advocates. Observers commonly report that the public was largely excluded from the bargaining table."); Yochai Benkler, *Free as the Air to Common Use: First Amendment Constraints on Enclosure of the Public Domain*, 74 N.Y.U. L. REV. 354, 422 (1999) (noting that the hearings on the anticircumvention provisions of the DMCA suggest they were enacted in response "to concerns expressed primarily by the motion picture and musical recording industries").

16. *See First Amendment Skein*, supra note 15, at 28. ("Copyright's benefits inure disproportionately to large media firms that already own vast inventories of copyrighted expression. Copyright's burdens fall most heavily on individuals, nonprofits, and small independents that do not.") In a recent book, author David Bollier has observed that copyright actually works to the disadvantage of individual creators who need to be empowered more than ever. DAVID BOLLIER, BRAND NAME BULLIES: THE QUEST TO OWN AND CONTROL CULTURE 8 (2005). *See also* KEMBREW MCLEOD, FREEDOM OF EXPRESSION®: OVERZEALOUS COPYRIGHT BOZOS AND OTHER ENEMIES OF CREATIVITY (2005) (recommending that artists and authors aggressively exercise their intellectual property rights in the face of threats and legal challenges from overbearing copyright holders). *Cf.* William Cornish, *The Author as Risk-Sharer*, 26 COLUM.-VLA J.L. & ARTS 1, 12 (2002) (calling for increased recognition of "the author" in copyright law).

17. Benkler, supra note 15, at 408.

18. Two examples of such politically influential entities are Disney and Turner Entertainment. *See Moral Rights in Our Copyright Laws: Hearings on S. 1198 and S. 1253 Before the Subcomm. on Patents, Copyrights and Trademarks on the S. Comm. on the Judiciary*, 101st Cong. 1038, 1061 (1990) (statement of Peter Nolan, representative of both the Disney Corporation and the Motion Picture Association of America).

19. *See* Neil Netanel, *Copyright Alienability Restrictions and the Enhancement of Author Autonomy: A Normative Evaluation*, 24 RUTGERS L.J. 347, 414–15 (1993).

20. *See generally* Sheldon Halpern, *Of Moral Right and Moral Righteousness*, 1 MARQ. INTELL. PROP. L. REV. 65 (1997) (cautioning that we need to design moral rights laws that are consistent with our particular culture and legal framework).

21. U.S. CONST. art I, § 8, cl. 8.

22. Edward C. Walterscheid, *To Promote the Progress of Science and Useful Arts: The Background and Origin of the Intellectual Property Clause of the United States Constitution*, 2 J. INTELL. PROP. L. 1, 32–33 (1994).

23. Edward C. Walterscheid, *To Promote the Progress of Science and Useful Arts: The Anatomy of a Congressional Power*, 43 IDEA 1, 3 (2003) [hereinafter *The Anatomy of a Congressional Power*].

24. DAVID P. CURRIE, THE CONSTITUTION IN CONGRESS: THE FEDERALIST PERIOD 1789–1801, at 93 (1997). *See also* Andres Hetherington, *Constitutional Purpose and*

Inter-Clause Conflict: The Constraints Imposed on Congress by the Copyright Clause, 9 MICH. TELECOMM. & TECH. L. REV. 457, 467 (2003) (noting this probably is the most common interpretation).

25. *See, e.g., The Anatomy of a Congressional Power*, supra note 23, at 5.

26. Dotan Oliar, *Making Sense of the Intellectual Property Clause: Promotion of Progress as a Limitation on Congress's Intellectual Property Power*, 94 GEO. L.J. 1771, 1818 (2006).

27. I take the position that the enactment of appropriately crafted federal moral rights legislation is a valid exercise of Congressional authority under the Copyright Clause, and therefore I do not discuss at length the issue of whether moral rights laws could be enacted pursuant to other constitutional provisions. Recent courts have concluded that the Copyright Clause does not forbid Congress from extending copyright-like protection to works of authorship that are not fixed pursuant to other constitutional clauses such as the Commerce Clause. *See, e.g., United States v. Moghadam*, 175 F.3d 1269 (11th Cir. 1999) (assuming, without deciding, that the Copyright Clause cannot serve as the constitutional authority for the criminal anti-bootlegging statute but sustaining this legislation pursuant to the Commerce Clause despite its protection of unfixed musical performances), *cert. denied*, 529 U.S. 1036 (2000); *United States v. Martignon*, 492 F.3d 140 (2d Cir. 2007) (sustaining the criminal liability provision of the anti-bootlegging provision as validly enacted under the Commerce Clause).

It should also be noted that another potential source of authority for moral rights protection is the treaty power. For an examination of whether Congress can invoke the treaty power to enact legislation that otherwise would be beyond the scope of its enumerated powers, see Richard B. Graves III, *Globalization, Treaty Powers, and the Limits of the Intellectual Property Clause*, 50 J. COPYRIGHT SOC'Y U.S.A. 199, 218 n.119 (2003) (citing several articles supporting the general principle that Congress cannot bypass the restrictions in the Copyright Clause by legislating pursuant to another clause).

28. For example, in *Burnett v. Chetwood*, (1720) 35 Eng. Rep. 1008 (Ch.), the executor of the author obtained an injunction against the printing of the author's work in English on the ground that prior excerpts of his work published in English without his permission caused him great embarrassment. The essence of the plaintiff's claim in this suit was proprietary rather than economic. MARK ROSE, AUTHORS AND OWNERS: THE INVENTION OF COPYRIGHT 50–51 (1993). The work at issue concerned the author's attempt to reconcile his theory of the earth's creation with Genesis, and the excerpts causing him embarrassment contained a facetious conversation between Eve and the serpent. Id. at 49. The author, while living, attempted to prevent any future translations or reprintings of his work. Id. Similarly, in *Pope v. Curl*, (1741) 26 Eng. Rep. 608 (Ch.), a seminal Anglo-American copyright law case establishing the writer's right to the copyright in his letters, the plaintiff's concern was both proprietary and commercial. ROSE, supra, at 60–64. Also, in *Millar v. Taylor*, (1769) 98 Eng. Rep. 201 (K.B.), the court upheld the author's rights in his work subsequent to its publication, invoking both personal and economic justifications for this conclusion. Specifically, *Millar* held that the denial of an author's post-publication right would result in the denial of profits to the author as well as a loss of control over the content and direction of his work. *See also* ROSE, supra, at 78–82.

29. *Donaldson v. Beckett*, (1774) 1 Eng. Rep. 837 (H.L.) (appeal taken from England), available at: www.llmcdigital.org/docdisplay.aspx?textid=9219997 (last visited Oct. 1, 2008).

30. Mark Rose, *Nine-Tenths of the Law: The English Copyright Debates and the Rhetoric of the Public Domain*, 66 LAW & CONTEMP. PROBS. 75, 81 (2003).

31. *Cf.* Jane Ginsburg, *A Tale of Two Copyrights: Literary Property in Revolutionary France and America*, 64 TUL. L. REV. 991, 1006–10 (1990) (noting that recognition for authors' rights began in France as early as 1791 but asserting the initial purpose of such laws was to promote access to the public domain rather than concern for authors' rights). *See also* supra Chapter 4 notes 21–22 and accompanying text.

32. One exception in this regard in the Anglo-American copyright tradition was the British Engravers' Act of 1735, which manifested a concern for poor quality copies that prejudiced the original artists. *See* Susan P. Liemer, *How We Lost Our Moral Rights and the Door Closed on Non-Economic Values in Copyright*, 5 J. MARSHALL REV. INTELL. PROP. L. 1, 15 (2005); *see also* supra Chapter 3 note 3.

33. *See* supra Chapter 3 notes 6 & 10–11 and accompanying text.

34. Hetherington, supra note 24, at 469. *See also* Orrin G. Hatch & Thomas R. Lee, *"To Promote the Progress of Science": The Copyright Clause and Congress's Power to Extend Copyrights*, 16 HARV. J.L. & TECH. 1 (2002). ("The founding-era understanding of 'progress' clearly extends to the dissemination or distribution of existing artistic works and is not limited to an increase in quantity or quality.")

35. Additionally, one of the most frequently articulated policy arguments favoring stronger moral rights protections is the need for global uniformity. The absence of meaningful moral rights laws in the United States represents a significant gap between United States' authors and their counterparts worldwide. *See, e.g.*, Michael B. Gunlicks, *A Balance of Interests: The Concordance of Copyright Law and Moral Rights in the Worldwide Economy*, 11 FORDHAM INTELL. PROP. MEDIA & ENT. L.J. 601, 604 (2001). This lack of harmony is especially compelling in light of Congress's decision to enact the Copyright Term Extension Act as an amendment to the 1976 Copyright Act, a decision that was influenced by the European Union's directive to establish a life plus seventy-year copyright term. The Supreme Court affirmed the constitutionality of this amendment in *Eldred v. Ashcroft*, relying largely on the need for global norms in this area. *See Eldred v. Ashcroft*, 537 U.S. 186, 205–6 (2003). *But see* id. at 259–60 (Breyer, J., dissenting) (expressing doubts regarding the extent to which uniformity has been achieved). See infra notes 47–50 for a discussion of *Eldred*.

36. Oliar, supra note 26, at 1818.

37. *See* Cyrill P. Rigamonti, *Deconstructing Moral Rights*, 47 HARV. INT'L L.J. 353, 360 (2006). *See also* supra Chapter 4 note 35 and accompanying text.

38. *See* supra Chapter 3 note 9 and accompanying text.

39. *See* supra Chapter 2 notes 56–65 and accompanying text.

40. *See* supra Chapter 2 note 69 and accompanying text.

41. *Cf.* David Nimmer, *The Moral Imperative Against Academic Plagiarism (Without a Moral Right Against Reverse Passing Off)*, 54 DEPAUL L. REV. 1, 74 (2004). ("The laws of the marketplace are ill served by allowing authors who no longer enjoy copyright protection to assert ersatz ownership through the vehicle of reverse passing off.")

42. *See Golan v. Gonzales*, 501 F.3d 1179, 1187 (10th Cir. 2007). ("Legislation promulgated pursuant to the Copyright Clause must still comport with other express limitations of the Constitution.")

43. *Wheaton v. Peters*, 33 U.S. 591, 663–64 (1834) (affirming that the importance of copyright's formalities was solely within the legislature's prerogative).

44. This abdication of judicial authority is somewhat ironic in light of the likelihood that the Framers gave Congress explicit authority in this area only because they feared that an absence of directive would preclude any Congressional activity concerning copyrights. It is not clear, however, that the Framers intended Congress to be the primary arbiter of authors' rights at the expense of the judiciary; the Court in *Wheaton* could have taken measures to expand its power under the Copyright Clause and thereby limit Congress's power. Marci A. Hamilton, *Copyright at the Supreme Court: A Jurisprudence of Deference*, 47 J. COPYRIGHT SOC'Y U.S.A. 317, 326 (2000). ("Copyright law . . . began and persisted as the special provenance of the Congress, not the Court.")

45. *Wheaton*, 33 U.S. at 661.

46. For a more complete analysis of this deference, see Hamilton, supra note 44, at 326–35. *See also* Willliam Patry, *The Enumerated Powers Doctrine and Intellectual Property: An Imminent Constitutional Collision*, 67 GEO. WASH. L. REV. 359, 363–64 (1999) (discussing the Supreme Court's reconceptualization of the Copyright Clause by allowing Congress to grant creators monopolies in original works of authorship and the public a right to copy unprotected material). For a discussion by the Supreme Court regarding the extent to which the Court defers to Congress in matters pertaining to copyright law, see *Eldred v. Ashcroft*, 537 U.S. 186, 211–13, 218 (2003). See Paul M. Schwartz & William Michael Treanor, *Eldred and Lochner: Copyright Term Extension and Intellectual Property as Constitutional Property*, 112 YALE L.J. 2331 (2003) for a thoughtful defense of deferential judicial review with respect to constitutional challenges to copyright laws.

47. *Eldred*, 537 U.S. at 204. Somewhat surprisingly, little scholarly discussion exists regarding whether the enactment of moral rights protection can be sustained from a constitutional standpoint. No cases have yet challenged VARA on this ground, and there have been only a few law review articles discussing this issue in any depth. *See, e.g.*, Eric Bensen, Note, *The Visual Artists' Rights Act of 1990: Why Moral Rights Cannot Be Protected Under the United States Constitution*, 24 HOFSTRA L. REV. 1127 (1996).

48. *See Eldred*, 537 U.S. at 232 n.8.

49. Id. at 205 n.10.

50. Id. at 218 (quoting *Graham v. John Deere Co. of Kansas City*, 383 U.S. 1, 6 [1966]).

51. *See* Jed Rubenfeld, *The Freedom of Imagination: Copyright's Constitutionality*, 112 YALE L.J. 1, 30–31 (2002).

52. *See generally* Lawrence Adam Beyer, *Legal Theory: Intentionalism, Art, and the Suppression of Innovation: Film Colorization and the Philosophy of Moral Rights*, 82 NW. U. L. REV. 1011, 1070 (1988) ("Expanding the contours of copyright as requested by moral rights advocates might also infringe upon first amendment rights."); Robert A. Gorman, *Copyright Courts and Aesthetic Judgments: Abuse or Necessity?* 25 COLUM. J.L. & ARTS 1, 10 (2001) (asserting Congress limited VARA's moral rights protection to works of visual art because granting moral rights for other works posed potential conflict with the First Amendment); Kathryn A. Kelly, *Moral Rights and the First Amendment: Putting Honor Before Free Speech?* 11 U. MIAMI ENT. & SPORTS L. REV. 211, 243 (1994) (noting a "potential constitutional clash" between the First Amendment and moral rights); Geri J. Yonover, *Artistic Parody: The Precarious Balance: Moral Rights, Parody, and Fair Use*, 14 CARDOZO ARTS & ENT. L.J. 79, 93 (1996) (stating First Amendment concerns may be the reason for American reluctance toward moral rights).

53. *See generally Golan v. Gonzales*, 501 F.3d 1179 (10th Cir. 2007).

54. Id.

55. Id. at 1187 (citing *Eldred*, 537 U.S. at 221).

56. Section 514 of the Uruguay Round Agreements Act (URAA) vests copyright in a restored work to the original author for the term the copyright would have been in effect in the United States had the work not fallen into the public domain due to lack of compliance with our formalities or for other specified reasons. This section of the URAA is codified at 17 U.S.C. §§ 104A and 109.

57. *Golan*, 501 F.3d at 1197. The court in *Golan* also held, however, that § 514 did not violate the Copyright Clause. *See* id. at 1186. On remand, the district court granted the plaintiffs' motion for summary judgment on the ground that the statutory provision did not pass First Amendment review. *Golan v. Holder*, 611 F. Supp.2d 1165 (D. Colo. 2009).

58. *See* supra notes 33–42 and accompanying text.

59. *See* Ginsburg, supra note 31, 995, 999–1001 & n.44 (1990).

60. *See Golan*, 501 F.3d at 1184.

61. *See* infra notes 91–108 and accompanying text.

62. Scholars have demonstrated that exempting copyright law from the strictures of the First Amendment not only is unfounded but also inconsistent with the approach courts have taken with respect to other areas of intellectual property. *See, e.g., Zacchini v. Scripps-Howard Broad. Co.*, 433 U.S. 562 (1977) (the right of publicity); *L.L. Bean, Inc. v. Drake Publishers, Inc.*, 811 F.2d 26 (1st Cir. 1987) (trademark law). For a full treatment of this issue, see *First Amendment Skein*, supra note 15. *See also* Michael Birnhack, *The Copyright Law and Free Speech Affair: Making-Up and Breaking-Up*, 43 IDEA 233, 288 n.245 (2003).

63. *See Golan*, 501 F.3d at 1197; ERWIN CHEMERINSKY, CONSTITUTIONAL LAW: PRINCIPLES AND POLICIES § 11.2.1, at 902–3 (2d ed. 2002).

64. *Golan*, 501 F.3d at 1197 (quoting *Grace United Methodist Church v. City of Cheyenne*, 451 F.3d 643, 657 (10th Cir. 2006) ([internal citations and quotations omitted])).

65. Id. (quoting *Ward v. Rock Against Racism*, 491 U.S. 781, 791 [1989]).

66. *See* Martin H. Redish, *The Content Distinction in First Amendment Analysis*, 34 STAN. L. REV. 113, 140 (1981) [hereinafter Redish, *The Content Distinction*] (noting that "the assumption that the courts can recognize and distinguish between these two kinds of regulations has proven incorrect in numerous instances").

67. Strict scrutiny requires that the government action be justified by a compelling state interest and achieved through the least restrictive alternative. *See Simon & Schuster, Inc. v. N.Y. State Crime Victims Bd.*, 502 U.S. 105, 118 (1991).

68. Some scholars maintain that because copyright law operates to restrict individuals' speech content on the basis of the words or content they choose, it should be seen as content based and therefore subject to strict scrutiny. *See, e.g.*, Baker, supra note 15, at 922, 936–39; Mark A. Lemley & Eugene Volokh, *Freedom of Speech and Injunctions in Intellectual Property Cases*, 48 DUKE L.J. 147, 186 (1998).

69. *See* Redish, *The Content Distinction*, supra note 66, at 141.

70. Nonetheless, among some scholars who have argued that copyright is content-neutral, there is a sentiment that copyright should be subjected to heightened scrutiny because its application results in the government's distribution of speech-related entitlements in accordance with the rent-seeking demands of politically powerful groups. *See, e.g., First Amendment Skein*, supra note 15, at 67 (advocating a type of scrutiny that would require the government to demonstrate "that the regulation serves a substantial, legitimate governmental purpose and is narrowly tailored to minimize the burden on speech"); Rebecca

Tushnet, *Copyright as a Model for Free Speech Law: What Copyright Has in Common with Anti-Pornography Laws, Campaign Finance Reform, and Telecommunications Regulation*, 42 B.C. L. Rev. 1, 76 (2000) (suggesting the use of intermediate scrutiny, which would require Congress to explain how the current copyright laws do not substantially limit more speech than necessary).

71. *Cf. First Amendment Skein*, supra note 15, at 50, 54 (asserting that copyright law is content-neutral since it lacks a content-based purpose such as suppressing expression). It could also be argued that the disclaimer remedy I am advocating, *see* infra note 76 and accompanying text, is content based because it becomes operative only upon a finding that the author disapproves of the manner in which a user is employing her work, and therefore amounts to a viewpoint-based regulation. Case law suggests, however, that when legislation is enacted for a legitimate purpose other than suppressing speech or discriminating among subject matter, it is likely to be treated as content-neutral. *See, e.g., Turner Broad. Sys., Inc. v. FCC*, 512 U.S. 622 (1994) (finding must-carry rules content-neutral as "Congress's overriding objective was not to favor programming of a particular content, but rather to preserve access to free television programming. . . ."); *Universal City Studios, Inc. v. Reimerdes*, 111 F. Supp. 2d 294, 326–30 (S.D.N.Y. 2000) (concluding that the DMCA is content-neutral on the ground that the government's purpose was to prevent copyright infringement rather than "to regulate the expression of ideas"). For a skeptical view of the prevailing approach that content-neutral regulations should be upheld if they "reasonably" further an "insignificant" state interest, see Zimmerman, supra note 1, at 364 (invoking First Amendment theory to advocate for a mandatory public domain).

72. *See generally* Martin H. Redish, *Commercial Speech, First Amendment Intuitionism and the Twilight Zone of Viewpoint Discrimination*, 41 Loy. L.A. L. Rev. 101 (2008). ("Classical viewpoint discrimination selectively regulates (or protects) speech on the basis of regulatory hostility to a specific social, political, or moral position sought to be expressed by the speaker.")

73. *Golan v. Gonzales*, 501 F.3d 1179, 1196 (10th Cir. 2007).

74. *Ward v. Rock Against Racism*, 491 U.S. 781, 791 (1989) (quoting *Clark v. Cmty. for Creative Non-Violence*, 468 U.S. 288, 293 [1984]).

75. However, there may be some instances in which a right of attribution should not be recognized. *See* infra Chapters 6 and 7.

76. It could be argued that requiring attribution triggers strict scrutiny because such a law not only impacts the content of speech but also conceivably represents compelled speech. Similarly, requiring a disclaimer can be viewed as compelled speech. A disclaimer is "a repudiation or denial of responsibility or connection." American Heritage Dictionary of the English Language 515 (4th ed. 2000). These arguments are unlikely to withstand scrutiny, however, because a finding of compelled speech usually implicates speech involving ideological beliefs or mandating a particular viewpoint. *See, e.g., W. Va. Sate Bd. of Educ. v. Barnette*, 319 U.S. 624 (1943) (holding the government could not enforce a mandatory pledge and flag salute in opposition to individuals' religious beliefs); *Pruneyard Shopping Ctr. v. Robins*, 447 U.S. 74 (1980) (holding an order to allow a student petition at a private shopping center did not constitute compelled speech because the viewpoint expressed by the students was unlikely to be associated with the shopping center, and the shopping center could post a disclaimer).

77. *See* Lee, supra note 7, at 148–49 (noting that the First Amendment and the Copyright Clause share the goal of free access by the public to materials important to learning).

Patterson and Joyce also discuss why the Copyright Clause is consistent with the First Amendment: "The promotion of learning was a free speech policy because copyright required a new work; the condition of publication was a free speech policy because it ensured access; and the limited copyright term was a free speech policy because it protected and enlarged the public domain." L. Ray Patterson & Craig Joyce, *Copyright in 1791: An Essay Concerning the Founders' View of the Copyright Power Granted to Congress in Article I, Section 8, Clause 8 of the U.S. Constitution*, 52 EMORY L.J. 910, 945 (2003). *See also First Amendment Skein*, supra note 15, at 50 ([C]opyright's constitutional pedigree has purchase."); Michael D. Birnhack, *More or Better? Shaping the Public Domain*, in THE FUTURE OF THE PUBLIC DOMAIN, supra note 4, at 85 (noting how copyright and free speech share the same democratic goal).

78. *See* infra notes 121–24 and accompanying text. *See also* Catherine L. Fiske, *Credit Where It's Due: The Law and Norms of Attribution*, 95 GEO. L.J. 49, 91–92 (2006).

79. *Cf.* Baker, supra note 15, at 941–42 (suggesting that the First Amendment does not protect a situation in which "the purported infringer does or should know that, even after viewing, hearing, or reading her asserted transformation, people are likely to mistake it for the original author's work").

80. *See* supra notes 33–35 and accompanying text.

81. C. Edwin Baker, *Scope of the First Amendment Freedom of Speech*, 25 UCLA L. REV. 964, 990 (1978) [hereinafter Baker, *Scope of Freedom*].

82. Id. at 991.

83. Martin H. Redish, *The Value of Free Speech*, 130 U. PA. L. REV. 591, 593 (1982).

84. Id. at 593, 602–3.

85. Baker, *Scope of Freedom*, supra note 81, at 992.

86. Redish takes issue with Baker's theory on the ground that is too narrowly confined and therefore results in the exclusion of expression that should otherwise be protected. *See* Redish, *The Value of Free Speech*, supra note 83, at 620–22.

87. *See* id. at 624.

88. Baker, *Scope of Freedom*, supra note 81, at 996. Ironically, however, Baker sees copyright protection as content based. *See* supra note 68.

89. Baker, *Scope of Freedom*, supra note 81, at 1000.

90. Id. at 1002.

91. Redish, *The Value of Free Speech*, supra note 83, at 624.

92. Id. at 625.

93. David Lange, *Reimagining the Public Domain*, 66 LAW & CONTEMP. PROBS. 463, 476 (2003).

94. Id. at 475.

95. Id. at 479.

96. Id. at 470, 479. Lange sees "no suppression at all" with respect to "the business of acknowledgments . . . at least not if reasonable precautions are taken to avoid imposing liability for inadvertence, or conditioning appropriation upon the adequacy of acknowledgment, or doing something of that sort. . . ." E-mail from David Lange, Melvin G. Shimm Professor of Law, Duke University School of Law, to Roberta Kwall, Raymond P. Niro Professor of Intellectual Property Law, DePaul University College of Law (Apr. 4, 2007) (on file with author).

97. Lange, supra note 93, at 479 (citing David Lange & Jennifer Lange Anderson, *Copyright, Fair Use and Transformative Critical Appropriation* [2001], available at: www .law.duke.edu/pd/papers/langeand.pdf) (last visited Oct. 6, 2008). In a new book, Lange and his co-author Jefferson Powell reaffirm this view of moral rights. *See* DAVID L. LANGE & H. JEFFERSON POWELL, NO LAW—INTELLECTUAL PROPERTY IN THE IMAGE OF AN ABSO-LUTE FIRST AMENDMENT 57–60, 184–85 (2009).

98. Malla Pollack, *Towards a Feminist Theory of the Public Domain, or Rejecting the Gendered Scope of Unites States Copyrightable and Patentable Subject Matter*, 12 WM. & MARY J. WOMEN & L. 603, 619 (2006).

99. Id.

100. Id. at 621 (quoting LEWIS HYDE, THE GIFT 103 [1983]).

101. Id. at 621–23.

102. *See* supra Chapter 2 notes 27–32, 56–63, and accompanying text.

103. *See* Lee, supra note 7, at 163–64; Birnhack, supra note 77, at 85–86.

104. *See* Lee, supra note 7, at 165.

105. R. Anthony Reese, *Public but Private: Copyright's New Unpublished Public Domain*, 85 TEX. L. REV. 585 (2007).

106. *See* id. for a complete treatment of this issue. Reese notes that this aspect of our copyright law places the United States in uncharted territory. *See* id. at 611 (noting also that "the United States cannot rely on the experience of other nations in addressing issues that arise from the new public domain status of old unpublished works").

107. Id. at 615.

108. Id. at 609. *See* supra Chapter 4 at notes 89–90 and accompanying text. Code de la Propriété Intellectuelle (Intellectual Property Code) art. L.121-2 (Fr.), available at: http:// 195.83.177.9/code/liste.phtml?lang=uk&c=36&r=2497 (last visited Oct. 6, 2008).

109. *See* Samuelson, supra note 2, at 830.

110. *See* supra notes 6–13 and accompanying text.

111. Larry Lessig, *The Architecture of Innovation*, 51 DUKE L.J. 1783, 1788 (2002).

112. *Cf.* Zimmerman, supra note 1, at 370 (noting that there is a "baseline presumption" that the contents of the public domain can be used "without permission and without charge").

113. Other scholars object to the characterization of works that are regulated as part of the public domain. *See, e.g.*, Samuelson, supra note 2, at 832 (noting that open-source and other licensed content are more appropriately termed *contractually constructed commons*); Lee, supra note 7, at 118 (noting the importance of unrestricted access to the public domain).

114. *See* LAWRENCE LESSIG, THE FUTURE OF IDEAS: THE FATE OF THE COMMONS IN A NETWORKED WORLD 20 (2001); Lessig, supra note 111, at 1788. *See also* James Boyle, *The Second Enclosure Movement and the Construction of the Public Domain*, 66 LAW & CONTEMP. PROBS. 33, 68 (2003) (interpreting Lessig's position).

115. *See* Lessig, supra note 111, at 1788.

116. James Boyle elaborates upon these themes in Boyle, supra note 114, at 68–69 n.145.

117. Id. at 66.

118. Mark F. Schultz, *Copynorms: Copyright Law and Social Norms*, in 1 INTELLEC-TUAL PROPERTY AND INFORMATION WEALTH: ISSUES AND PRACTICES IN THE DIGITAL AGE 210 (Peter K. Yu ed., 2007). In contrast, norms also can be descriptive in that they reflect

individual behavior on a grand scale and thus achieve a sense of legitimacy. *See* id. at 213. File sharing is an excellent example to the extent the prevalence of this practice creates the perception that unauthorized file sharing is even more common than the reality suggests. Id. *See also* Lior Jacob Strahilevitz, *Charismatic Code, Social Norms, and the Emergence of Cooperation on the File-Swapping Networks,* 89 VA. L. REV. 505, 542–43 (2003). *See also* infra Chapter 9 notes 44–45 and accompanying text.

119. Robert Merges, *A New Dynamism in the Public Domain,* 71 U. CHI. L. REV. 183 (2004) (discussing these private initiatives in the context of both copyright and patent law).

120. Schultz, supra note 118, at 211. *See also* Nimmer, supra note 41, at 69 (discussing the "house rules" concerning plagiarism within the academy and elsewhere); Fiske, supra note 78, at 92–94 (discussing the varying norms of attribution in print and broadcast journalism). *See also* infra Chapter 9 notes 85–90 and accompanying text.

121. *See* supra Chapter 1 notes 22–24 and accompanying text.

122. GNU Software License, Version 3, art. 7, available at: www.gnu.org/copyleft/gpl .html (last visited Oct. 6, 2008). Some scholars have been critical of governance models such as Creative Commons and open source as public domain models on the ground that they are burdened by underlying intellectual property rights and license terms. *See, e.g.,* Samuelson, supra note 2, at 832; Elkin-Koren, supra note 5.

123. GNU Software License, Version 3, art. 7, available at: www.gnu.org/copyleft/gpl .html (last visited Oct. 6, 2008).

124. But see infra Chapter 7 for a consideration of situations in which community or industry norms effectively preclude applying certain moral rights protections.

CHAPTER 6

1. Henry Hansmann & Marina Santilli, *Authors' and Artists' Moral Rights: A Comparative Legal and Economic Analysis,* 26 J. LEGAL STUD. 95, 103–4 (1997).

2. Id. (questioning the conventional rationales for moral rights and positing that much of what drives the adoption of moral rights derives from "important reputational externalities" that attach to works we label "art").

3. Andre Lucas & Pascal Kamina Robert Plaisant, *France,* in 1 INTERNATIONAL COPYRIGHT LAW AND PRACTICE § 7[2][a] (Paul Edward Geller ed., 2007). This idea also accounts for the special rules governing moral rights in connection with computer programs. *See also* supra Chapter 4 note 55 and accompanying text.

4. *See* Edward C. Walterscheid, *To Promote the Progress of Science and Useful Arts: The Anatomy of a Congressional Power,* 43 IDEA 1, 61 (2002) (noting that the term *writings* may have been used by the Framers because it had been used in the Statute of Anne as well as in several previously existing state copyright statutes).

5. Id. at 62.

6. Id. at 63. "[O]ver time both Congress and the Supreme Court engaged in a series of legal fictions by which the interpretation given to 'writings' has been constantly expanded until today, until it bears little relationship to either the common dictionary definition at the end of the eighteenth century or to the modern dictionary definition." Id.

7. Id.

8. Id.

9. In 1802, "designs, engravings, etchings, cuts, and other prints" were added to the copyright statute as covered works. Id. at 64. The entire history of the Clause and its judicial

interpretation suggests that from the outset, "Congress and the courts have been operating outside and in violation of an express power delegated to Congress." Id. at 59 (quoting Study No. 3, *The Meaning of "Writings" in the Copyright Clause of the Constitution, (1956)*, reprinted in COPYRIGHT LAW REVISION, STUDIES PREPARED FOR THE SUBCOMMITTEE ON PATENTS, TRADEMARKS, AND COPYRIGHTS OF THE SENATE COMMITTEE ON THE JUDICIARY, 86TH CONG., 1ST SESS. 71, 86–87 [1960]). For a concise summary of the expanded scope of copyright protection, see Michael Birnhack, *The Copyright Law and Free Speech Affair: Making-Up and Breaking-Up*, 43 IDEA 233, 290 n.260 (2003).

10. *See* Copyright Act of Mar. 4, 1909, ch. 320, 35 Stat. 1075.

11. *See* Walterscheid, supra note 4, at 65–66.

12. 17 U.S.C. § 102(a) (2000). The legislative history for the 1976 Act notes that by omitting a definition of originality, the statute intended to "incorporate without change the standard of originality established by the courts" under the 1909 Act. S. REP. NO. 94-473, at 50 (1975).

13. 499 U.S. 340 (1991).

14. Id. at 345.

15. Id.

16. *See, e.g., Jon Woods Fashions, Inc. v. Curran*, No. 85 Civ. 3203(MJL), 1988 U.S. Dist. LEXIS 3319, at *5–6 (S.D.N.Y. Apr. 13, 1988) (quoting M. NIMMER, NIMMER ON COPYRIGHT § 2.08[B][3], at 2–85, 86 [1979 ed.]).

17. *Alfred Bell & Co. v. Catalda Fine Arts, Inc.*, 191 F.2d 99, 102–3 (2d Cir. 1951).

18. *See* Russ VerSteeg, *Originality and Creativity in Copyright Law*, in 1 INTELLECTUAL PROPERTY AND INFORMATION WEALTH: ISSUES AND PRACTICES IN THE DIGITAL AGE, 20 (Peter K. Yu ed., 2007) (recommending a definition for "creativity" as a "material or distinguishable variation"). For a pre-*Feist* critique of originality as a "legal fiction" that is "inherently unascertainable," see Jessica Litman, *The Public Domain*, 39 EMORY L.J. 965, 969, 1004–7 (1990).

19. *See* Diane L. Zimmerman, *It's An Original!(?): In Pursuit of Copyright's Elusive Essence*, 28 COLUM. J.L. & ARTS 187, 211 (2005). Additionally, she ponders whether judges should be required to "distinguish among works, based on qualitative or equivalent norms." Id.

20. *Feist*, 499 U.S. at 345. *Feist's* articulation of the originality standard is vulnerable to criticism on the ground that it fails the objectives of the Copyright Clause by including works that will not necessarily promote progress. *See* Walterscheid, supra note 4, at 71 (advocating a standard of novelty and observing that it is simply not apparent "how granting an exclusive right in a writing that is not novel in any way promotes the progress of science").

21. *Feist*, 499 U.S. at 348.

22. Id. at 359.

23. *See* Willliam Patry, *The Enumerated Powers Doctrine and Intellectual Property: An Imminent Constitutional Collision*, 67 GEO. WASH. L. REV. 359, 377 n.104 (1999). Interestingly, the standard for copyright originality varies within the European Community. *See* Herman Cohen Jehoram, *The EC Copyright Directives, Economics and Authors' Rights*, 25 INT'L REV. INDUS. PROP. & COPYRIGHT L. 821, 829 (1994) (noting that, historically, Germany's standard was among the most stringent to the extent "courts require more than just personal expression").

24. *See* supra Chapter 5 at notes 33–41 and accompanying text.

25. *See* supra notes 6–12 and accompanying text; supra notes 43–50 in Chapter 5. Indeed, "the task of definition, of inclusion and exclusion, upon deliberation and compromise, is precisely the type of line drawing that is the function of the legislature." Ilhyung Lee, *Toward an American Moral Rights in Copyright*, 58 WASH. & LEE L. REV. 795, 839 (2001).

26. *Feist*, 499 U.S. at 363.

27. Id. at 345–47.

28. *See* id. at 349. Some courts, in fact, invoke a more stringent test for infringement when the work at issue has a narrow range of protectable and unauthorized expression. *See also Dyer v. Napier*, 81 U.S.P.Q.2d 1035, 1044 (D. Ariz. 2006); *see* infra notes 73–76 and accompanying text; *Trek Leasing, Inc. v. United States*, 75 U.S.P.Q.2d 1449 (Fed. Cir. 2005) (test for infringement of copyright in a post office building constructed in particular architectural style requires "supersubstantial similarity" since plaintiff's copyright is "thin"); *Apple Computer, Inc. v. Microsoft Corp.*, 35 F.3d 1435 (invoking the "virtual identity" test rather than the more lenient "substantial similarity" test for infringement).

29. As Elliot Silverstein of the Directors Guild of America testified before Congress in 1987 against film colorization, "some values are more important than material reward . . . some things are just not for sale." *Legal Issues That Arise When Color Is Added to Films Originally Produced, Sold, and Distributed in Black and White: Hearings on Legal Issues That Arise When Color Is Added to Black-and-White Movies, Before the Subcomm. on Tech. and the Law, of the Senate Comm. on the Judiciary*, 100th Cong. 7–12 (1987) (statement of Elliot Silverstein, Directors Guild of America).

30. Christine Haight Farley, *Judging Art*, 79 TUL. L. REV. 805, 811–15 (2005) [hereinafter *Judging Art*].

31. Id.

32. 188 U.S. 239, 351 (1903).

33. *Judging Art*, supra note 30, at 818.

34. *See, e.g., Veeck v. S. Bldg. Code Cong. Int'l, Inc.*, 293 F.3d 791 (5th Cir. 2002) (en banc decision holding that building codes are copyrightable until they become enacted as law, after which they enter the public domain).

35. *See* Lee, supra note 25, at 839–40 (recognizing legitimate criticism of a moral rights system that would protect subject matter such as office memos and cabinets); *see also* Greg R. Vetter, *The Collaborative Integrity of Open-Source Software*, 2004 UTAH L. REV. 563 (discussing the moral right of integrity and the parallel system of open-source licensing in software).

36. Lee, supra note 25, at 839–40.

37. *See* Vetter, supra note 35, at 662–69 (questioning the application of conventional moral rights protection with respect to software).

38. 188 U.S. 239 (1903).

39. *See* Sarah Kutner & Holly Rich, Note, *Dirty Dancing: Attributing the Moral Right of Attribution to American Copyright Law: The Work for Hire Doctrine and the Usurping of the Ultimate Grand Dame and Founder of Modern Dance, Martha Graham*, 22 HOFSTRA LAB. & EMP. L.J. 325, 349 (2004) (urging that VARA be expanded to cover performing arts and noting that the creativity of choreography is particularly "the most misunderstood and underestimated" due to its seemingly effortless and undisciplined physical appeal). *Cf.* David Nimmer, *Copyright in the Dead Sea Scrolls: Authorship and Originality*, 38 HOUS. L. REV. 1, 184 (2001) (noting how works of "low authorship . . . flood the theoretical

portholes for federal copyright protection" despite the small degree of attention they attract in practice since few people attempt to copyright such works); *Open Source Yoga Unity v. Choudhury*, No. C 03-3182 PJH, 2005 WL 756558, at *4 (N.D. Cal. Apr. 1, 2005) (observing that if the selection and arrangement of the yoga sequence at issue is entitled to copyright protection, the resulting protection would be considered "thin").

40. 17 U.S.C. § 101 (2000).

41. *See* id.

42. 17 U.S.C. § 106A(a)(3)(B).

43. *Carter v. Helmsley-Spear, Inc.*, 861 F. Supp. 303, 325 (S.D.N.Y. 1994), rev'd and vacated in part, aff'd in part, 71 F.3d 77 (2d Cir. 1995). One commentator has observed, however, that the "recognized stature" standard is controversial to the extent it requires courts "to make distinctions based on aesthetic considerations." Christopher J. Robinson, *The "Recognized Stature" Standard in the Visual Artists Rights Act*, 68 FORDHAM L. REV. 1935, 1965 (2000).

44. 17 U.S.C. § 101 (2000). In the case of multiple cast, carved, or fabricated sculptures, the statute covers 200 or fewer as long as they are "consecutively numbered by the author and bear the signature or other identifying mark of the author." Id.

45. Id.

46. VISUAL ARTISTS RIGHTS ACT OF 1990, H.R. REP. NO. 101-514, at 6922 (1990) (testimony of Professor Jane Ginsburg).

47. *See, e.g., Silberman v. Innovation Luggage Inc.*, 67 U.S.P.Q.2d 1489 (S.D.N.Y. 2003).

48. *See, e.g., Nat'l Ass'n for Stock Car Auto Racing, Inc. (NASCAR) v. Scharle*, 184 Fed. App'x 270 (3d Cir. 2006).

49. *Phillips v. Pembroke Real Estate, Inc.*, 288 F. Supp. 2d 89 (D. Mass. 2003), aff'd, 459 F.3d 128, 129, 143 (1st Cir. 2006). The district court left open the question whether a park could ever be a "work of visual art" as defined by VARA, holding instead this particular park did not qualify.

50. 459 F.3d 128 (1st Cir. 2006).

51. *Flack v. Friends of Queen Catherine Inc.*, 139 F. Supp. 2d 526, 529–34 (S.D.N.Y. 2001).

52. In a novel VARA case, a district court in Illinois ruled that a sculpture of native wildflowers located on Chicago's lakeside Grant Park could qualify as a painting or sculpture within the meaning of VARA, but that the work in question is not subject to copyright protection for lack of demonstrated originality, and therefore, not protected under VARA. *See Kelley v. Chi. Park Dist.*, No. 04-C-07715, 2008 WL 4449886 (N.D. Ill. Sept. 29, 2008).

53. *See* supra note 45 and accompanying text. *See also* Russ VerSteeg, *Federal Moral Rights for Visual Artists: Contract Theory and Analysis*, 67 WASH. L. REV. 827, 840–41 (1992) (questioning this standard and suggesting that it "should not be interpreted as mutually exclusive of 'for purposes of selling'").

54. 384 F. Supp. 2d 83 (D.D.C. 2005).

55. Id. at 85.

56. Id. at 87.

57. Jennifer Olsson, Note, *Rights in Fine Art Photography: Through a Lens Darkly*, 70 TEX. L. REV. 1489, 1490 (1992).

58. Copyright Act of 1865, ch. 126, § 1, 13 Stat. 540 (extending protection to "photographs and the negatives thereof").

59. *Burrow-Giles Lithographic Co. v. Sarony*, 111 U.S. 53, 60 (1884) (internal quotation marks omitted).

60. Id.

61. Id.

62. Christine Haight Farley, *The Lingering Effects of Copyright's Response to the Invention of Photography*, 65 U. PITT. L. REV. 385, 437 (2004) [hereinafter *Lingering Effects*].

63. Id. at 419.

64. Id. at 417, 427–28.

65. Id. at 389–91.

66. *See Burrow-Giles Lithographic Co.*, 111 U.S. at 59.

67. *See Lingering Effects*, supra note 62, at 430.

68. Id. at 438.

69. Olsson, supra note 57, at 1497 (discussing the later work of Garry Winogrand).

70. *Lingering Effects*, supra note 62, at 388.

71. Id. at 432.

72. 36 F. Supp. 2d 191 (S.D.N.Y. 1999).

73. *Dyer v. Napier*, 81 U.S.P.Q.2d 1035, 1044 (D. Ariz. 2006).

74. Id. at 1042.

75. Id. at 1043 (internal quotation marks omitted).

76. Id. at 1044. According to the evidence in the case, the plaintiff hired animal trainers to assist him in manipulating the animals so that they would present themselves in the desired pose. Id. at 1037. Specifically, the trainers "placed a baby mountain lion on the end of a boulder near a drop-off. When the mother mountain lion was released, she instinctively walked over to the boulder and used her mouth to pick up the kitten." Id. To produce the photograph in question, this procedure was repeated more than twelve times. Id.; *see also Satava v. Lowry*, 323 F.3d 805 (9th Cir. 2003) (holding that no copyright protection exists for common elements in glass-in-glass jellyfish sculpture and typical jellyfish physiology). In *Bleistein v. Donaldson Lithographing Co.*, 188 U.S. 239, 249 (1903), Judge Holmes observed: "Others are free to copy the original. They are not free to copy the copy. The copy is the personal reaction of an individual upon nature. Personality always contains something unique." Id. at 249–50 (internal citations omitted).

77. *Lingering Effects*, supra note 62, at 434; *see also Time, Inc. v. Bernard Geis Assocs.*, 293 F. Supp. 130, 143 (S.D.N.Y 1968) (finding "many elements of creativity" in the Zapruder pictures, namely, selection of the type of camera, type of film, type of lens, area of the subject matter, timing, and the shooting location); *Pagano v. Chas. Beseler Co.*, 234 F. 963, 964 (S.D.N.Y. 1916) (describing the photographer's timing as a creative choice that "undoubtedly requires originality").

78. *See Lingering Effects*, supra note 62, at 390, 435–37.

79. *See* Michael Kimmelman, *Walker Evans. Or Is It?* N.Y. TIMES, Aug. 25, 2006, at E27.

80. Id.; *see* 17 U.S.C. § 105 (disallowing copyright protection for any work of the government of the United States).

81. Kimmelman, supra note 79.

82. Id.

83. Interestingly, the Berne Convention differentiates the term of protection for photographic works and works of applied art by stating that the individual members should

make this determination, although protection should last at least "twenty-five years from the making of such a work." Berne Convention for the Protection of Literary and Artistic Works art. 7(4), Sept. 9, 1886, 828 U.N.T.S. 221 (as last revised in Paris on July 24, 1971 and amended Sept. 28, 1979).

84. Randy Kennedy, *Lessons in New Ways to See: Troubled Girls Learn an Art of Examination*, N.Y. Times, July 5, 2006, at E1.

85. Kimmelman, supra note 79, at E30.

86. Id.

87. *See* supra notes 59–65 and accompanying text; *cf. Marco v. Accent Publ'g Co.*, 969 F.2d 1547 (3d Cir. 1992) (engaging in a similar ad hoc evaluation of a photograph's creativity in the context of a work for hire determination).

88. Simon Frith, *Pop Music*, in The Cambridge Companion to Pop and Rock Music 93, 94–95 (Simon Frith et al. eds., 2001).

89. Tim Smith, The NPR Curious Listener's Guide To Classical Music 2–3 (2002). Smith explains:

> Typically, the pop music composer is finished after creating a tune with chords (harmony) underneath it. By contrast, the classical composer's task is far from over with the writing of a melody or a chord or a rhythmic pattern; that's only the beginning. The classical composer is interested in developing the full potential of the melodic and harmonic ideas.

Id. at 3. *But see* Julie E. Cohen, *Copyright, Commodification, and Culture: Locating the Public Domain*, in The Future Of The Public Domain—Identifying The Commons In Information Law 143 (Lucie Guibault & P. Bernt Hugenholtz eds., 2006) (noting that musicologists have documented borrowings and reworkings among classical composers). An interesting comparison is presented in *Montgomery v. Montgomery*, 60 S.W.3d 524 (Ky. 2001). The court there was faced with the question whether music videos should be considered commercial for purposes of a right of publicity claim. Id. The majority observed that music videos display the same artistic and creative elements as motion pictures, whereas the dissent argued that music videos are merely profit-driven and essentially lack artistic quality.

90. *See* supra notes 36–39 and accompanying text.

91. *Cf.* Paul Edward Geller, *Toward an Overriding Norm in Copyright: Sign Wealth*, 159 Revue Internationale du Droit d'Auteur 3 (1994) (proposing that authorship norms require "some personal imprint" as opposed to marketplace norms that require "at most, minimal creativity").

92. 111 U.S. 53 (1884).

93. Id. at 59–60.

94. *But see* Litman, supra note 18, at 1004–5 (arguing that despite its "esteem" in copyright jurisprudence, "originality . . . is irrelevant to the resolution of actual cases").

95. David Lange, *Reimagining the Public Domain*, 66 Law & Contemp. Probs. 463, 481 (2003).

96. Id.

97. *See* 17 U.S.C. § 101 (defining "derivative work"). *See also L. Batlin & Son, Inc. v. Snyder*, 536 F.2d 486, 491 (2d Cir. 1976) (en banc); *Durham Indus., Inc. v. Tomy Corp.*, 630 F.2d 905 (2d Cir. 1980); *Gracen v. Bradford Exch.*, 698 F.2d 300, 305 (7th Cir. 1983); *Entm't Research Group, Inc. v. Genesis Creative Group, Inc.*, 122 F.3d 1211 (9th Cir. 1997). At least one commentator has suggested that this view "represent[s] a considerable

departure from traditional copyright doctrine." Peter Jaszi, *Toward a Theory of Copyright: The Metamorphoses of "Authorship,"* 1991 DUKE L.J. 455, 461.

98. *Batlin,* 536 F.2d at 491. In calling for "at least some substantial variation, not merely a trivial variation," *Batlin* is seemingly inconsistent with *Bell's* "merely trivial" standard. *See Alfred Bell & Co. v. Catalda Fine Arts, Inc.,* 191 F.2d 99, 102–3 (2d Cir. 1951) (internal citations omitted); supra note 17 and accompanying text. On the other hand, *Bell* also uses the phrase "distinguishable variation." *Bell,* 191 F.2d at 102.

99. *See Gracen,* 698 F.2d at 305. ("[A] derivative work must be substantially different from the underlying work to be copyrightable.") More recent cases in the Seventh Circuit suggest somewhat of a retraction from *Gracen's* heightened originality standard, although that standard has not been explicitly overruled. *See, e.g., Saturday Evening Post Co. v. Rumbleseat Press, Inc.,* 816 F.2d 1191, 1192 (7th Cir. 1987) (observing that derivative works are copyrightable if they have *some incremental originality* and the copyright "is limited to that increment") (emphasis added). *Cf. Gaiman v. McFarlane,* 360 F.3d 644, 658 (7th Cir. 2004). ("There has to be *some* original expression contributed by anyone who claims to be a coauthor. . . .")

100. *Burrow-Giles Lithographic Co. v. Sarony,* 111 U.S. 53, 60 (1884); *Lingering Effects,* supra note 62, at 431–32.

101. *Burrow-Giles,* 111 U.S. at 60; *Lingering Effects,* supra note 62, at 426. Sarony's narrative with respect to his creative choices was intended not only to inform the Court but also to distinguish his work from that of the numerous non-art photographers. *Lingering Effects,* supra note 62, at 429.

102. *See* 17 U.S.C. § 101 (2000). The 1976 Act was intended "to draw as clear a line as possible between copyrightable works of applied art and uncopyrighted works of industrial design." H.R. REP. NO. 94-1476, at 55 (1976).

103. H.R. REP. NO. 94-1476, at 55 (1976).

104. *See, e.g., Pivot Point Int'l, Inc. v. Charlene Prods., Inc.,* 372 F.3d 913, 926 (7th Cir. 2004) (invoking conceptually separable test to uphold copyrightability for the "hungry look" on the face of a mannequin); *Brandir Int'l, Inc. v. Cascade Pac. Lumber Co.,* 834 F.2d 1142 (2d Cir. 1987) (applying Professor Denicola's conceptually separable test to reject copyright protection for a thick, interwoven wire initially constructed as artwork but later modified into a bicycle rack); *Norris Indus., Inc. v. Int'l Tel. & Tel. Corp.,* 696 F.2d 918 (11th Cir. 1983) (holding wire wheel covers not copyrightable because they did not contain physically or conceptually separable works of art); *Animal Fair, Inc. v. AMFESCO Indus., Inc.,* 620 F. Supp. 175, 186–88 (D. Minn. 1985) (holding bear-paw designs on slippers conceptually separable), aff'd mem., 794 F.2d 687 (8th Cir. 1986); *Trans-World Mfg. Corp. v. Al Nyman & Sons, Inc.,* 95 F.R.D. 95 (D. Del. 1982) (invoking conceptually separable test to support copyright in eyeglass display cases).

105. *See Pivot Point,* 372 F.3d at 917.

106. *See id.* at 922 (noted in Robert C. Denicola, *Applied Art and Industrial Design: A Suggested Approach to Copyright in Useful Articles,* 67 MINN. L. REV. 707, 744 [1983]). *See also Parfums Givenchy, Inc. v. C & C Beauty Sales, Inc.,* 832 F. Supp. 1378, 1392 (C.D. Cal. 1993) (holding artistic packaging physically separable from the utilitarian aspects of the perfume inside); *Ted Arnold, Ltd. v. Silvercraft Co.,* 259 F. Supp. 733 (S.D.N.Y. 1966) (holding copyrightable a simulated antique telephone encasing a pencil sharpener based on physical separability test).

107. In addition to the "test design process" test adopted in *Brandir*, 834 F.2d at 1142, and discussed infra in the text, other tests have been suggested by courts and commentators. One formulation determines conceptual separability from the standpoint of the ordinary reasonable observer by looking to whether "the article . . . stimulate[s] in the mind of the beholder a concept that is separate from the concept evoked by its utilitarian function." *Carol Barnhart, Inc. v. Econ. Cover Corp.*, 773 F.2d 411, 419–24 (2d Cir. 1985) (Newman, J., dissenting); *see* infra note 115 and accompanying text. Other tests include whether the primary use of the work is artistic or utilitarian, and whether the work is marketable as art. *See Brandir*, 834 F.2d at 1144 (calling neither one of these tests "very satisfactory"); *Galiano v. Harrah's Operating Co.*, 416 F.3d 411, 421 (5th Cir. 2005) (adopting "the likelihood-of-marketability standard *for garment design only*"). In addition, Professor Goldstein has proposed a test positing that a particular "feature incorporated in the design of a useful article is conceptually separable if it can stand on its own as a work of art traditionally conceived, and if the useful article in which it is embodied would be equally useful without it." Paul Goldstein, International Copyright: Principles, Law & Practice 109 (2001). Several courts have adopted the Goldstein test. *See, e.g., Collezione Europa U.S.A., Inc. v. Hillsdale House, Ltd.*, 243 F. Supp. 2d 444 (M.D. N.C. 2003) (holding sculpted leaves of a furniture collection sufficiently separable to be copyrightable); *Celebration Int'l, Inc. v. Chosun Int'l, Inc.*, 234 F. Supp. 2d 905 (S.D. Ind. 2002) (finding the sculptural aspects of a tiger costume conceptually separable from its utilitarian functions).

108. 834 F.2d 1142 (2d Cir. 1987).

109. 17 U.S.C. § 102(5) (2000).

110. *Brandir*, 834 F.2d at 1145–46.

111. Id. The dissent in *Brandir* objected to the majority's test for conceptual separability in part on the ground that a work's copyrightability should not "depend upon largely fortuitous circumstances concerning the creation of the design in issue." Id. at 1151 (Winter, J., concurring in part and dissenting in part).

112. To further illustrate the operation of this bifurcation, garment designs can be compared with decorative quilts. Garment designs, even those that are quite elaborate, historically have been denied copyright protection on the ground that they are useful articles that are the product of a craft or trade, rather than art. *See, e.g., Galiano v. Harrah's Operating Co.*, 416 F.3d 411, 419–22 (5th Cir. 2005) (denying copyrightability to casino uniforms). Courts have, however, held that patterns or other artistic elements featured on a fabric may be eligible for copyright protection if they can be identified separately from the useful purpose of the clothing. *See, e.g., Express, LLC v. Fetish Group, Inc.*, 424 F. Supp. 2d 1211 (C.D. Cal. 2006) (upholding copyright protection for the arrangement, placement, and look of lace trim on a tunic). In contrast to clothing for humans, clothing for a toy bear has been held copyrightable given the absence of a utilitarian function. *Boyds Collection, Ltd. v. Bearington Collection, Inc.*, 365 F. Supp. 2d 612 (M.D. Pa. 2005). As of this writing, discussions have occurred with respect to federal legislation that will afford a form of sui generis, or copyright-like, protection for the overall appearance of new and original fashion designs. *See* Design Piracy Prohibition Act, H.R. 2033, 110th Cong. (2007); S. 1957, 110th Cong. (2007).

On the other hand, copyright protection has been afforded to quilt tops (the artistically decorated top cover of a quilt), as well as to the individual quilt blocks, which sewn together comprise the quilt top. *See Brown v. McCormick*, 23 F.2d 594 (D. Md. 1998) (upholding original elements in a quilt block depicting a "black bird flying over a man and a woman holding hands"); *Boisson v. Banian, Ltd.*, 273 F.3d 262 (2d Cir. 2001) (upholding copyright protection of the layout and color scheme of quilts consisting of square blocks containing the capital letters of the alphabet displayed in order). In her book *Who Owns Culture*, Susan Scafidi notes that in 1971, a New York museum mounted an exhibition of quilts from diverse communities and "was perhaps the first curatorial recognition of quilts as American women's artwork." SUSAN SCAFIDI, WHO OWNS CULTURE? APPROPRIATION AND AUTHENTICITY IN AMERICAN LAW 27 (2005). In a similar vein, courts have held that artistic designs woven or imprinted onto rugs qualify for copyright protection. *See, e.g., Peel & Co. v. Rug Market*, 238 F.3d 391, 395 (5th Cir. 2001).

113. *See Pivot Point Int'l Inc. v. Charlene Prods., Inc.*, 372 F.3d 926, 931 (7th Cir. 2004) (quoting *Carol Barnhart, Inc. v. Econ. Cover Corp.*, 773 F.2d 411, 418 [2d Cir. 1985] [Newman, J., dissenting]) (holding copyrightable the face of a mannequin with particular types of features); *see also Stanislawski v. Jordan*, 337 F.Supp. 2d 1103, 1112 (E.D. Wis. 2004) (adopting *Pivot Point* standard).

114. *See Carol Barnhart, Inc. v. Econ. Cover Corp.*, 773 F.2d 411, 423 (1985) (Newman, J., dissenting) (discussing the type of evidence relevant to "conceptual separability"); *Poe v. Missing Persons*, 745 F.2d 1238, 1243 (9th Cir. 1984) (identifying evidence pertinent to the district court's determination of whether a soft sculpture was a utilitarian article of clothing or a work of art).

115. *Carol Barnhart*, 773 F.2d at 422 (Newman, J., dissenting). In *Carol Barnhart*, the majority held that life-size, anatomically correct human torso forms were not copyrightable.

116. Id.

117. *Judging Art*, supra note 30, at 837.

118. Id.

119. *See Lingering Effects*, supra note 62, at 451 n.252 (citing Constance Lewallen & Sherry Levine, J. CONTEMP. ART, available at: www.jca-online.com/slevine.html [last visited June 6, 2008]).

120. *Blanch v. Koons*, 467 F.3d 244 (2d Cir. 2006).

121. Id. at 247.

122. Id. at 253 (quoting *Campell v. Acuff-Rose Music, Inc.*, 510 U.S. 569, 579 [1994]).

123. Id. at 247 (quoting Koons Aff., dated June 10, 2005, at ¶ 10). The court further quoted Koons as stating: "By re-contextualizing these fragments as I do, I try to compel the viewer to break out of the conventional way of experiencing a particular appetite as mediated by mass media." Id. (internal citation omitted).

124. *See infra* Chapter 7 at notes 132–34 and accompanying text.

CHAPTER 7

1. 497 F. Supp. 304, 312 (S.D.N.Y. 1980) (holding that a misleading attribution of authorship violated § 43(a) of the Lanham Act).

2. Laura A. Heymann, *The Birth of the Authornym: Authorship, Pseudonymity, and Trademark Law*, 80 NOTRE DAME L. REV. 1377, 1381, 1446 (2005).

3. Id. at 1446.

4. Catherine L. Fisk, *Credit Where It's Due: The Laws and Norms of Attribution*, 95 GEO. L.J. 49, 63 (2006) [hereinafter Fisk, *Credit Where It's Due*].

5. Greg Lastowka, *The Trademark Function of Authorship*, 85 B.U. L. REV. 1171, 1241 (2005).

6. *See* Alan Feuer, *Jury Finds Writer's Alias Was Fraud*, N.Y. TIMES, June 23, 2007, at A12; Alan Feuer, *Judge Orders Author to Pay Film Company $350,000 in Legal Fees*, N.Y. TIMES, Aug. 1, 2007, at B5.

7. Henry Hansmann & Marina Santilli, *Authors' and Artists' Moral Rights: A Comparative Legal and Economic Analysis*, 26 J. LEGAL STUD. 95, 131 (1997).

8. Id. at 132.

9. The House Report states that the right of attribution contained in § 106A (a)(1) extends "to the right to publish anonymously or under a pseudonym." H.R. REP. NO. 101-514 (1990), reprinted in 1990 U.S.C.C.A.N. 6915, 6924. The authority cited for this proposition is the *Final Report of the Ad Hoc Working Group on U.S. Adherence to the Berne Convention*, 10 COLUM.-VLA J.L. & ARTS 513, 550 (1985–86). The Working Group Report does not, however, establish that VARA covers anonymous and pseudonymous works. It simply mentions that Article *6bis* of Berne encompasses this right, citing as support the WORLD INTELLECTUAL PROP. ORG., GUIDE TO THE BERNE CONVENTION FOR THE PROTECTION OF LITERARY AND ARTISTIC WORKS (PARIS ACT 1971) 41 (1978). In fact, VARA explicitly requires that works be signed in certain instances. *See* 17 § 101 U.S.C. (2007) (definition of a "work of visual art"). The legislative history on the signature requirement is muddied but it has been suggested that the real reason for the signature requirement was to meet "unreasonable demands by the book publishing industry, which was determined to eliminate even the most implausible hypothetical scenario for liability." William Patry, *The Visual Artists Rights Act of 1990*, in PATRY ON COPYRIGHT § 16:14 (2006).

10. David Nimmer, *The Moral Imperative Against Academic Plagiarism (Without a Moral Right Against Reverse Passing Off)*, 54 DEPAUL L. REV. 1, 15 (2004). Countries vary in their approach as to whether moral rights extend to anonymous or pseudonymous works. *See* supra Chapter 4.

11. Hansmann & Santilli, supra note 7, at 131–32.

12. Heymann, supra note 2, at 1406.

13. 514 U.S. 334 (1995) (holding unconstitutional a state law prohibiting any individual from distributing material designed to promote or defeat a political issue unless the author's name and address were listed).

14. Heymann, supra note 2, at 1430.

15. Id.

16. Fisk, *Credit Where It's Due*, supra note 4, at 92.

17. Id.

18. Hansmann & Santilli, supra note 7, at 136.

19. Id.

20. *See* Fisk, *Credit Where It's Due*, supra note 4, at 65, 95.

21. Id. at 65.

22. *See* JENNIE ERDAL, GHOSTING: A DOUBLE LIFE (2003) (discussed in Fisk, *Credit Where It's Due*, supra note 4, at 96, noting that "the memoir makes clear that both the writer and the person who hired her were ghosting").

23. Id. at xii.

24. Lastowka, supra note 5, at 1222.

25. Id. at 1225–26.

26. Clancy apparently made a modest contribution to the *Op-Center* books by discussing in a telephone conversation the general concept of a television series upon which they were based, after which he subsequently agreed to allow Rovin to write the series under his name. Unfortunately for Clancy, poor reviews and consumer disappointment resulted in his alleging damage to his authorial reputation in subsequent litigation. Lastowka, supra note 5, at 1223–26.

27. Id. at 1223.

28. For a discussion of the doctrine's theoretical application in the Netherlands, see Jane C. Ginsburg, *The Concept of Authorship in Comparative Copyright Law*, 52 DePaul L. Rev. 1063, 1088–90 (2003) [hereinafter Ginsburg, *The Concept of Authorship*]. Interestingly, Russian copyright law also has a work for hire doctrine. See *Itar-Tass Russian News Agency v. Russian Kurier, Inc.*, 153 F.3d 82 (2d Cir. 1998); see also Copyright Act, 1968, No. 63, § 35(6) (Austl.) (providing that the employer of an author owns the copyright in certain instances).

In contrast, French law does not recognize the work made for hire concept except with regard to computer programs, a position that also is shared by some other countries. *See, e.g.*, Jane C. Ginsburg, *Reforms and Innovations Regarding Authors' and Performers' Rights in France: Commentary on the Law of July 3, 1985*, 10 Colum.-VLA J.L. & Arts 83, 88–89 (1985); Council Directive on Protection of Computer Software 91/250, art. 2.1, 1991 O.J. (L122). In addition, French law has special provisions for collective works that resemble the operation of works made for hire. See Andre Lucas & Pascal Kamina Robert Plaisant, *France*, in 1 International Copyright Law and Practice § 4 [1](b)(ii)(C) (Paul Edward Geller & Melville B. Nimmer eds., 18th ed. 2006). Interestingly, Jane Ginsburg cites French sources from the early to middle nineteenth century supporting a broader view of "author" as including "not only those who themselves created a literary work, but also those who have had the work composed by others, and who undertake to pay for its composition." *See* Ginsburg, *The Concept of Authorship*, supra, at 1088–90.

The civil law tradition exemplified by the French perspective regarding works for hire does, however, look to other means to achieve a comparable result in certain situations. Such means "include rules of presumed transfers of exploitation rights, statutory limitations on moral rights, and judicially tailored rules for commissioned works or works created in an employment relationship." Marina Santilli, *United States' Moral Rights Developments in European Perspective*, 1 Marq. Intell. Prop. L. Rev. 89, 96–99 (1997) (providing a comprehensive discussion of these issues). By way of comparison, the British Copyright Act provides that "where a work . . . is made by an employee . . . his employer is the first owner of any copyright in the work subject to any agreement to the contrary." Copyright, Designs & Patents Act, 1988, ch. 48, § 11(2) (U.K.). According to this provision, only ownership rather than authorship is attributed to the employer. Id. Nevertheless, §§ 79(3) and 82 of the British Act essentially negate this distinction by diminishing the attribution and integrity rights of employed authors. Id. at §§ 79(3), 82. Germany lacks a direct work for hire rule but § 43 of the Copyright Law manifests a presumption of transfer of rights to use works of employed authors in favor of employers. Urheberrechtsgesetz [Copyright Law], Sept. 9, 1965, BGBl. I at 1273, § 43 (F.R.G.). *See also* supra Chapter 4 notes 36–38.

29. E-mail from Adolf Dietz to Roberta Kwall (July 18, 2005) (on file with author).

30. *See* Catherine L. Fisk, *Authors at Work: The Origins of the Work-for-Hire Doctrine*, 15 Yale J.L. & Human. 1, 68 (2003) [hereinafter Fisk, *Authors at Work*]. ("If Ameri-

can law had recognized moral rights as French law does, it might have been more difficult to imagine how the corporation could acquire all the rights to the employee's works.")

31. *See Martha Graham Sch. & Dance Found., Inc. v. Martha Graham Ctr. of Contemporary Dance, Inc.*, 380 F.3d 624, 634 (2d Cir. 2004) (discussing both the 1909 and 1976 Copyright Acts).

32. *Shapiro, Bernstein & Co. v. Bryan*, 123 F.2d 697, 699 (2d Cir. 1941).

33. Fisk, *Credit Where It's Due*, supra note 4, at 54; *see also* Nimmer, supra note 10, at 73. ("Far more threatening . . . than divesting economic rights into their employees under the work-made-for-hire doctrine would be to vest exclusive attribution in the employers.")

34. For a comprehensive analysis of the history of the work for hire doctrine in the nineteenth and early twentieth centuries, see Fisk, *Authors at Work*, supra note 30.

35. 17 U.S.C. § 26 (repealed). Under judicial interpretations of the 1909 Act, the work for hire doctrine vested copyright ownership in the person at whose "instance and expense" the work was created, regardless of whether the work was created by an employee or an independent contractor. *See, e.g., Brattleboro Publ'g Co. v. Winmill Publ'g Corp.*, 369 F.2d 565, 567–68 (2d Cir. 1966); *Lin-Brook Builders Hardware v. Gertler*, 352 F.2d 298, 300 (9th Cir. 1965). Although the 1909 Act's work for hire doctrine initially was confined to works created by traditional "employees" in the scope of their employment, the doctrine later was expanded to include independent contractors. *See, e.g., Forward v. Thorogood*, 985 F.2d 604, 606 (1st Cir. 1993) (citing *Murray v. Gelderman*, 566 F.2d 1307, 1310 (5th Cir. 1978); *Brattleboro Publ'g Co.*, 369 F.2d at 567–68).

36. *See* Jessica D. Litman, *Copyright, Compromise, and Legislative History*, 72 CORNELL L. REV. 857, 889 (1987). *Cf. Cmty. for Creative Non-Violence v. Reid*, 490 U.S. 730, 749–50 (1989) (noting that Congress's "paramount goal in revising the 1976 Act" was to enhance "predictability and certainty of copyright ownership").

37. 17 U.S.C. § 201(b) (2000).

38. Id. § 101.

39. Id.; *see Compaq Computer Corp. v. Ergonome, Inc.*, 210 F. Supp. 2d 839 (S.D. Tex. 2001) (summarizing the split among the circuits on the question of the appropriate timing of the execution of the written agreement in § 101(2)).

40. *But see* Fisk, *Authors at Work*, supra note 30, at 64 (noting, in the context of the legislative history of the 1909 Act, some sensitivity to the distinction between authorship and copyright ownership on the part of Robert Underwood Johnson, Secretary of the American Authors' Copyright League). *See also* id. at 68 (observing that one of the drafters of the 1909 Act "worried that employer ownership might allow a firm to alter and degrade a work after its creation and injure the reputation of the individual employee who was known to have been its creator").

41. *See* Rochelle Cooper Dreyfuss, *The Creative Employee and the Copyright Act of 1976*, 54 U. CHI. L. REV. 590, 600 (1987) (noting that "a signed writing can, at most, have the effect of rebutting the presumption that the employer is the copyright owner").

42. See supra Chapter 3 notes 31–35 and accompanying text for a brief discussion of the legislative history of VARA.

43. *See* 17 U.S.C. § 101 (2000) (definition of "work of visual art"). In the context of visual art specifically, this exclusion can have a tremendous impact in practice since works made for hire "may account for a number of major art works, including major commissions,

installed works, and works incorporated into buildings." *See* REGISTER OF COPYRIGHTS, FINAL REPORT: WAIVER OF MORAL RIGHTS IN VISUAL ART WORKS xv (1996).

44. Those states that exclude works for hire from coverage are California, Connecticut, Massachusetts, Nevada, New Mexico, and New York.

45. It is important to note, however, that under the current statute, the determination that a work is one for hire affects issues other than just ownership of the copyright. For example, when a work for hire has been licensed, that license is not subject to termination under §§ 203 & 304 of the Act. The original rationale underlying the termination provisions was to provide additional benefits to authors. In *Marvel Characters, Inc. v. Simon*, the court noted that because the statutory author of a work for hire historically was an employer–publisher, this rationale is not as directly applicable since "an employer–publisher does not face the same potential unequal bargaining position as an individual author." 310 F.3d 280, 291 (2d Cir. 2002). Also, the employer of a work for hire can exercise the renewal right under § 304(a), as opposed to the colloquial author or her statutory successors. The number of years copyright protection subsists also varies between ordinary works and works for hire pursuant to §§ 302(a) and (c). According to § 302(a), copyright protection in general lasts for the life of the author plus seventy years. Section 304(c) provides that in the case of works made for hire (as well as anonymous and pseudonymous works), protection lasts "for a term of ninety-five years from the date of first publication, or a term of 120 years from the year of" the work's creation, "whichever expires first." To the extent all of these provisions are concerned with the economic value of the author's copyright, rather than the dignity interests of authors, their continued application may not present difficulties from a moral rights standpoint.

46. 17 U.S.C. § 101(2) (2000).

47. § 101(1).

48. 490 U.S. 730 (1989); *see also* Justin Hughes, *The Personality Interest of Artists and Inventors in Intellectual Property*, 16 CARDOZO ARTS & ENT. L.J. 81, 151 (1998) (noting that the "employee" prong "has remained the battleground for work-for-hire disputes—so much so that the 1909 law and 1976 law cases look much the same").

49. 490 U.S. at 730.

50. According to the Court's analysis, the level of CCNV's participation in the project was not sufficiently high to merit its being designated as the legal author for purposes of the work for hire doctrine. The overall consideration, according to the Court, is whether the hiring party has the "right to control the manner and means by which the product is accomplished." *Reid*, 490 U.S. at 751. In applying the *Reid* factors, the Court concluded that Reid was an independent contractor given his level of skill, the use of his own tools and studio, his discretion in hiring assistants, the relatively short period of time in which he was retained by CCNV, the payment to Reid upon the completion of the job, CCNV's lack of being in the sculpting business, and CCNV's failure to pay taxes or provide any other employee benefits to Reid. Id. at 752–53.

51. Id. at 750–51.

52. *See* RESTATEMENT (SECOND) OF AGENCY § 220(2) (2007).

53. *MacLean Assocs., Inc. v. Wm. M. Mercer-Meidinger-Hansen, Inc.*, 952 F.2d 769, 777–78 (3d Cir. 1991).

54. Id. at 776 (quoting *Reid*, 490 U.S. at 751–52).

55. Of course, "the right to control the manner and means by which the product is accomplished" does relate to whose meaning and message the work conveys. *Reid*, 490 U.S.

at 751. Still, of all the more specific *Reid* factors enumerated by the Supreme Court, only the skill required of the hired party and perhaps "the extent of the hired party's discretion over when and how long to work" may have a bearing on whether the work reflects the meaning and message of the hired party. *See id.*

As a general matter, a major problem with the application of the *Reid* factors is that a court may readily manipulate them if inclined toward a particular result. For example, the court in *Carter v. Helmsley-Spear* may have reached the result it did because it was troubled by the prospect of allowing the work to remain in a lobby for a long period of time when the original agreement was entered into by a net lessee of the building, rather than by the building's owner. *See* infra notes 72–74 and accompanying text. Similarly, in *Martha Graham School and Dance Foundation, Inc. v. Martha Graham Center of Contemporary Dance, Inc.*, 380 F.3d 624 (2d Cir. 2004), *see* infra notes 75–76 and accompanying text, the court manipulated the *Reid* factors, particularly the exercise of creative control, to arrive at a desired result. In that case, had the dances not been classified as works for hire, the copyrights to them would have passed under Graham's will to her long-time companion, who was many years the dancer's junior, rather than to the Martha Graham Center of Contemporary Dance. *Martha Graham*, 380 F.3d at 631.

56. *Cf.* Michael P. Matesky II, Note, *Whose Song Is It Anyway? When Are Sound Recordings Used in Audiovisual Works Subject to Termination Rights and When Are They Works Made for Hire?* 5 VA. SPORTS & ENT. L.J. 63 (2005) (advocating that when sound recordings are commissioned for "the primary purpose" of being used in audiovisual works, they should qualify as works made for hire).

57. Hughes, supra note 48, at 153. Although his discussion of commissioned works is for the purpose of explicating when a creator should be considered an "employee" under the first prong of the statute, this objective does not detract from the relevance of his observations to works falling under the specially commissioned prong.

58. Id.

59. Id. at 154.

60. Hughes posits that "the relationship between the artist's creativity and patron's intentionality is or is often close to a zero sum game," and typically "we will never know the score in that game" because the parties' ideas are often incapable of being clearly differentiated. Id. at 157.

61. *See* 17 U.S.C. § 101 (2000) (definitions of "work made for hire," including "supplementary" works, and "instructional" texts).

62. Hughes, supra note 48, at 150. I tracked thirty-three federal cases that applied the "specially commissioned" prong of the Copyright Act of 1976. *See* supra note 46 and accompanying text. Nineteen of these cases were decided solely on the presence or absence of a clearly written "work for hire" agreement. None of the courts sought to determine whose meaning and message the work reflected.

63. *Cmty. for Creative Non-Violence v. Reid*, 490 U.S. 730, 751–53 (1985).

64. Toward the end of its opinion, the Court indicated that perhaps CCNV might be considered a joint author of the sculpture if the district court subsequently found on remand that the parties prepared the work so as to comply with the statutory requirements for joint authorship. *Reid*, 490 U.S. at 753; *see* 17 U.S.C. § 101 (2000) (defining a "joint work"). On remand following the Supreme Court's opinion, the district court determined that Reid should be recognized as the sole author of the sculpture and that he has sole ownership rights under § 106 regarding all three-dimensional reproductions of the sculpture.

Cmty. for Creative Non-Violence v. Reid, No. 86-1507, 1991 WL 415523, at *1 (D.D.C. 1991). The court also concluded that CCNV is the sole owner of the original copy of the sculpture, and that both parties are co-owners of all § 106 rights respecting two-dimensional reproductions of the sculpture. Id.

65. The sculpture at issue in *Reid* was created prior to the effective date of VARA, and therefore not subject to the statute. *See* 17 U.S.C. § 106A(d)(2) (2000). Further, note that VARA only prevents destruction of works that are "of recognized stature." § 106A(a) (3)(B). The "recognized stature" caveat regarding destruction is not present in the prohibition involving mutilation. *See also* supra Chapter 3 notes 36, 38, and accompanying text.

66. According to the appellate court, "Co-ownership (or even sole ownership) of the copyright does not appear to carry with it a right to stop or limit CCNV's tour or to gain possession of the unique work of art." *Reid*, 846 F.2d 1485, 1498 (D.C. Cir. 1995).

67. *Reid*, 1991 WL 415523, at *1.

68. 539 U.S. 23 (2003).

69. *Twentieth Century Fox Film Corp. v. Entm't Distrib.*, 429 F.3d 869 (9th Cir. 2005), cert. denied sub nom., *Dastar Corp. v. Random House, Inc.*, 126 S. Ct. 2932 (2006). Under the 1909 Act, in the case of a work that is not one for hire, only the author could renew the copyright in the final year of the initial twenty-eight-year period. Doubleday had renewed the copyright and Dastar thus attempted to argue that the work was not a work for hire, and therefore the publisher's renewal was ineffective to vest it with ownership of the copyright. Id. at 876.

70. Id. at 880.

71. *See* Lastowka, supra note 5, at 1201 (quoting Allan Nevins).

72. 71 F.3d 77 (2d Cir. 1995).

73. In applying the *Reid* factors, *see* supra notes 53–55 and accompanying text, the district court concluded that the plaintiffs were independent contractors. *Carter v. Helmsley-Spear, Inc.*, 861 F. Supp. 303, 317–21 (S.D.N.Y. 1994).

74. The Second Circuit apparently felt the need to defend its work for hire conclusion against the strong showing of artistic freedom enjoyed by the plaintiffs: "Again, we emphasize that despite the conclusion reached we do not intend to marginalize factors such as artistic freedom and skill, making them peripheral to the status inquiry. The fact that artists will always be retained for creative purposes cannot serve to minimalize this factor of the *Reid* test, even though it will usually favor VARA protection." *Carter*, 71 F.3d at 87. The Second Circuit essentially predicated its opinion that the sculpture was a work for hire on the combination of the existence of payroll formalities, the existence of additional projects assigned to the plaintiffs, the defendants' furnishing the plaintiffs with needed supplies, and the need for the plaintiffs to obtain the defendants' consent to hire assistants. Id. at 88.

75. 380 F.3d 624 (2d Cir. 2004).

76. Id. at 642.

77. *See* Hughes, supra note 48, at 156 ("As much as the patron intervenes—or can intervene—in the process of intellectual production, the artist may feel that *less* of their personalities are involved in the creation.") (emphasis added); Hansmann & Santilli, supra note 7, at 134. ("[W]ork for hire, in general, is work that is subject to substantial control by the person who commissions the work [and] as such, it has less connection with the personality of its creator.")

78. *See* Hughes, supra note 48, at 154–57 (discussing cases in which the patron is a sufficient cause for the creation and exhibits control over the artistic direction); Hansmann & Santilli, supra note 7, at 134. ("[T]he interests of the artist that are protected by moral rights doctrine are less in evidence in work- for- hire than they are in other forms of creative work.")

79. Hansmann & Santilli, supra note 7, at 134.

80. *See* supra notes 18–27 and accompanying text.

81. Steve Friess, *History Claims Her Artwork, But She Wants it Back*, N.Y. TIMES, Aug. 30, 2006, at B1, B6 (quoting an e-mail by museum deputy director Teresa Swiebocka).

82. Id. at B6. Babbitt passed away in 2009, just as this book was going to press, without getting back her artwork.

83. I tracked nearly seventy federal cases applying the "employee" prong of the work for hire doctrine post *Cmty. for Creative Non-Violence v. Reid*. *See* supra note 48 and accompanying text. Twenty-one cases involved computer software. Other subject matter included photographs for catalogues or trade publications, architectural drawings, instructional texts and materials, fabric designs, musical jingles for advertisements, quilt designs, a state license plate, and a manual for making pasta. Only a small percentage of the litigated work for hire cases involved subject matter that arguably would meet the proposed heightened originality standard. *See, e.g.*, *Gaiman v. McFarlane*, 360 F.3d 644 (7th Cir. 2004) (a comic book script); *Metcalf v. Bochco*, 294 F.3d 1069 (9th Cir. 2002) (a screenplay); *Marco v. Accent Publ'g Co.*, 969 F.2d 1547 (3d Cir. 1992) (highly creative photographs taken for a trade journal); *Marshburn v. United States*, 20 Cl. Ct. 706 (Cl. Ct. 1990) (a painted mural in the employee cafeteria); *Brown v. Flowers*, 297 F. Supp. 2d 846 (M.D.N.C. 2003) (a musical composition); *Staggers v. Real Authentic Sound*, 77 F. Supp. 2d 57 (D.D.C. 1999) (music compositions). *Cf.* Hansmann & Santilli, supra note 7, at 108–9 (positing that the right of integrity should be extended to work for which the "the artist's name is considered informative or useful in assessing the work," and where "the reputation of the artist is . . . based on the entire body of work [the artist] has created").

84. 71 F.3d 77 (2d Cir. 1995); 517 U.S. 1208 (1996).

85. 380 F.3d 624 (2d Cir. 2004).

86. *See* supra note 36–37 and accompanying text.

87. *See* Fisk, *Credit Where It's Due*, supra note 4, at 93 (mentioning *The Economist* as the most well-known example of a publication maintaining a norm of nonattribution).

88. *See generally* supra Chapter 4.

89. *Cf.* H.R. REP. NO. 101-514 (1990), reprinted in 1990 U.S.C.C.A.N. 6918, 6918–19 (noting that collaborative works such as audiovisual works are typically works made for hire, and therefore granting attribution and integrity rights to such authors might "conflict with the distribution and marketing of these works").

90. 147 F.3d 195 (2d Cir. 1998).

91. Id. at 198.

92. Id. at 197.

93. Lynn Thomson, *The Rewards of Collaboration, Parabasis*, J.A.S.K. THEATER PROJECTS, Spring 1997, at 12.

94. *Thomson*, 147 F.3d at 198 n.11.

95. Id. at 198 n.10.

96. Lynn Thomson, *And an Artist Is an Artist Is an Artist*, AM. THEATRE, Sept. 1998, at 9.

97. 17 U.S.C. § 101 (2000) (definition of "joint work").

98. *See, e.g., Thomson,* 147 F.3d at 195; *Childress v. Taylor,* 945 F.2d 500 (2d Cir. 1991).

99. *See Erickson v. Trinity Theatre, Inc.,* 13 F.3d 1061 (7th Cir. 1994).

100. *See Aalmuhammed v. Lee,* 202 F.3d 1227 (9th Cir. 2000).

101. *See* Rochelle Cooper Dreyfuss, *Collaborative Research: Conflicts on Authorship, Ownership, and Accountability,* 53 VAND. L. REV. 1161, 1206 (2000) (noting, in the context of the *Thomson* decision, that "the statutory reference to intent is quite different from the court's").

102. The requirement that a contribution must be independently copyrightable to serve as a basis for joint authorship has the advantages of simplicity and predictability. On the other hand, this standard does not have a definitive basis in the statutory definition of "joint work," or the accompanying legislative history. For other criticism of this standard, see id. at 1208.

103. *See* id. at 1206. ("The court's test creates a great deal of mischief, for it allows one collaborator—the dominant party—to lure others into contributing material to a unitary work, all the while withholding the intent to share in its economic and reputational benefits.")

104. Id. at 1206–7.

105. *Thomson v. Larson,* 147 F.3d 195, 199 (2d Cir. 1998).

106. 846 F.2d 1485, 1497 (D.C. Cir. 1988), aff'd on other grounds, 490 U.S. 730 (1989).

107. H.R. REP. NO. 94-1476, at 121 (1976), reprinted in 1976 U.S.C.C.A.N. 5659, 5736–37.

108. EDWARD H. RABIN, ROBERTA ROSENTHAL KWALL & JEFFREY L. KWALL, FUNDAMENTALS OF MODERN PROPERTY LAW 279 (5th ed. 2006).

109. Section 201 of the Act simply provides: "[c]opyright in a work protected under this title vests initially in the author or authors of the work. The authors of a joint work are co-owners of copyright in the work." 17 U.S.C. § 201(a) (2000).

110. *See* Mary LaFrance, *Authorship, Dominance, and the Captive Collaborator: Preserving the Rights of Joint Authors,* 50 EMORY L.J. 193, 193 (2001).

111. *See* Avner D. Sofer, *Joint Authorship: An Uncomfortable Fit with Tenancy in Common,* 19 LOY. L.A. ENT. L. REV. 1, 19 (1998).

112. Christopher A. Harkins, *Tattoos and Copyright Infringement: Celebrities, Marketers, and Businesses Beware of the Ink,* 10 LEWIS & CLARK L. REV. 313, 316 (2006). For a general discussion of tattoos and moral rights under VARA, see Thomas F. Cotter & Angela M. Mirabole, *Written on the Body: Intellectual Property Rights in Tattoos, Makeup, and Other Body Art,* 10 UCLA ENT. L. REV. 97, 111–17 (2003).

113. Harkins, supra note 112, at 316–17.

114. Id. at 315, 325–26.

115. Id. at 316.

116. Id. at 318.

117. *Cf.* 17 U.S.C. § 109(c) (2000) (providing that public display of a copyrighted work is permissible "either directly or by the projection of no more than one image at a time, to viewers present at the place where the copy is located").

118. Margaret Chon, *New Wine Bursting from Old Bottles: Collaborative Internet Art, Joint Works, and Entrepreneurship,* 75 OR. L. REV. 257, 264–65 (1996). ("The reader

(or user) in a digitized networked environment often in turn becomes an 'Author' even as to works that are not intended to be collaborative.") This dynamic relationship has been termed "intertext," which signifies a state in which each author operates as both creator and user. Id.

119. Id. at 274.

120. Id. at 266.

121. Id. at 274.

122. Id.

123. Id. at 274 n.59 (quoting Bonnie Mitchell).

124. Id. at 274.

125. *See* Sofer, supra note 111, at 17.

126. Id. at 16 (advocating the establishment of a fiduciary relationship between joint authors).

127. *Cf.* JANICE M. STEIL, MARITAL EQUALITY 35 (1997) (discussing the status of partners in romantic relationships and how their relative power affects the relationships between the partners themselves and between the partners and their children).

128. *See* Fisk, *Credit Where It's Due*, supra note 4, at 73 (discussing the importance of "transparency" in attribution regimes).

129. Mary LaFrance has proposed a similar "originality with teeth" standard for resolving coauthorship disputes in the context of copyright's joint works doctrine discussed above. LaFrance, supra note 110, at 259. Under her proposal, a putative coauthor must satisfy an initial burden that she has made "a *substantial copyrightable* contribution." Id. at 261 (also noting that once a putative coauthor satisfies this burden, the party seeking to deny coauthorship status should bear the burden of demonstrating that the other litigant's contribution was used pursuant to an express or implied license"). Although Judge Richard Posner has argued, in the context of joint authorship, that sometimes it does not make sense to adopt a standard requiring that each contribution to a collaborative work be independently copyrightable, *see Gaiman v. McFarlane*, 360 F.3d 644, 659 (7th Cir. 2004) (holding a comic book character to have been jointly authored), the situation is completely different with respect to moral rights protections.

130. Fisk, *Credit Where It's Due*, supra note 4, at 77.

131. *See* supra Chapter 6 note 37 and accompanying text.

132. It is considered a complete taboo to remove a person's name from a project's history or credits. Fisk, *Credit Where It's Due*, supra note 4, at 89.

133. Id. at 90–91 (discussing the terms of various open-source licensing agreements).

134. *Cf.* Greg R. Vetter, *The Collaborative Integrity of Open-Source Software*, 2004 UTAH L. REV. 563, 570 (proposing a system of collaborative integrity protection for open-source software in order to preserve the open and royalty-free nature of the software).

135. *See* supra note 111 and accompanying text.

136. 17 U.S.C. § 106A(e)(1) (2000).

137. H.R. REP. NO. 101-514, at 19 (1990), reprinted in 1990 U.S.C.C.A.N. 6915, 6929.

138. When VARA was enacted, Congress directed the Copyright Office to commission a report on the impact of the waiver provisions. Among the recommendations in the Final Report was one suggesting that VARA be amended to provide that one joint author cannot waive the moral rights of the other joint authors absent their written consent. REGISTER OF COPYRIGHTS, supra note 43, at 192.

139. Robert J. Sherman, *The Visual Artists Rights Act of 1990: American Artists Burned Again*, 17 CARDOZO L. REV. 373, 416–17 (1995).

140. Aside from objectionable modifications, one joint author also can use the work in a manner deemed objectionable by the other joint authors. Examples include: "if a vegetarian's coauthored work is used to endorse beef; if a serious noncommercial artist's work is licensed for use in an advertising campaign." Sofer, supra note 111, at 19.

141. 811 F.2d 1091, 1092 (7th Cir. 1987) (affirming dismissal of a suit by a professor coauthor against the university, its trustees, and employees, alleging that the publication of an article with the authors' names in the wrong order violated the due process clause of the Fourteenth Amendment).

142. Id. at 1095; *see also* supra notes 107–8 and accompanying text.

143. *Weinstein*, 811 F.2d at 1095.

144. Id. at 1095 n.3.

145. Id.

146. The court concluded that Weinstein's coauthors could publish the article in its revised form, that Weinstein was not deprived of property in violation of due process, and that his claim based on his unlawful discharge was frivolous. Id. at 1098.

147. To the plaintiff, the order in which his name appeared on the article was significant for several reasons having to do with his professional standing. Id. at 1092. For example, Weinstein argued that his not being listed as the first author precluded his use of this topic for a dissertation, diminished his accomplishments among other professors, and hampered his ability to demonstrate citations under his name given the prevalent practice of listing citations only under the name of the first author. Id. at 1093.

CHAPTER 8

1. JIB FOWLES, STARSTRUCK: CELEBRITY PERFORMERS AND THE AMERICAN PUBLIC 261 (1992).

2. U.S. CONST. art. I, § 8, cl. 8. *See* supra Chapter 6 at notes 4–12 and accompanying text.

3. *Goldstein v. California*, 412 U.S. 546, 559 (1973).

4. Id. at 562.

5. The Trade-Mark Cases, 100 U.S. 82, 94 (1879).

6. *Goldstein*, 412 U.S. at 562.

7. *See Burrow-Giles Lithographic Co. v. Sarony*, 111 U.S. 53, 57–58 (1884).

8. *See, e.g., Toney v. L'Oreal USA, Inc.*, 406 F.3d 905 (7th Cir. 2005); *Brown v. Ames*, 201 F.3d 654 (5th Cir. 2000). *See also* RESTATEMENT (THIRD) OF UNFAIR COMPETITION § 46 cmt. i (1995) ("Personal identities and the indicia by which they are recognized . . . are not generally within the subject matter of copyright."); 2 J. THOMAS MCCARTHY, THE RIGHTS OF PUBLICITY AND PRIVACY § 11:52 (2d ed. 2007).

9. According to § 301 of the 1976 Copyright Act, preemption of a state law will result when both the content at issue falls within the subject matter of copyright law and the law in question provides a right that is "equivalent" to any of the exclusive rights provided by federal copyright law. 17 U.S.C. § 301 (2000).

10. *See, e.g., KNB Enterprises v. Matthews*, 92 Cal. Rptr. 2d 713, 723 (Cal. Ct. App. 2000) (stating that the plaintiff models' right of publicity claims, as asserted under the California state statute, were not preempted under federal copyright law because the mod-

els' likenesses are not copyrightable and the right of publicity does not fall within the subject matter of copyright). *But see Stanford v. Caesars Entm't Inc.*, 430 F. Supp. 2d 749 (W.D. Tenn. 2006) (holding state publicity action preempted because it was based on the plaintiff's fictional character, the performance of which was a fixed "dramatic work" and thus within the scope of copyright protection); *Laws v. Sony Music Entm't, Inc.*, 448 F.3d 1134 (9th Cir. 2006) (holding plaintiff's state law claims based on misappropriation of her name and voice preempted because they derived from defendant's use of copyrighted work).

11. *Lavery v. Westwood One, Inc.*, No. BC287916, 2005 WL 2327320 (Cal. Ct. App. Sept. 23, 2005). *Lavery* treated the plaintiff's persona as a work for hire, and therefore found the plaintiff's employer to be the "'author' of her creation," thus suggesting that personas can be considered within the scope of copyright protection. Id. at *5–6. *See also* supra Chapter 7 for a discussion of work for hire. This court also reached a different result regarding the preemption issue. The plaintiff was suing to recover for the unauthorized use of her name, voice, and likeness in rebroadcasts of the show, and the court held that her action was preempted under copyright law because the show was within the subject matter of copyright and the rights at issue were equivalent to those under copyright law. *Lavery*, 2005 WL 2327320, at *6. *Lavery* distinguished *KNB*, supra note 10, on the ground that "*KNB* made it clear that its holding would not extend to a cause of action against the copyright holder by an actor . . . and that under such circumstances, any state cause of action for violation of the right of publicity would be preempted by federal copyright law." Id. at *7.

12. *But see* 1 MELVIN B. NIMMER & DAVID NIMMER, NIMMER ON COPYRIGHT § 1.01[B][1][c] (2004). ("A *persona* can hardly be said to constitute a 'writing' of an 'author' within the meaning of the Copyright Clause of the Constitution. *A fortiori*, it is not a 'work of authorship' under the Act. Such name and likeness do not become a work of authorship simply because they are embodied in a copyrightable work such as a photograph.")

13. 17 U.S.C. § 102 (2000). Further, the definition of "fixed" contained in § 101 requires that the work must be fixed "by or under the authority of the author." § 101.

14. *See* H.R. REP. No. 94-1476, at 52 (1976), reprinted in 1976 U.S.C.C.A.N. 5659, 5665. ("[I]t makes no difference what the form, manner or medium of fixation may be. . . .") Note that in *Baltimore Orioles, Inc. v. Major League Baseball Players Ass'n*, 805 F.2d 663, 678 n.26 (7th Cir. 1986), the Seventh Circuit held that once a persona has been "fixed" in a tangible form, it can come within the scope of copyrightable subject matter. *Toney v. L'Oreal USA, Inc.*, subsequently decided by the same circuit, see supra note 8, arguably implicitly overruled this aspect of *Baltimore Orioles* by noting that an individual's "likeness—her persona—is not authored and it is not fixed" despite the fact that it might be fixed in a tangible format that is copyrightable. 406 F.3d 905, 910 (7th Cir. 2005). Still, the *L'Oreal* court was careful to clarify its holding in *Baltimore Orioles* as "state laws that intrude on the domain of copyright are preempted even if the particular expression is neither copyrighted nor copyrightable." Id. at 911. *See also Nat'l Basketball Ass'n v. Motorola, Inc.*, 105 F.3d 841 (2d Cir. 1997) (holding that misappropriation claims based in part on the copyrighted broadcasts of games satisfies the subject matter preemption requirement even though the misappropriation action involves both copyrighted and non-copyrightable subject matter).

15. *See* LEO BRAUDY, THE FRENZY OF RENOWN: FAME AND ITS HISTORY 66 (1986).

16. Id.

17. *See* JOHN O'SHAUGHNESSY & NICHOLAS JACKSON O'SHAUGHNESSY, PERSUASION IN ADVERTISING 147 (2004) (noting examples of political success hinging on the politician's appearing to be connected to the masses).

18. RICHARD DYER, STARS 39 (1979).

19. Id. at 19.

20. *See* O'SHAUGHNESSY & O'SHAUGHNESSY, supra note 17, at 148 (noting that celebrities, "in adding something of their own persona to the brand, allow people to fantasize that if they use the product, some of the celebrity's persona will rub off onto them").

21. *See* FOWLES, supra note 1, at 24.

22. Id. at 169.

23. Id. at 178.

24. STUART EWEN, ALL CONSUMING IMAGES: THE POLITICS OF STYLE IN CONTEMPORARY CULTURE 99 (1988).

25. *See* O'SHAUGHNESSY & O'SHAUGHNESSY, supra note 17, at 148.

26. Marcelle S. Fischler, *"Grey's Anatomy"* . . . *and Closet*, N.Y. TIMES, Feb. 25, 2007, § 9, at 1, 13.

27. *See* FOWLES, supra note 1, at 176–77 (describing the charitable efforts of celebrities); IRVING REIN ET AL., HIGH VISIBILITY: TRANSFORMING YOUR PERSONAL AND PROFESSIONAL BRAND 11 (1987) (noting how celebrity also means power and money not just for the celebrities themselves, but also for businesses, charities, political parties, etc.).

28. *See* infra notes 48–59 and accompanying text.

29. DANIEL J. BOORSTIN, THE IMAGE: A GUIDE TO PSEUDO-EVENTS IN AMERICA 53 (Antheneum 1987) (1961). Boorstin's observation is even more true today than when his book was first published in 1961.

30. *See* FOWLES, supra note 1, at 28; JAMES MONACO, CELEBRITY: THE MEDIA AS IMAGE MAKERS 3 (1978).

31. *See* MONACO, supra note 30, at 6.

32. *See* Robert S. Cathcart, *From Hero to Celebrity: The Media Connection*, in AMERICAN HEROES IN A MEDIA AGE 45 (Susan J. Drucker & Robert S. Cathcart eds., 1994).

33. *See* DYER, supra note 18, at 9–10.

34. *See* JOSHUA GAMSON, CLAIMS TO FAME: CELEBRITY IN CONTEMPORARY AMERICA 25–26 (1994).

35. Id.

36. Id. at 75–107, 115–20 (suggesting that celebrity teams cater just to the media rather than to the ultimate audience).

37. *See* ROSEMARY J. COOMBE, THE CULTURAL LIFE OF INTELLECTUAL PROPERTIES: AUTHORSHIP, APPROPRIATION, AND THE LAW 88–129 (1998).

38. SUSAN SCAFIDI, WHO OWNS CULTURE? APPROPRIATION AND AUTHENTICITY IN AMERICAN LAW 131 (2005); Justin Hughes, *The Personality Interest of Artists and Inventors in Intellectual Property*, 16 CARDOZO ARTS & ENT. L.J. 81 (1998).

39. *McFarland v. Miller*, 14 F.3d 912 (3d Cir. 1994).

40. Id. at 920–21.

41. Id. at 920. The court remanded on the ground that there exists "a triable issue" as to whether the plaintiff met this standard.

42. *Landham v. Lewis Galoob Toys, Inc.*, 227 F.3d 619, 625 (6th Cir. 2000).

43. *Wendt v. Host Int'l, Inc.*, 197 F.3d 1284, 1286–87 (9th Cir. 1999) (Kozinski, J., dissenting from the order rejecting the suggestion for rehearing en banc).

44. *See generally* 1 McCarthy, supra note 8, § 4:72 (discussing the difficulties presented by close cases involving character portrayals).

45. For example, John Rawls' writings on egalitarian justice have sparked a debate over "how much of an individual's [talents and tastes] are a result of his or her choices, and how much a result of unchosen circumstances." Andrew Stark, *Beyond Choice: Rethinking the Post-Rawlsian Debate over Egalitarian Justice*, 20 Pol. Theory 36, 36 (2002).

46. Mark P. McKenna, *The Right of Publicity and Autonomous Self-Definition*, 67 U. Pitt. L. Rev. 225, 279 (2005).

47. Alice Haemmerli, *Whose Who? The Case for a Kantian Right of Publicity*, 49 Duke L.J. 383, 431 (1999).

48. *See* Restatement (Third) of Unfair Competition § 46 cmt. b (1995); id. § 49 cmt. b. *Cf.* Restatement (Second) of Torts §§ 652C, 652H (1977) (providing that the measure of damages for an invasion of privacy is the harm to the plaintiff's privacy resulting from the invasion, the mental distress proved, and special damages resulting from the invasion). *See also* McKenna, supra note 46, at 285 n.257.

49. In the landmark decision, *Pavesich v. New England Life Insurance Co.*, 50 S.E. 68 (Ga. 1905), the Supreme Court of Georgia upheld the plaintiff's invasion of privacy claim against an insurance company that had utilized the plaintiff's picture, without his consent, in an advertisement for insurance. The court observed that because the "form and features of the plaintiff are his own," the defendant invaded "the rights of his person" by displaying them in public for advertising purposes. *Pavesich*, 50 S.E. at 79.

50. *See, e.g., Munden v. Harris*, 134 S.W. 1076 (Mo. Ct. App. 1911) (holding that an individual has a property right in her picture); *Edison v. Edison Polyform & Mfg. Co.*, 67 A. 392, 394 (N.J. Ch. 1907). ("[I]t is difficult to understand why the peculiar cast of one's features is not also one's property, and why its pecuniary value, if it has one, does not belong to its owner, rather than to the person seeking to make an unauthorized use of it.")

51. 202 F.2d 866, 868 (2d Cir. 1953). For a discussion of some pre-*Haelan* decisions that implicitly recognize a right of publicity, see Harold R. Gordon, *Right of Property in Name, Likeness, Personality and History*, 55 Nw. U. L. Rev. 553, 560–65 (1960); Melville Nimmer, *The Right of Publicity*, 19 Law & Contemp. Probs. 203, 218–21 (1954).

52. Nimmer, supra note 51, at 204–10.

53. 124 F.2d 167 (5th Cir. 1941).

54. McKenna, supra note 46, at 243.

55. *Martini Luther King, Jr. Ctr. for Soc. Change, Inc. v. Am. Heritage Prods., Inc.*, 296 S.E.2d 697, 704 (Ga. 1982).

56. *See* Restatement (Third) of Unfair Competition § 46 cmt. b (1995). *See, e.g., Waits v. Frito-Lay, Inc.*, 978 F.2d 1093 (9th Cir. 1992); infra note 66 and accompanying text.

57. *See, e.g., Fanelle v. LoJack Corp.*, No. CIV. A. 99-4292, 2000 WL 1801270 (E.D. Pa. Dec. 7, 2000) (noting that the majority view is that noncelebrities can bring a cause of action based on the right of publicity).

58. *See* Restatement (Third) of Unfair Competition § 46 cmt. b (1995).

59. *Ryan v. Volpone Stamp Co.*, 107 F. Supp. 2d 369, 391 (S.D.N.Y. 2000). Elsewhere, however, recovery for both commercial and personal losses must be obtained through a

companion suit rather than a single cause of action. *See* RESTATEMENT (THIRD) OF UNFAIR COMPETITION § 46 cmt. b (1995).

60. *See* SCAFIDI, supra note 38, at 147.

61. This reference is derived from Andy Warhol's famous quip: "In the future everybody will be world famous for fifteen minutes." THE OXFORD DICTIONARY OF QUOTATIONS 803 (Elizabeth Knowles ed., 5th ed. 1999). *See also* Gloria Franke, *The Right of Publicity vs. The First Amendment: Will One Test Ever Capture the Starring Role?* 79 S. CAL. L. REV. 945, 989 (2006) (noting how the Internet and reality programming have fostered "the democratization of celebrity").

62. McKenna, supra note 46, at 229. Mark McKenna has termed this interest one of "autonomous self-definition," and argues that "every individual should be able to control uses of her identity that interfere with her ability to define her own public character." Id. at 285.

63. 737 F. Supp. 826, 839–40 (S.D.N.Y. 1990) (upholding the look-alike claim as within the scope of the state statute but reaching the opposite conclusion with respect to the sound-alike claim; also dismissing defamation claims because no ordinary person viewing the commercial could draw the inference that the underage band members were manufacturing, selling, or trafficking in alcoholic beverages in violation of state law).

64. In some jurisdictions such as New York, the unauthorized appropriation of protected attributes is actionable under the state statutory right of privacy.

65. *See Grant v. Esquire, Inc.*, 367 F. Supp. 876, 880 (S.D.N.Y. 1973) (stating that Grant had asserted that he did not want himself or others "to profit by the publicity value of his name and reputation"); *Onassis v. Christian Dior-New York, Inc.*, 472 N.Y.S.2d 254, 257 (N.Y. Sup. Ct. 1984) (arguing that defendants hired a look-alike because they "knew there was little or no likelihood" that the plaintiff "would ever consent to be depicted in this kind of advertising campaign"), aff'd mem., 110 A.D.2d 1095 (N.Y. App. Div. 1985).

66. *Waits v. Frito-Lay, Inc.*, 978 F.2d 1093, 1093 (9th Cir. 1992).

67. *Comedy III Prods., Inc. v. Gary Saderup, Inc.*, 21 P.3d 797, 803 (Cal. 2001).

68. 408 So. 2d 619 (Fla. Dist. Ct. App. 1981).

69. Id. at 620.

70. FLA. STAT. § 540.08 (2006). Florida's commercial misappropriation law explicitly excludes media uses having a "legitimate public interest and where such name or likeness is not used for advertising purposes." § 540.08(3)(a).

71. 698 F.2d 430 (11th Cir. 1983).

72. Id. at 431–33.

73. 464 F. Supp. 426 (S.D.N.Y. 1978).

74. Id. at 429.

75. Id. at 430.

76. *Ruffin-Steinback, v. dePasse*, 267 F.3d 457, 462 (6th Cir. 2001).

77. Michiko Kakutani, *Is It Fiction? Is It Nonfiction? And Why Doesn't Anybody Care?* N.Y. TIMES, July 27, 1993, at C13.

78. Id.

79. *Tyne v. Time Warner Entm't Co.*, 901 So. 2d 802, 810 (Fla. 2005) (holding that the term *commercial purpose* does not apply to subject matter, such as motion pictures, that do not directly promote a good or service). At issue in *Tyne* was the same state statute as in *Loft v. Fuller*. *See* supra notes 68–70 and accompanying text.

80. *Tyne*, 901 So. 2d at 804.

81. Dareh Gregorian, *Jackie: "Jesus" Heist!—Comic Sues Over Ad*, N.Y. POST, Aug. 25, 2006, at 19.

82. *See* supra Chapter 1.

83. In its brief, the defendant argued that "the combination of exclamation point and question mark signals the incredulous tone of the question." Defendant Jews for Jesus' Memorandum in Opposition to Plaintiff's Motion for Preliminary Injunction, at 20. I would submit, however, that the defendant's pamphlet, particularly the cover, involved a use of Mason's identity to depict him saying something he does not believe. The "incredulous tone" of the legend is not as clear-cut as the defendant suggests. *See* Leslie Kim Treiger-Bar-Am, *The Moral Right of Integrity: A Freedom of Expression*, in 2 NEW DIRECTIONS IN COPYRIGHT 150 (Fiona Macmillan ed., 2006) (observing that freedom of expression supports the right of integrity's "protection against distortion of expression").

84. *See Mason v. Jews for Jesus*, No. 06 Civ. 6433, 2006 U.S. Dist. LEXIS 81707 (S.D.N.Y. Nov. 8, 2006).

85. No. 108446/05, 2006 N.Y. Misc. LEXIS 230 (N.Y. Sup. Ct. Feb. 8, 2006).

86. 434 N.E.2d 1319 (N.Y. 1982).

87. N.Y. CIV. RIGHTS LAW §§ 50–51 (McKinney 2006).

88. *Nussenzweig*, 2006 N.Y. Misc. LEXIS 230, at *7.

89. *Arrington*, 434 N.E.2d at 1320.

90. *Nussenzweig*, 2006 N.Y. Misc. LEXIS 230, at *7.

91. Carey Lening, *Legal Issues Likely to Increase with the Commercialization of User-Generated Content*, 73 PAT. TRADEMARK & COPYRIGHT J. (BNA) 702, 702 (2007).

92. Joel Anderson, *What's Wrong with This Picture? Dead or Alive: Protecting Actors in the Age of Virtual Reanimation*, 25 LOY. L.A. ENT. L. REV. 155, 184 (2005).

93. Id. at 170–71.

94. *Hirsch v. S.C. Johnson & Son, Inc.*, 280 N.W.2d 129 (Wis. 1979) (upholding athlete's right of publicity in his nickname "Crazylegs" in action against manufacturer of shaving gel for misappropriation of the nickname).

95. *Motschenbacher v. R.J. Reynolds Tobacco Co.*, 498 F.2d 821 (9th Cir. 1974) (holding that California law protected an individual's proprietary interest in his identity in a case involving a television commercial featuring the unique decorations of plaintiff's racing car).

96. *White v. Samsung Elecs. Am., Inc.*, 971 F.2d 1395 (9th Cir. 1992).

97. *Cf.* RESTATEMENT (THIRD) OF UNFAIR COMPETITION § 46 cmt. d (1995). ("The use must therefore be sufficient to identify the person whose identity the defendant is alleged to have appropriated.")

98. TENN. CODE ANN. §§ 47-25-1103 to -1104 (2006). In Tennessee, these rights terminate after two years of nonuse subsequent to the initial ten-year period. However, the rights extend indefinitely if use continues.

99. IND. CODE §§ 32-36-1-1 to -20 (2006); OKLA. STAT. tit. 12, § 1448 (2006).

100. *See* WASH. REV. CODE ANN. § 63.60.020(3), (7) (West 2006); § 63.60.040(1)–(2).

101. The California law took effect on January 1, 2008. CAL. CIV. CODE § 3344.1(h) (Deering 2008). Similar legislation was considered by the New York Legislature in 2007 but never was enacted. *See Bill Creating Postmortem Right of Publicity Considered in New York Senate Assembly*, 74 PAT. TRADEMARK & COPYRIGHT J. (BNA) 211 (June 15, 2007).

102. *See Prima v. Darden Rests., Inc.*, 78 F. Supp. 2d 337, 345 (D.N.J. 2000) (recognizing a right of publicity as a property right that can descend to the person's estate upon death).

103. *See* supra note 59 and accompanying text.

104. *Compare* N.Y. CIV. RIGHTS LAW §§ 50–51 (relatives of a deceased are precluded from suing under the statute since the right of privacy is deemed personal in nature), with VA. CODE ANN. § 8:01-40 (providing relief to the relatives of a decedent whose name or likeness is appropriated for commercial purposes).

105. In *Tennessee ex rel. Elvis Presley International Memorial Foundation v. Crowell*, 733 S.W.2d 89 (Tenn. Ct. App. 1987), the court articulated several justifications for a descendible right of publicity that focus on economic benefit. These justifications include: (1) promoting an individual's right of testamentary distribution; (2) preventing unjust enrichment; (3) promoting a celebrity's expectation that she is creating something of value to pass on to her heirs and assigns after her death; (4) promoting the expectations of any licensees with whom the celebrity might have contracted; and (5) furthering the public interest in truthful representations regarding sponsorship of goods. Id. at 97–99.

106. *Cf.* RESTATEMENT (THIRD) OF UNFAIR COMPETITION § 46 cmt. h (1995). ("As a general matter . . . the dignity and proprietary interests that support the recognition of a right of publicity become substantially attenuated after death.")

107. Alternatively, the economic aspects of publicity rights could be protected through an amendment to section 43(a) of the Lanham Trademark Act, 15 U.S.C. § 1125(a) (2000), that would govern instances where personas are misappropriated for commercial purposes causing consumer confusion. Various groups including a subcommittee of the American Bar Association's Intellectual Property Law Section and the International Trademark Association have worked on such an endeavor.

108. *See* supra notes 63–90 and accompanying text.

109. *See* Judge Kozinski's opinions in *Wendt v. Host Int'l, Inc.*, 197 F.3d 1284 (9th Cir. 1999) (Kozinski, J., dissenting from denial of petition for rehearing); *White v. Samsung Elecs. Am., Inc.*, 989 F.2d 1512, 1519 (9th Cir. 1993) (Kozinski, J., dissenting from the denial of hearing en banc). *See also* Diane Leenheer Zimmerman, *Fitting Publicity Rights into Intellectual Property and Free Speech Theory: Sam, You Made the Pants Too Long!* 10 DePAUL-LCA J. ART & ENT. L. & POL'Y 283 (2000).

CHAPTER 9

1. Laurence R. Helfer, *Human Rights and Intellectual Property: Conflict or Coexistence?* 5 MINN. INTELL. PROP. REV. 47 (2003).

2. Universal Declaration of Human Rights, G.A. Res. 217A, at 71, U.N. GAOR, 3d Sess., 1st plen. mtg., U.N. Doc. A/810 (Dec. 12, 1948), available at: www.un.org/Overview/rights.html [hereinafter UDHR] (last visited Dec. 8, 2008).

3. David Shiman, *Economic and Social Justice: A Human Rights Perspective*, available at: www1.umn.edu/humanrts/edumat/hreduseries/tb1b/Section1/tb1-3.htm (last visited Dec. 8, 2008).

4. *See* infra notes 13–19 and accompanying text.

5. MARY ANN GLENDON, A WORLD MADE NEW (2001); *see also* JAMES W. NICKEL, MAKING SENSE OF HUMAN RIGHTS 1 (1987). ("Today's idea of human rights is a compound that was brewed in the cauldron of World War II.") Professor Paul Torremans has stated that the UDHR came about based on a recognition that during the war, "science and technology as well as copyright based propaganda had been abused for atrocious purposes by those who lost the war" and that such abuses "had to be prevented for the future." Paul

Torremans, *Copyright as a Human Right*, in COPYRIGHT AND HUMAN RIGHTS: FREEDOM OF EXPRESSION—IP—PRIVACY 5 (Paul L.C. Torremans ed., 2004).

6. *See* supra Chapter 7 notes 81–82 and accompanying text.

7. The balancing provision, Article 27, Paragraph 1, provides that "[e]veryone has the right to freely participate in the cultural life of the community, to enjoy the arts and to share in scientific advancement and its benefits." *See* infra notes 23, 101 & 102 and accompanying text. Additionally, Article 19 of the UDHR protects the right to freedom of opinion and expression. The right to the protection of interests in intellectual creations was discussed in four of the seven formal sessions in which the UDHR was drafted. Peter K. Yu, *Reconceptualizing Intellectual Property Interests in a Human Rights Framework*, 40 U.C. DAVIS L. REV. 1039, 1051 (2007).

8. Yu, supra note 7, at 1052–54.

9. Id. at 1056–58.

10. Id. at 1070.

11. Yu notes the following distinct rationales at play during the voting process in addition to concern for authors' rights: a populist view that 27(2) also safeguards the interests of everyone; the idea that these rights were already included in the American Declaration on the Rights and Duties of Man that was adopted by more than twenty-one Latin American countries and the United States; a concern for the internationalization of copyright law; and an instrumentalist view that recognition of this right ultimately would support other important goals such as intellectual freedom. Id. at 1056–58.

12. Torremans, supra note 5, at 7 (discussing French cases involving Charlie Chaplin and John Huston).

13. International Covenant on Economic, Social and Cultural Rights, G.A. Res. 2200, U.N. GAOR, 21st Sess., Supp. No. 16, U.N. Doc. A/6316 (1966), available at: www.unhchr .ch/html/menu3/b/a_cescr.htm [hereinafter ICESCR] (last visited Dec. 8, 2008). ICESCR entered into force on January 3, 1976.

14. Office of the United Nations High Commissioner for Human Rights, Status of Ratifications of the Principal International Human Rights Treaties (June 18, 2006), available at: www.unhchr.ch/pdf/report.pdf (last visited Dec. 8, 2008).

15. "According to the law of treaties, a government that has signed but not ratified a treaty (like the Covenant) must 'refrain from acts which would defeat the object and purpose of [the] treaty . . . until it shall have made its intention clear not [to] become a party. . . .' Unfortunately, courts in the USA are not likely to attach much importance to this rule if an action were brought before that claims the USA is defeating the object and purpose of the Covenant." Shiman, supra note 3.

16. ICESCR, supra note 13, art. 15(1)(c).

17. At the time, few observers considered the rights of authors and inventors to be human rights, yet "these rights were recognized at the birth of the international human rights movement." *See* Laurence R. Helfer, *Collective Management of Copyright and Human Rights: An Uneasy Alliance*, in COLLECTIVE MANAGEMENT OF COPYRIGHT AND RELATED RIGHTS 85 (Daniel J. Gervais ed., 2006) [hereinafter Helfer, *An Uneasy Alliance*].

18. International Covenant on Civil and Political Rights, G.A. Res. 2200A (XXI), U.N. Doc A/6316 (Dec. 16, 1966), available at: www.unhchr.ch/html/menu3/b/a_ccpr.htm [hereinafter ICCPR] (last visited Dec. 8, 2008). This covenant addresses freedom of expression and the right to "receive and impart information and ideas of all kinds . . . either orally, in writing, or in print, in the form of art, or through any other media of . . . choice." Id. art.

19, para. 2. The "International Bill of Human Rights" also includes two Optional Protocols, neither of which was signed by the United States.

19. Article 19, Paragraph 3 is the balancing provision, stating that the exercise of rights in Paragraph 2 may be subject to restrictions to respect the right or reputations of others.

Some scholars see freedom of expression as the key to understanding moral rights protection. *See* Leslie Kim Treiger-Bar-Am, *The Moral Right of Integrity: A Freedom of Expression*, in 2 NEW DIRECTIONS IN COPYRIGHT 128 (Fiona Macmillan ed., 2006). In addition, recall that in the *Hugo* case discussed in Chapter 4, the court relied on Article 10 of the European Convention of Human Rights, which is an effort by the Council of Europe to strengthen human rights commitments. Substantively, the European Convention is comparable to the ICCPR and it includes protection for freedom of expression. Compliance with the European Convention is achieved through the Court of Human Rights. *See* LOUIS HENKIN ET AL., HUMAN RIGHTS 339, 552 (1999). Of course, freedom of expression can be used not only as a justification for moral rights, but also as a defense by those who seek to violate the moral rights of others. *See* Treiger-Bar-Am, supra, at 158 (noting that "while understanding section 80 [the codified right of integrity in the UK Copyright, Designs and Patents Act of 1988] as a freedom of expression would entail a liberal reading of claims, it would entail a liberal reading of defences as well").

20. The Committee "is a supervisory body of eighteen human rights experts who monitor the implications of the Covenant." Helfer, *An Uneasy Alliance*, supra note 17, at 87.

21. U.N. Comm. on Econ., Soc. & Cultural Rights [CESCR], *Substantive Issues Arising in the Implementation of the International Covenant on Economic, Social and Cultural Rights* [ICESCR], 27th Sess., U.N. Doc. E/C12/2001/15 (Dec. 14, 2001), available at: www .unhchr.ch/tbs/doc.nsf/0/1e1f4514f85124232c1256ba6003b2cc6/$FILE/G0146641.pdf [hereinafter CESCR 2001 Statement] (last visited Dec. 8, 2008).

22. CESCR, *General Comment No. 17: The Right of Everyone to Benefit from the Protection of the Moral and Material Interests Resulting from any Scientific, Literary or Artistic Production of Which He Is the Author*, 35th Sess., U.N. Doc. E/C.12/GC/17 (Jan. 12, 2006), available at: www.unhchr.ch/tbs/doc.nsf/(Symbol)/E.C.12.GC.17.En?Open Document [hereinafter *General Comment No. 17*] (last visited Dec. 8, 2008).

23. CESCR 2001 Statement, supra note 21, ¶ 4. *See also* infra note 102 and accompanying text.

24. CESCR 2001 Statement, supra note 21, ¶ 4.

25. Id. CESCR also contrasted intellectual property rights that "may be allocated, limited in time and scope, traded, amended and even forfeited," with human rights that "are fundamental, inalienable, and universal entitlements belonging to individuals and in some situations groups of individuals and communities." Id. ¶ 6.

26. Laurence Helfer notes that such comments by the CESCR are interpretations rather than binding law and thus can be viewed by governments as "aspirational." Laurence R. Helfer, *International Rights Approaches to Intellectual Property: Toward a Human Rights Framework for Intellectual Property*, 40 U.C. DAVIS L. REV. 971, 999 (2007) [Helfer, *Toward a Human Rights Framework*].

27. *General Comment No. 17*, supra note 22, ¶ 1.

28. Id. ¶ 2.

29. Id. ¶ 12.

30. Id. ¶ 13. "[T]he Committee considers that 'moral interests' in article 15, paragraph 1(c) include the right of authors to be recognized as the creators of their scientific, literary and artistic productions and to object to any distortion, mutilation or other modification of, or other derogatory action in relation to, such productions, which would be prejudicial to their honour or reputation," citing article *6bis* of the Berne Convention for the Protection of Literary and Artistic Works.

31. Id. ¶ 7. Here, CESCR reiterates that its definition of "authors" was limited in scope to natural persons or groups of individuals and thus it precludes human rights recognition of corporate authorship such as works made for hire. It does, however, acknowledge that communities might be authors in some situations. Id. ¶ 8. Moreover, according to the Comment, ICESCR provides a floor for human rights protection, which makes up the "core obligations" of the Covenant. The list of core obligations under *General Comment No. 17*, supra note 22, ¶ 39 includes:

(a) To take legislative and other necessary steps to ensure the effective protection of the moral and material interests of authors;

(b) To protect the rights of authors to be recognized as the creators of their scientific, literary and artistic productions and to object to any distortion, mutilation or other modification of, or other derogatory action in relation to, their productions that would be prejudicial to their honour or reputation;

(c) To respect and protect the basic material interests of authors resulting from their scientific, literary or artistic productions, which are necessary to enable those authors to enjoy an adequate standard of living;

(d) To ensure equal access, particularly for authors belonging to disadvantaged and marginalized groups, to administrative, judicial or other appropriate remedies enabling authors to seek and obtain redress in case their moral and material interests have been infringed;

(e) To strike an adequate balance between the effective protection of the moral and material interests of authors and States parties' obligations in relation to the rights to food, health and education, as well as the rights to take part in cultural life and to enjoy the benefits of scientific progress and its applications, or any other right recognized in the Covenant.

These specific obligations may be more generally categorized into three "levels" or "types" of obligations by member states toward the rights of authors: to respect, to protect, and to fulfill. *See* id. ¶ 39.

32. Yu, supra note 7, at 1142.

33. Id. at 1077.

34. *See* Torremans, supra note 5, at 16–17. ("From a Human Rights perspective the author or creator assumes also a lot of importance" that "manifests itself in the work produced . . . being acknowledged as having an intrinsic value as an expression of human dignity and creativity"). *Cf.* Rochelle Cooper Dreyfuss, *Patents and Human Rights: Where Is the Paradox?* Molengrafica Series, (forthcoming), available at: http://ssrn.com/abstract= 929498 (last visited Dec. 8, 2008) (differentiating copyrights from patents on the ground that human dignity concerns may be implicated with respect to works of authorship but not inventions).

35. *See* Helfer, *Toward a Human Rights Framework*, supra note 26, at 996 (noting the existence of a core material right for authors and that any additional intellectual property protections beyond these core rights must balance public access considerations).

36. Torremans, supra note 5, at 19.

37. Peter Drahos, *The Universality of Intellectual Property Rights: Origins and Development*, at 14, available at: www.wipo.int/tk/en/hr/paneldiscussion/papers/pdf/drahos.pdf (last visited Dec. 8, 2008).

38. Id. at 15.

39. H. G. Schemers, *The International Protection of the Right of Property*, in PROTECTING HUMAN RIGHTS: THE EUROPEAN DIMENSION 579 (F. Matscher & H. Petzold eds., 1988).

40. Drahos disputes that universal recognition translates into a universal, human rights norm. Instead, with respect to intellectual property rights as a general matter, he argues that such rights should be seen as instrumental rights through which other types of human rights can be fashioned. Drahos, supra note 37, at 22.

41. Justin Hughes, *American Moral Rights and Fixing the Dastar "Gap,"* 2007 UTAH L. REV. 659, 712.

42. Id. at 706 (noting that "most major common law countries—and several significant civil law countries—were members of the Berne Convention for decades before they passed moral rights statutes for the two Article 6*bis* rights").

43. *See* supra Chapter 4 notes 8–9 and accompanying text.

44. Jennifer E. Rothman, *The Questionable Use of Custom in Intellectual Property*, 93 VA. L. REV. 1899, 1903 (2007).

45. Id. at 29 (discussing the incorporation of customary law into IP decisions); *see* Mark F. Schultz, *Copynorms: Copyright Law and Social Norms*, in 1 INTELLECTUAL PROPERTY AND INFORMATION WEALTH 201, 206–7 (Peter K. Yu ed., 2006) (focusing on the compliance aspects of file-sharing).

46. Drahos, supra note 37, at 2. Roman law, which was heavily influenced by Greek thought, was the source for both the common and civil law European systems. *See* Mladen Vukmir, *The Roots of Anglo-American Intellectual Property Law in Roman Law*, 32 IDEA 123, 127, 151–52 (1991–92).

47. *See* Neil Netanel, *Maharam of Padua v. Giustiniani: The Sixteenth-Century Origins of the Jewish Law of Copyright*, 44 HOUS. L. REV. 821 (2007) for a detailed account of this case. One of the complicating features of this situation was that the defendant was not Jewish, thus forcing the judge to grapple with the thorny issue of the extent to which Jewish law could govern the conduct of a Gentile.

48. ETZ HAYIM, TORAH AND COMMENTARY 15 (2001).

49. Id. at 18.

50. MOSHE WEISSMAN, THE MIDRASH SAYS 45–46 (Bnay Yakov Publications, 1980). According to this interpretation, Adam violated God's right of attribution through misattribution by attributing to God words that He did not speak (specifically, the injunction not to touch the fruit). He also violated God's right of integrity by modifying God's original commandments.

51. *See* supra Chapter 2 notes 16–21 and accompanying text.

52. PIRKEI AVOS, ETHICS OF THE FATHERS (Mesorah Publications 1984); *see also* Berel Wein, PIRKEI AVOS, TEACHINGS FOR OUR TIMES (Shar Press 2003) (noting that chapter 6 is a later addition to the rest of the text dating back to around the fourth or fifth century rather than around 200 CE).

53. PIRKEI AVOS, supra note 52, at Ch. 6, § 6, 59.

54. Id. at 59 n.6 (commentary by Rabbi Meir Zlotowitz).

55. Ethics of the Fathers, BABYLONIAN TALMUD, *Nezikin*.

56. *See generally* Sacha Stern, *Attribution and Authorship in the Babylonian Talmud*, 45 J. JEWISH STUD. 28 (1994).

57. Id. at 47–48.

58. Id. at 47.

59. Stern notes that since any "sayer" of a saying in the Talmud was always seen as "the bearer . . . of his masters' teachings and of other earlier traditions," it is inappropriate to consider "any attributee . . . as an 'author' in the full, modern Western sense of the term." Id. at 51.

60. Id. at 46.

61. Id. at 50–51.

62. Id. at 47.

63. SIVA VAIDHYANATHAN, COPYRIGHTS AND COPYWRONGS: THE RISE OF INTELLECTUAL PROPERTY AND HOW IT THREATENS CREATIVITY 37–38 (2001).

64. Susan P. Liemer, *How We Lost Our Moral Rights and the Door Closed on Non-Economic Values in Copyright*, 5 J. MARSHALL REV. INTELL. PROP. L. 1, 11 (2005).

65. *See* supra notes 22–34 and accompanying text in Chapter 4.

66. Pluridictionnaire Larousse: Dictionnaire Encyclopedique De L'enseignement 911 (1st ed. 1975) (defining "moral" as (1) "qui concerne les regles de conduites en usage dans une societe determine" [pertaining to rules of behavior in a particular society], and (2) "se dit de ce qui est relatif a l'esprit, de ce qui est intellectuel (par opposition materiel, physique)" [pertaining to the spirit, concerned with the intellect (rather than material and physical)]). The English definition of "moral" encompasses this same idea. *See* Merriam Webster's Dictionary (defining "moral" as "of or relating to principles of right and wrong in behavior," or as "perceptual or psychological rather than tangible or practical in nature or effect"), available at: www.merriam-webster.com/dictionary/moral (last visited Dec. 8, 2008).

67. *See* supra text preceding note 3 in Chapter 3.

68. The novelty of the perspective developed in the text is reflected in the recent statement by a district court that "[c]opyight and trademark law are not matters of strong moral principle." Rather, "[i]ntellectual property regimes are economic legislation based on policy decisions that assign rights based on assessments of what legal rules will produce the greatest economic good for society as a whole." *Louis Feraud Int'l S.A.R.L. v. Viewfinder, Inc.*, 406 F. Supp. 2d 274, 281 (S.D.N.Y. 2005).

69. Yu, supra note 7, at 1137.

70. Madhavi Sunder, *IP³*, 59 STAN. L. REV. 257, 331 (2006).

71. Id. at 331.

72. Drahos, supra note 37, at 24.

73. Id. at 25; *see also* Torremans, supra note 5, at 9 (noting that copyright and intellectual property rights were included in the human rights instruments only because they were viewed "as tools to give effect to and to protect other stronger Human Rights").

74. *MGM Studios, Inc. v. Grokster, Ltd.*, 545 U.S. 913 (2005).

75. The Court observed "that one who distributes a device with the object of promoting its use to infringe copyright, as shown by clear expression or other affirmative steps taken to foster infringement, is liable for the resulting acts of infringement by third parties." Id. at 936–37.

76. The lower courts also concluded that no vicarious liability resulted because, given the lack of a centralized mechanism, the defendants lacked the ability to supervise and control the infringing conduct, which occurred after the products had passed to the end-users. *See MGM Studios, Inc. v. Grokster, Ltd.,* 259 F. Supp. 2d 1029, 1041, 1045 (D. Cal. 2003), aff'd, 380 F.3d 1154, 1165 (9th Cir. 2004), vacated, 545 U.S. 913 (2005). In light of the Supreme Court's holding regarding inducement, it did not determine the appropriate prospective application of third party liability principles.

77. *See* Mark A. Lemley, *Inducing Patent Infringement,* 39 U.C. DAVIS L. REV. 225, 233 (2005). ("The Court's opinion can be read merely to adopt the common law patent principle that those who advertise or affirmatively encourage others to infringe are liable for inducement.")

78. *Grokster,* 545 U.S. at 924.

79. Immediately after the opinion was issued, Asher Meir, the Research Director at the Business Ethics Center in Jerusalem (an independent institute located in the Jerusalem College of Technology) wrote the following in an editorial in the *Jerusalem Post*: "I can't comment on whether the court's ruling is good law, but I *can* say that it is good ethics. A firm can't take a 'see no evil, hear no evil, speak no evil' approach to the use of its product if there is a significant chance it is being improperly used, or if there is any active connivance in such improper use. . . . I believe that the clear ethical message of this ruling will be helpful in clarifying the importance of intellectual property rights." Asher Meir, *Grokster File-Sharing and Glue-Sniffing,* JERUSALEM POST, July 3, 2005, at 17. According to Julie Sigall, the Associate Registrar for Policy and International Affairs at the Copyright Office, most participants in the *Grokster* decision are "reasonably satisfied" with the ruling and Congress has not been besieged with requests to modify the ruling. 71 PAT. TRADEMARK & COPYRIGHT J. (BNA) 667 (Apr. 14, 2006).

80. *See* Sunder, supra note 70, at 286–88.

81. John Henry Merryman, *The Refrigerator of Bernard Buffet,* 27 HASTINGS L.J. 1023, 1043 (1976).

82. Id.

83. *Final Report of the Ad Hoc Working Group on U.S. Adherence to the Berne Convention,* 10 COLUM.-VLA J.L. & ARTS 513, 552 n.19 (1985–86) (suggesting that an express contractual provision allowing omission of the author's name would be unenforceable as against copyright policy).

84. Id. at 555.

85. Rebecca Tushnet, *Naming Rights: Attribution and Law,* 2007 UTAH L. REV. 781, 783 n.11 [hereinafter Tushnet, *Naming Rights*]; Greg Lastowka, *The Trademark Function of Authorship,* 85 B.U. L. REV. 1171, 1184–85 (2005) (stating that "even in this postmodern era, anti-plagiarism norms remain quite strong"); Stuart P. Green, *Plagiarism, Norms, and the Limits of Theft Law: Some Observations on the Use of Criminal Sanctions in Enforcing Intellectual Property Rights,* 54 HASTINGS L.J. 167, 175 (2002) (noting that people view attribution as similar to a "moral obligation"). *See also* Henry Hansmann & Marina Santilli, *Authors' and Artists' Moral Rights: A Comparative Legal and Economic Analysis,* 26 J. LEGAL STUD. 95, 130–31 (1997) (noting that the negative right of attribution is "relatively unproblematic" and "has obvious utility in protecting artists from theft of the reputation they have cultivated and in protecting the public at large from being misled"). *But see* Michael Landau, *Dastar v. Twentieth Century Fox: The Need for Stronger Protection of*

Attribution Rights in the United States, 61 N.Y.U. ANN. SURV. AM. L. 273, 298 (2005) (stating that "copying a work without giving attribution is plagiarism, and the Court . . . is giving its blessing to the practice").

86. Green, supra note 85, at 174. He traces the concept of plagiarism back to both Jewish and Roman law. Id. at 177; *see also* Harold C. Streibich, *The Moral Right of Ownership to Intellectual Property: Part I—From the Beginning to the Age of Printing*, 6 MEM. ST. U. L. REV. 1, 5–6 (1975) (noting that both Greek and Roman culture "'stigmatized' plagiarism as a crime," despite little enforcement "of the 'moral right' of a creator to his work" [citing G.H. PUTNAM, AUTHORS AND THEIR PUBLIC IN ANCIENT TIMES 68 (3rd ed. rev. 1896)]). Recall also that the term *plagiarism* is derived from the Latin term for kidnapping. *See* supra note 26 and accompanying text in Chapter 2.

87. Green, supra note 85, at 195.

88. *But see* supra Chapter 4 notes 88–89 and accompanying text.

89. Green, supra note 85, at 199; David Nimmer, *The Moral Imperative Against Academic Plagiarism (Without a Moral Right Against Reverse Passing Off)*, 54 DEPAUL L. REV. 1 (2004) (endorsing the result in *Dastar* with respect to reverse passing off as a general matter but approving the norms of plagiarism in specialized settings such as the academy); Rebecca Tushnet, *Payment in Credit: Copyright Law and Subcultural Creativity*, LAW & CONTEMP. PROBS., Spring 2007, at 135, 155 (noting that among the community of fan creators, plagiarism is "one of the most serious offenses" and that when such conduct surfaces, "fans are likely to publicly excoriate the plagiarist").

90. Green, supra note 85, at 201; *see also* Landau, supra note 85, at 307–10.

91. Green, supra note 85, at 219.

92. Catherine L. Fisk, *Credit Where It's Due: The Laws and Norms of Attribution*, 95 GEO. L.J. 49, 52 (2006).

93. *See, e.g.*, Jane C. Ginsburg, *The Right to Claim Authorship in U.S. Copyright and Trademark Law*, 41 HOUS. L. REV. 263 (2004).

94. Tushnet, *Naming Rights*, supra note 85, at 785.

95. Rothman, supra note 44, at 47–48.

96. *See, e.g.*, Greg Lastowka, *Digital Attribution: Copyright and the Right to Credit*, 87 B.U. L. REV. 41 (2007).

97. *See* id. at 60–61 (noting that according to a survey of French chefs, the most important norm governing recipe sharing was the expectation of proper attribution, and positing that law professors also are motivated by reputational profits); *see also* Emmanuelle Fauchart & Eric von Hippel, *Norms-Based Intellectual Property Systems: The Case of French Chefs*, 19 ORG. SCI. 187, 193 (2008). Recall also the discussion in Chapter 7 regarding the development of prevalent attribution norms by various communities.

The momentum for attribution rights was reflected in a previously proposed attribution rule by the Copyright Office that would allow people to copy "orphan works" whose copyright owners are known but not capable of being located, as long as attribution to *both* the author and the copyright owner is provided. *See* REGISTER OF COPYRIGHTS, REPORT ON ORPHAN WORKS 110–11 (2006), available at: www.copyright.gov/orphan/orphan-report -full.pdf (last visited Dec. 8, 2008). As of this writing, the 2006 bill has been withdrawn but an amended Orphan Works Reform Bill is working its way through Congress. The current version specifies attribution only "to the legal owner of the infringed copyright." S. 2913, 110th Cong. (as passed by Senate, Sept. 26, 2008).

98. *See* Charles Beitz, *The Moral Rights of Creators of Artistic and Literary Works*, 13 J. POL. PHIL. 330, 349 (2005).

99. Id. at 349.

100. *See* supra Chapter 1 notes 13–17 and accompanying text.

101. *See* supra notes 7 & 16 and accompanying text.

102. *See* supra notes 7 & 23 and accompanying text. Helfer notes that balancing the public's interests with those of creators and inventors represents "one of the most challenging tasks" for the CESCR. Helfer, *An Uneasy Alliance*, supra note 17, at 88. To date, the CESCR has not drafted general comments interpreting the other subsections of Article 15 that protect the public's rights. Id. at 112.

CHAPTER 10

1. 17 U.S.C. § 113(d) (2006).

2. At least one appellate court has held that VARA does not protect site-specific art. *See Phillips v. Pembroke Real Estate, Inc.*, 459 F.3d 128 (1st Cir. 2006).

3. The Copyright Act provides that all civil actions (including those under VARA) must be brought "within three years after the claim accrued." *See* §§ 501(a), 507. For a critique of this standard, see Peter Karlen, *Moral Rights and Real Life Artists*, 15 HASTINGS COMM. & ENT. L.J. 929, 948–49 (1993) (urging running of the statute of limitations from the time of discovery).

4. *See* Karlen, supra note 3, at 949 (noting that "[a] disproportionate number of moral rights cases involve claims against government entities"). *See, e.g., Kelley v. Chi. Park Dist.*, No. 04-C-07715, 2008 WL 4449886 (N.D. Ill. Sept. 29, 2008), discussed in note 52 in Chapter 6. This area is further complicated by the uncertain constitutional status of the Copyright Remedy Clarification Act (CRCA), which expressly eliminated state immunity for copyright infringement. *See* § 511(a). Some courts have ruled that the CRCA is unconstitutional. *See, e.g., Chavez v. Arte Publico Press*, 204 F.3d 601 (5th Cir. 2000); *Mktg. Info. Masters, Inc. v. Bd. of Trs. of the Cal. State Univ. Sys.*, 552 F. Supp. 2d 1088 (S.D. Cal. 2008); *Nat'l Ass'n of Bds. of Pharmacy v. Bd. of Regents of the Univ. Sys. of Ga.*, No. 3:07-CV-084, 2008 U.S. Dist. LEXIS 32116 (M.D. Ga. Apr. 18, 2008). Although subsequent bills have been introduced, as of this writing no such legislation has been enacted.

5. *See* supra text following note 112 in Chapter 6.

6. *See* supra notes 113–16 and accompanying text in Chapter 6.

7. *See* supra notes 44–45 and accompanying text in Chapter 6.

8. *See* supra note 5 and accompanying text in Chapter 4.

9. 17 U.S.C. § 201(a).

10. As David Nimmer notes, the United States Supreme Court vindicated the first publication right as a component of copyright law in *Harper & Row, Publishers, Inc. v. Nation Enterprises*, 471 U.S. 539 (1985), which involved the unauthorized scoop of President Ford's forthcoming autobiography. *See* David Nimmer, *The Moral Imperative Against Academic Plagiarism (Without a Moral Right Against Reverse Passing Off)*, 54 DEPAUL L. REV. 1, 17 (2004) (recognizing that the relevant Berne provision "has some vitality under U.S. law"). Although my proposal advocates that colloquial authors of works made for hire retain the ability to assert the moral rights of attribution and integrity, I recognize that it does not specifically provide for a right of disclosure for colloquial authors of works made for hire.

11. This element also is actionable under VARA. 17 U.S.C. § 106A(a)(1)(B). *See also* supra notes 120–22 in Chapter 4 discussing a similar right in the United Kingdom.

12. *See* supra text following note 40 in Chapter 3.

13. *See* supra note 9 and accompanying text in Chapter 7.

14. *See* 17 U.S.C. § 106A(a)(1). *See* supra note 58 and accompanying text in Chapter 3 for a discussion of reverse passing off.

15. *See* supra text following note 10 in Chapter 7.

16. *See* supra note 10 and accompanying text in Chapter 7.

17. *See* supra notes 63–66 and accompanying text in Chapter 3; *see also* Jane C. Ginsburg, *The Right to Claim Authorship in U.S. Copyright and Trademarks Law*, 41 HOUS. L. REV. 263, 304, 307 (2004) (noting the uncertainty regarding authors' and performers' entitlement to name credit after *Dastar*). *But see* Nimmer, supra note 10, at 43 (arguing that the laws of passing off sufficiently protect authors' rights to compel recognition for their works even after *Dastar* but that *Dastar* properly refused relief for reverse passing off in situations involving both copyrightable works and those in the public domain).

18. C. Edwin Baker, *First Amendment Limits on Copyright*, 55 VAND. L. REV. 891, 941 (2002).

19. The potential for public harm also is diminished by the limited duration I propose. *See* infra notes 64–76 and accompanying text.

20. *Cf.* 17 U.S.C. § 504(c)(2) (2000) (providing that statutory damages under copyright law can be increased to a sum of up to $150,000 for cases involving willful conduct by the defendant). With respect to the availability of damages, my proposal is somewhat narrower than VARA, which does not confine the damage remedy. *Cf.* Catherine L. Fisk, *Credit Where It's Due: The Laws and Norms of Attribution*, 95 GEO. L.J. 49, 114–15 (2006) (noting the distinction between copyright infringement and wrongful attribution and observing that the remedy for failing to attribute should not be injunctive relief but rather "a right to share the reputation benefits of authorship").

21. *See* Rebecca Tushnet, *Naming Rights: Attribution and Law*, 2007 UTAH L. REV. 789, 800.

22. *Cf.* Paul Geller, *Toward an Overriding Norm in Copyright: Sign Wealth*, REVUE INTERNATIONALE DU DROIT D'AUTEUR, Jan. 1994, at 19–20 (arguing for a more limited right of integrity as compared to attribution). Writing in the context of fan fiction, Rebecca Tushnet demonstrates that the propriety of attribution is quite distinct from the potentially concerning claims for control over works that arise through strong integrity protections. *See* Rebecca Tushnet, *Payment in Credit: Copyright Law and Subcultural Creativity*, LAW & CONTEMP. PROBS., Spring 2007, at 135, 166. Her observations highlight the irony that absent any integrity protections, strong attribution rights actually can undermine the right of integrity to the extent authors can find themselves in the position of being credited when their works are used in ways they deem objectionable. Id. at 167. My proposed disclaimer remedy substantially ameliorates this concern because it would require both attribution as well as disclaimers in instances in which authors object to particular uses.

23. *See* supra text following note 13 in Chapter 5.

24. 17 U.S.C. § 106A(a)(2).

25. *See* supra Chapters 1, 2, and 5.

26. *See* supra notes 13–16 and accompanying text in Chapter 1; supra text following note 73 in Chapter 2.

27. *See* supra notes 13–17 and accompanying text in Chapter 1; supra text following note 73 in Chapter 2; *cf.* Ilhyung Lee, *Toward an American Moral Rights in Copyright*, 58 WASH. & LEE L. REV. 795, 840–42 (2001) (advocating a dignity-based right of integrity that would include procedural devices of prior notice of another's alteration or use of the author's work and the author's opportunity to object, along with a "balancing of the author's dignity interest and the competing interest of the opposing party").

28. *See* supra Chapter 5 notes 77–92 and accompanying text.

29. *See* supra Chapter 5 notes 87–90 and accompanying text.

30. A somewhat similar remedial structure was part of the National Film Preservation Act of 1988, Pub. L. No. 100-446, 102 Stat. 1782, amended by National Film Preservation Act of 2005, Pub. L. No. 109-9, 119 Stat. 218, which authorized the Library of Congress to designate twenty-five culturally significant films per year and to include a prominent label alerting the public to any material alterations. Id. § 3(a)(1)(C), (2)(A). This label also served as a warning that the alterations were done without the consent of the creative talent responsible for the film's creation. Subsequently, Congress repealed this statute. *See* Nimmer, supra note 10, at 26–27.

31. *Cf. Gilliam v. Am. Broad. Co.*, 538 F.2d 14, 25 n.13 (2d Cir. 1976) (arguing that a disclaimer would not have provided adequate relief under the facts of that case). See supra Chapter 3 for a further discussion of *Gilliam*.

32. *See* Greg Lastowka, *The Trademark Function of Authorship*, 85 B.U. L. REV. 1171, 1231 n.294 (2005) (citing MELVIN SIMENSKY ET AL., ENTERTAINMENT LAW 1005–1120 [3d ed. 2003]).

33. Id.

34. *See* Charles R. Beitz, *The Moral Right of Creators of Artistic and Literary Works*, 13 J. POL. PHIL. 330, 340 (2005) (quoting Samuel G. Freedman, *"Endgame" Opens in Wake of Pact*, N.Y. TIMES, Dec. 13, 1984, at C14). In his article, Beitz notes that Beckett's rights were being asserted pursuant to a copyright license. Id.

35. *Cf.* Peter K. Yu, *Reconceptualizing Intellectual Property Interests in a Human Rights Framework*, 40 U.C. DAVIS L. REV. 1039, 1103 (2007) (noting that "the protection of moral interests in intellectual creations" requires attribution and, where appropriate for modified works, disclaimers in order to protect "the personal link between authors and their creations").

36. *See* supra note 130 and accompanying text in Chapter 4.

37. *See* Copyright, Designs & Patents Act, 1988, ch. 48, § 205G(5)–(6) (U.K.); ELIZABETH ADENEY, THE MORAL RIGHTS OF AUTHORS AND PERFORMERS § 14.148, at 430 (2006). *See* supra notes 11–15 and accompanying text in Chapter 4 for a discussion of performers' moral rights. Recall also that in Australia, the false atttribution provision protects, in part, "the author from being associated with a work that is no longer entirely his own." ADENEY, supra, at 577; *see* supra note 123 and accompanying text in Chapter 4.

38. For example, the moral rights statutes in Louisiana, Maine, New Jersey, New York, and Rhode Island contain a provision to this effect. *See* LA. REV. STAT. ANN. § 51:2153 (2008); ME. REV. STAT. ANN. tit. 27, § 303(2) (2008); N.J. STAT. ANN. § 2A:24A-4 (West 2008); N.Y. ARTS & CULT. AFF. LAW § 14.03(1) (Consol. 2008); R.I. GEN. LAWS § 5-62-3 (2008). In contrast, other states such as California, Connecticut, and Pennsylvania

actually prohibit the act of modification. *Cf.* CAL. CIV. CODE § 987(c) (Deering 2008); CONN. GEN. STAT. ANN. § 42-116t(a) (West 2008); 73 PA. STAT. ANN. § 2104(a) (West 2008).

39. *See* 17 U.S.C. § 106A(a)(2) (2000).

40. *See* text following note 40 in Chapter 3.

41. Recall that some countries such as France and Germany do not maintain a "prejudicial to the author's honor or reputation" caveat. *See* supra note 53 and accompanying text in Chapter 4.

42. *See* supra Chapter 1 notes 29–33 and accompanying text.

43. *See* supra note 38 and accompanying text in Chapter 3; supra text accompanying note 71 in Chapter 4.

44. *See* supra note 73 and accompanying text in Chapter 4.

45. *See* supra note 74 and accompanying text in Chapter 4.

46. *See* supra notes 26–27 and accompanying text.

47. For a contrary perspective on the right of integrity, particularly with respect to destruction, see Amy Adler, *Against Moral Rights*, 97 CAL. L. REV. 263 (2009). *Cf.* CAL. CIV. CODE § 987(a)–(c), (f) (Deering 2008) (providing protection for works of fine art "of recognized quality" from physical alteration or destruction, where "recognized quality" is determined based "on the opinions of artists, art dealers, collectors of fine art, curators of art museums, and other persons involved with the creation or marketing of fine art"); ADENEY, supra note 37, at 521 (noting that "the 'recognized quality' limitation [of the California statute] does not, as under VARA, apply only when destruction is at issue"). It is also interesting to note that "[t]he 'recognized stature' standard [under VARA] is much more stringent than the 'recognized quality' requirement under some state statutes," including the California statute. Peter H. Karlen, *What's Wrong with VARA: A Critique of Federal Moral Rights*, 15 Hastings Comm. & Ent. L.J. 905, 916 (1993).

48. *Cf.* the Australian statute that protects against destruction of artistic works that are "prejudicial to the author's honour or reputation." Copyright Act, 1968, No. 63, § 195AJ (Austl.); ADENEY, supra note 37, at 583.

49. On its face, VARA is not specific as to whether the right to prevent destruction applies only to originals or also limited edition copies. *See* 17 U.S.C. § 101 (2000) (definition of work of visual art) and § 106A(a)(3)(B). The legislative history, however, suggests that the destruction right would apply to limited editions. *See* H.R. REP. NO. 101-514, at 21 (1990), reprinted in 1990 U.S.C.C.A.N. 6915, 6919. ("[T]he works of visual art covered by H.R. 2690 are limited to originals: works created in single copies or in limited editions.")

50. Jane Ginsburg has suggested that although the inability to waive attribution may be the best recognition of moral rights, this position may be "too extreme" for the United States. Ginsburg, supra note 17, at 300. She also notes that Berne does not require a prohibition on waivers. Id.; *see also* Michael B. Gunlicks, *A Balance of Interests: The Concordance of Copyright Law and Moral Rights in the Worldwide Economy*, 11 FORDHAM INTELL. PROP. MEDIA & ENT. L.J. 601, 624–26 (2001) (noting that there is a wide variation among Berne members regarding waiver).

51. *See* supra notes 70–71 and accompanying text in Chapter 3.

52. *Cf.* Hansmann & Santilli, *Authors' and Artists' Moral Rights: A Comparative Legal and Economic Analysis*, 26 J. LEGAL STUD. 95, 129 (1997) (noting that the more narrowly crafted the right of integrity, the more inefficient it is to allow waiver).

53. *Final Report of the Ad Hoc Working Group on U.S. Adherence to the Berne Convention*, 10 COLUM.-VLA J.L. & ARTS 513, 556 (1986) [hereinafter *Final Report of the Ad Hoc Working Group*].

54. *See* supra notes 85–87 and accompanying text in Chapter 4.

55. *See* supra notes 54–55 and accompanying text in Chapter 4; *see also Final Report of the Ad Hoc Working Group*, supra note 53, at 556 (discussing varying views on alienation and waiver).

56. 17 U.S.C. § 106A(e)(1) (2000); *see* supra notes 135–39 and accompanying text in Chapter 7.

57. *See* supra text following note 127 in Chapter 7.

58. *See* Fisk, supra note 20, at 66–67 (noting, for example, that in the music industry audiences "expect a certain 'authenticity' in the performers . . . [so that] the role of the producer in creating rock music cannot be too visible; the rock band is imagined by the audience to be the creation of the performing musicians, not the record company men in suits"). Fisk's overall point is that an intellectual property system concerning attribution must be subject to industry norms: "In the absence of legal protection for the important interests in attribution, norms govern credit, and many industries have attempted to embody the norms into enforceable contracts, professional regulation, and even certain laws." Id. at 116.

59. For a state statute with this language, see the Massachusetts moral rights statute, MASS. GEN. LAWS ANN. ch. 231, § 85S(d) (West 2008).

60. *See* 17 U.S.C. § 107 (providing that, notwithstanding VARA, "the fair use of a copyrighted work . . . is not an infringement of copyright").

61. *See* Ginsburg, supra note 17, at 304 (noting, in the context of attribution, that "the test for reasonableness [for omission of credit] . . . is not the same as for fair use").

62. *Cf. Louis Vuitton Malletier S.A. v. Haute Diggity Dog, LLC*, 507 F.3d 252, 260 (4th Cir. 2007) (noting that in order to be considered a parody, a trademark "must convey two simultaneous—and contradictory—messages: that it is the original, but also that it is *not* the original and is instead a parody" [quoting *People for the Ethical Treatment of Animals v. Doughney*, 263 F.3d 359, 366 (4th Cir. 2001)]).

63. For a somewhat contradictory perspective on parody and attribution, see Tushnet, supra note 22, at 162 (arguing that in light of the strong connection between an original and a markedly transformative parody, attribution may still be appropriate "even when the original author is appalled by what has been done to a work"). My problem with this idea is that attribution in these circumstances might be understood by the public as approval or authorization of the parodied work by the original author, which can create a sense of unnecessary confusion.

64. *See* supra notes 38–41 in Chapter 5.

65. *See also* infra note 74 and accompanying text.

66. Berne Convention for the Protection of Literary and Artistic Works art. *6bis*(2), Sept. 9, 1886, 828 U.N.T.S. 221 [hereinafter Berne Convention] (as last revised in Paris on July 24, 1971); *see also* supra notes 6 & 88 and accompanying text in Chapter 4.

67. The 1948 revision of the Berne Convention limited the duration of the covered rights to the author's lifetime. *See* Berne Convention for the Protection of Literary and Artistic Works art. *6bis*(1), Sept. 9, 1886, 331 U.N.T.S. 217 (as amended in Brussels on June 26, 1948).

68. *See* Berne Convention, supra note 66, art. *6bis*(2).

69. Id. art. *6bis*(3); supra Chapter 4 at note 7 and accompanying text.

70. WORLD INTELLECTUAL PROP. ORG., GUIDE TO THE BERNE CONVENTION FOR THE PROTECTION OF LITERARY AND ARTISTIC WORKS (PARIS ACT 1971) 42 (1978).

71. *Final Report of the Ad Hoc Working Group*, supra note 53, at 556 (noting § 106(2) of the Copyright Act and § 43(a) of the Lanham Act in particular). *But see* Justin Hughes, *American Moral Rights and Fixing the Dastar "Gap,"* 2007 UTAH L. REV. 659, 672 (stating that "VARA, by itself, is not a Berne-compliant moral rights regime for works of fine art").

72. 17 U.S.C. § 106A(d)(2) (2000).

73. H.R. REP. NO. 101-514, at 18 (1990), reprinted in 1990 U.S.C.C.A.N. 6915, 6928.

74. 17 U.S.C. § 106A(d)(3).

75. *See* infra text following note 80.

76. For example, the Louisiana statute covers visual and graphic works in any medium but for motion pictures, *see, e.g.,* LA. REV. STAT. ANN. § 51:2152(7) (2008). Louisiana also covers reproductions. *See* § 51:2153(2).

77. 17 U.S.C. § 301(f)(1).

78. § 301(f)(2)(A)–(C).

79. *See* Robert A. Gorman, *Visual Artists Rights Act of 1990*, 38 J. COPYRIGHT SOC'Y 233, 240 (1990). This view is also consistent with VARA's legislative history, see H.R. REP. NO. 101-514, at 21 (1990), reprinted in 1990 U.S.C.C.A.N. 6915, 6931, as well as the preemption law under the 1976 Act under which courts frequently adopt a strict standard requiring additional elements to negate preemption. *See, e.g., Rosciszewski v. Arete Assocs., Inc.,* 1 F.3d 225, 230 (4th Cir. 1993) (holding preempted claim under Virginia Computer Crimes Act because the statute's requirement of intent does not add a qualitatively different element from that of unauthorized copying); *see also* supra note 51 and accompanying text in Chapter 3.

80. *See* supra note 64 and accompanying text.

81. *Tyne v. Time Warner Entm't Co.,* 901 So. 2d 802, 810 (Fla. 2005) (holding that state commercial misappropriation law does not apply to a motion picture except in limited circumstances).

82. 95 F.3d 959 (10th Cir. 1996).

83. Id. at 969.

84. Id. at 970, 972.

85. Id. at 972. The court continued that "a parody of a celebrity does not merely lampoon the celebrity, but exposes the weakness of the idea of value that the celebrity symbolizes in society." Id.

86. Id. at 972.

87. *See Burnett v. Twentieth Century Fox Film Corp.,* 491 F. Supp. 2d 962 (C.D. Cal. 2007) (granting the defendant's motion to dismiss the plaintiff's copyright claim on the ground that the parody constitutes fair use).

88. In the *Burnett* case, the court also granted the defendant's motion to dismiss the plaintiff's § 43(a) claim because the nature of the use "does not explicitly mislead the viewer as to affiliation, connection, association with, or sponsorship or approval by plaintiffs." Id. at 973.

89. *See* supra notes 26–27 and accompanying text.

90. *See* Carey Lening, *Got Clearance? Why Failing to Clear a Song with the Artist May Spell More Than Just Political Embarrassment for Candidates*, 75 PAT. TRADEMARK & COPYRIGHT J. (BNA) 575 (Mar. 28, 2008) (noting that both John Mellencamp and the Swedish group Abba publicly objected to 2008 Presidential candidate John McCain using their respective hit songs, "Our Country" and "Take a Chance on Me"); *see also* Sarah Wheaton, *Theme Songs and Others*, N.Y. TIMES, Feb. 16, 2008, at 14 (providing other examples of presidential candidates who had to stop using certain songs in their campaigns).

91. *See* supra Chapter 1 notes 29–36 and accompanying text.

Index

Note to Reader: *Passim* indicates numerous mentions over the given range of pages.

access circumvention in U.S. copyright law, xv

Adeney, Elizabeth, 187–188n123, 189n148

advertising, copyright protection of, 74

agency relationship under work for hire doctrine, 96

Albert, Laura, 88

alienability. *See* waiver

Amabile, Teresa, 11, 22

American Repertory Theater, 154

Andrews, Virginia Cleo (V.C.), 91

anonymity: dignity and, 168n16; in international copyright law, 207n10; in moral rights reform, 149–150; overview, 87–90; right of, 48; under VARA, 28; waivers and, 46

appropriation art, copyright protection of, 83–85

architectural works, integrity rights in, 184n78

Arp, Jean, 16

Arrington v. New York Times, 126–127

art. *See under* appropriation; fine; reproduced; site-specific; visual

Art Against the Odds (Rubin), 20

Article *6bis*. *See* Berne Convention for the Protection of Literary and Artistic Works

artistry, 73, 81–84

The Asphalt Jungle (film), 41

assertion requirement in attribution, 48–49

attribution, dual quality of, 169n23

attribution, right of: in Australian copyright law, 232n37; author trademark, 87–88; as authorship

norm, 138–140; under the Berne Convention, 28; in civil law systems, 41–42, 44; in common law systems, 48–49; community norms and, 66; compelled speech and, 195n76; in copyright law, 142–145; under the DMCA, 26–27; false, 149, 187n123, 188n125; First Amendment challenge, 61–62; in functional works, 85; ghostwriting and, 90–91; industry norms and, 234n58; in joint authorship, 108–109; limits to, 182n43; in moral rights reform, 149–154, 157; in open-source software, 108–109; orphan works and, 229–230n97; overview, 5–9; parody and, 234n63; reasonableness criterion and, 188n125; under VARA, 28; waivers and, 46. *See also* Lanham Act

attribution violations: *Batiste v. Island Records, Inc.*, 7; damages, 151; distinguished from plagiarism, 143; in U.S. copyright law, xv

Auschwitz–Birkenau Memorial and Museum, 101

author: defined by the CESCR, 225n31; defined in case law, 112; defined in common law, 47–48; distinguished from copyright owner, 27

author trademark, 87–88

"authornym," 87

authorship: core rights, 225n31; distinguished from copyright ownership, 23, 214n109; ghostwriting, 46, 90–92; public, and copyright, 170n8; textual integrity

authorship (*continued*)
and, 1–9; under work for hire
doctrine, 93–99 *passim. See also*
anonymity; pseudonymity
authorship, joint, 102–110;
copyrightability and, 214n102,
215n129; in moral rights reform,
158–159; order of names, 216n147;
ownership and, 104–105,
211–212n64; of personas, 117–119;
use of the work and, 216n140; under
work for hire doctrine, 102–104
authorship norms, 133–145; attribution
and integrity in, 138–140, 142–145;
civil law tradition, 140–141; moral
rights as, 137–138; plagiarism and
attribution in, 143–144; property law
in, 141–142
autonomous self-definition, 220n62
autonomy in First Amendment protection,
62–63
Azoulay, Leon, 3

Babbitt, Dina Gottliebova, 100–101, 133
Baker, Edwin, 62–63
balancing provision of the UDHR, 223n7
Balzac, Honoré de, 39
Batiste v. Island Records, Inc., 7
Beckett, Samuel, 45, 153–154
Beitz, Charles: on meaning and message,
168n10; on moral rights protection, 3;
on privileging, 144
Benkler, Yochai, 55
Bereshit Micrography (Azoulay), 3
Berne Convention for the Protection of
Literary and Artistic Works: on
anonymity and pseudonymity, 89; on
the assertion requirement, 49; on
authorship norms, 142; compliance
with, 137; on duration of rights,
160–161; on ghostwriting, 158;
history of Article 6bis, 179n5; on
moral rights, 225n30; overview,
27–28; on photography, 202–203n83;
self-executing adherence to, 176n33;
U.S. noncompliance with, 37. *See also*
moral rights reform

Blanch v. Koons, 84
Bleistein v. Donaldson Lithographing, 73
Bloustein, Edward, 4
Bollier, David, 190n16
Boorstin, Daniel, 13, 115
"borrowing" and authorship, 2
*Brandir International v. Cascade Pacific
Lumber*, 81–82
breach of contract, 32–33
"breath of life," 15
Bridgeman Art Library v. Corel Corp.,
77
British Engravers' Act (1735), 192n32
Buffet, Bernard, 178n69
Burrow-Giles Lithographic v. Sarony,
76–77, 81, 112
bylines, 90

*Cardtoons v. Major League Baseball
Players Assoc.*, 163
*Carol Barnhart Inc. v. Economy Cover
Corp.*, 83
Carter v. Helmsley-Spear, 99, 101,
210–211n55
CDPA (Copyright, Designs, and Patents
Act), 47–51, 188n128
CESCR (Committee on Economic, Social
and Cultural Rights, United Nations,
2001), 135–136, 224n25
Chain Art Project, 107
Chalke, Sarah, 118
children's creativity, 20
Chinese Cultural Revolution, 168n3
Chon, Margaret, 107
Christie, Agatha, 125
civil law tradition: on destruction of
works, 156; in international copyright
law, 38–40; moral rights in, 140–141;
public domain and, 65; on work for
hire, 208n28
Claims to Fame (Gamson), 116
Clancy, Tom, 92
CMI (copyright management information),
26–27
Committee on Economic, Social and
Cultural Rights (United Nations,
CESCR, 2001), 135–136, 224n25

commodification of art: creativity and, 22, 53; under the dualist theory, 39–40; under Lockean theory, 25

common law copyright, 175n30, 178n69

common law doctrines, 32–35, 177n53

commons and public domain, 54

Community for Creative Non-Violence v. Reid, 95–98, 104, 108

compliance and public morality, 5

computer programs, copyright protection of, 183n55, 186n105

conceptual separability test of copyrightability, 81–82

content-neutrality of copyright law, 61, 194–195n70, 194n68, 195n71

contract. *See* breach of contract

contractor status under work for hire doctrine, 94–99, 210n50, 211n62

Coombe, Rosemary, 117

Copyright, Designs, and Patents Act (CDPA), 47–51, 188n128

Copyright Act (1909): in *Gilliam v. ABC*, 175n30; on work for hire, 93; on works of authorship, 70

Copyright Act (1976), 25–26; on art as utility, 204n102; on joint works, 103; overview, 23; on utilitarian function, 81; on work for hire, 93–95; on works of authorship, 70

Copyright Clause: Congressional authority under, 191n27; enhanced moral rights protection, 56–57; moral rights reform and, 152; overview, 23–24; on writings, 69, 111–112

copyright distinguished from moral rights, 55–56

copyright law, 23–35; common law and, 32–35, 175n30, 178n69; Copyright Act (1976), 25–26; criticism of, 1; DMCA, 26–27, 167n4; expanding in the public domain, 55; history, 23–25; infringement, 141–142, 200n28; intellectual property law and, 133–136; Lanham Act, 30–32; public authorship and, 170n8; relationship with First Amendment, 194n62; statute of limitations, 230n3; tests for,

205n107; United States compared with other countries, xiii–xv; VARA, 27–30

copyright law, international, 37–52; on anonymity and pseudonymity, 207n10; on attribution, 232n37; Berne Convention, 27–28; British, and property law, 57; British history, 140; in civil law systems, 40–47; in common law systems, 47–51; on destruction of works, 232n37; history, 38–40, 191n28; intellectual property law and, 133–136; Jewish history, 138–140; originality standard in, 199n23; restored works, 194n56; on work for hire, 208n28

copyright management information (CMI), 26–27

Copyright Office Report (1996), 29

copyright owner, ownership: distinguished from author, authorship, 23, 27, 214n109; joint authorship and, 104–105; moral rights vs. copyright, 55–57; under work for hire doctrine, 93–99 *passim*, 209n35

copyright protection: degree of originality and, 72; duration, in moral rights reform, 159–161; duration of, xv, 56–59, 192n35, 210n45; of personas, 112–113; type of work and, 69

Copyright Remedy Clarification Act (CRCA), 230n4

Copyright Term Extension Act, 192n35

Copyright Treaty (WIPO), 38

copyrightability: joint authorship and, 214n102, 215n129; of personas, 111–113, 217n14; tests for, 81–83, 205n107

craft or inspiration, 1

CRCA (Copyright Remedy Clarification Act), 230n4

Creation stories in Genesis, 13–14, 15, 17, 171n14, 172n54

Creative Commons Project, 6, 66

creative intent test of copyrightability, 82–83

creative thinking and information processing, xiv

creativity: authorship and, 2; commodification of art and, 21–22; degree of, 72; distinguished from originality, 71; fact or fiction, 1; freedom for, 43–44; gestational period, 12; inspiration of, xv, 20–21; in moral rights reform, 156; noneconomic incentives, 19–20; parental metaphor, 13–14, 107–108; play and, 11; random acts of, 82–83; unintended, 21. *See also* intrinsic creativity

Crusade in Europe (Eisenhower), 177n60

cultural factors of creativity, 12

Dacey, John, 15

damages: attribution violations, 151; persona violations, 111; under VARA, 176n47

dance as work for hire, 99, 210–211n55

Dastar Corp. v. 20th Century Fox Films: copyright infringement, 177n60; public domain and, 177n63; reverse passing off, 31–32; under work for hire doctrine, 98–99

Dead Sea Scrolls case, 41–42

deceased people, copyright duration for, 160–161

deceased people, personas of, 129–130, 222n105

deciphered text, copyright protection of, 182n48

defamation and copyright, 33

Defoe, Daniel, 14

derivative work: defined and protection of, 27; fictional characters as, 118; in *Gilliam v. ABC*, 175n30; originality in, 80; variation in, 204n98

design process test of copyrightability, 82–83

destruction of works, 44–45, 156, 212n65, 233n48, 233n49

The Devil's Advocate (film), 7, 156

Dietz, Adolf, 92

digital media, 141–142

Digital Millennium Copyright Act (DMCA, 1998), 26–27, 167n4

digitization and creativity, 78–79

dignity, authorship: anonymity and, 168n16; in human rights law, 133; in moral rights reform, 152, 156–157; silence and, 4; through textual integrity, 3–5; under work for hire doctrine, 99–100

Directors Guild of America, 200n29

disclaimer remedy: content-neutrality and, 195n71; in moral rights reform, 151–155, 159; right of attribution and, 61–66

disclosure, right of, 44–45, 65, 149

DMCA (Digital Millennium Copyright Act, 1998), 26–27, 167n4

Donaldson v. Beckett, 57

Drahos, Peter, 136, 141

Dreyfuss, Rochelle, 104

dualist theory of copyright, 39–40

Durham, Alan, 16, 21

duty distinguished from right, 139

Dyer v. Napier, 77

economic incentive: in intellectual property law, 227n68; joint authorship and, 104–105; originality and, 72–73

Eisenhower, Dwight. *See Dastar Corp. v. 20th Century Fox Films*

Eldred v. Ashcroft, 59, 192n35

Elkin-Koren, Niva, 182n48

employee status under work for hire doctrine, 99–102, 211n57, 213n83

Endgame (Beckett), 154

Engravers' Act of 1735, 174n3

Erdal, Jennie, 91

Ernst, Max, 17

"eureka" moment, 21

European Convention on Human Rights, 43–44, 224n19

Evans, Walker, 78

Ex Nihilo (Hart), 7, 13, 19, 156

exhibition purposes under VARA, 75–76

expression, freedom of, 223–224n18, 224n19

extrinsic motivation, 11

fabric design, copyright protection of, 205–206n112

factual use of personas, 125–128

fair use doctrine, 159

false attribution. *See under* attribution

false designation of origin, 30

fame phenomenon, 111

Farley, Christine, 76

Facsimile Edition of the Dead Sea Scrolls (Shanks), 42

Feist Publications v. Rural Telephone Service, 70–72

feminism in public domain theory, 64

fictional use of personas, 124–128

file sharing, xv, 197–198n118

film, 48, 181n39, 186n104

film colorization, 14, 31, 41, 200n29, 232n30

Film Disclosure Act, 31

fine art, 69, 198n9

First Amendment: moral rights protection and, 59–63, 152; relationship with copyright law, 194n62; use of persona and, 123–128 *passim. See also* speech entitlements

Fisk, Catherine: on attribution, 93, 234n58; on an author trademark, 88; on byline stories, 90; on speechwriting, 91

Fowles, Jib, 111

Francis, Connie, 8–9, 126, 154, 164

free speech. *See* First Amendment; speech entitlements

Frith, Simon, 79

Fromm, Erich, 15–16

Fuller, Robert, 167n1 (Intro.)

Gamson, Joshua, 116–117

garment design, copyright protection of, 205–206n112

General Comment (2005). *See* Committee on Economic, Social and Cultural Rights (United Nations, 2001)

Genesis: Creation stories, 171n14; on the gift of inspiration, 15; parental metaphor of creation, 13–14; on self-transcendence, 17

gestational period of creativity, 12

ghostwriting, 46, 90–92, 157–158

gifted theory of creativity, 14–16, 172n36

Gilliam v. American Broadcasting Company, Inc.: common law copyright and, 32–33; Copyright Act (1909), 175n30; disclaimer remedy, 154; false designation of origin, 30

Ginsburg, Jane: on the assertion requirement, 49, 187n119; on attribution, 187n115; on misattribution, 32; on U.S. compliance with Berne, 179n4; on visual art, 74–75; on waivers, 51, 233n50

Glendon, Mary Ann, 133

global uniformity in copyright duration, 192n35

GNU software license, 66–67

Golan v. Gonzales, 62

Goldman, Fred, 121

Goldman, Ron, 121

Goldstein test of copyrightability, 205n107

Goranson, Lecy, 118

Gordon, Wendy, 168n10

Grant, Cary, 123

Green, Stuart, 143

Halprin, Anna, 16–17

Hansmann, Henry: on anonymity and pseudonymity, 89; on duration of rights, 47; on ghostwriting, 90; on pseudonymity, 88–89; on work for hire, 40–41, 99–100

Hart, Frederick: creative process, 13; disclaimer remedy, 154; integrity violation, 7–8, 156; persona violation, 126, 164; Wolfe's view, 19

Hegel, Georg, 39–40

Helfer, Laurence, 136

Heymann, Laura, 87, 89–90

Hicks v. Casablanca Records, 125

Holmes, Justice, 73

"Honey Don't" (Perkins), 8

Hughes, Justin: on Berne compliance, 137; on CMI, 27; on commissioned works, 96; on ownership, 1; on persona creation, 117; on unintended creativity, 21

Hugo, Victor, 39, 43–44, 224n19
human rights laws. *See* authorship norms; *under* moral rights
humanism in public domain theory, 64
Huston, John, 41
Hyde, Lewis: on commodification of art, 22; on creativity, 17; on the gift of inspiration, 14–15; on self-transcendence, 16; on stewardship, 18

ICCPR (International Covenant on Civil and Political Rights, 1966), 134–135, 223–224n18, 224n19
ICESCR. *See* International Convention on Economic, Social and Cultural Rights (1966)
identity, control of, 119
industrial design, copyright protection of, 81–83
informational use of personas, 123–124
infringement and degree of originality, 200n28
inmates' creativity, 20
inspiration, inspirational: creativity, 13–14; defined, xiii–xiv; economic incentive contrasted, 72–73; motivation of creativity, xv, 20–21
inspiration or craft, 1
integrity, right of: authorship and, 1–9; as authorship norms, 138–140; under the Berne Convention, 28; in civil law systems, 42–44; in common law systems, 49–50; community norms and, 66; under the Copyright Act (1976), 27; in copyright law, 142–145; destruction of work and, 233n47; First Amendment challenge, 61–62; in Irish copyright law, 188n127; in moral rights reform, 148–154, 155–156; in open-source software, 109–110; overview, 5–9; personal vs. intellectual interests, 182–183n53; similarity to right of publicity, 111; violations, xv; waivers and, 45
integrity violations, 7–9, 156
intellectual property law: in the CESCR, 224n25; disclaimer remedy, 154–155;

as economic legislation, 227n68; human rights and, 133–136. *See also* copyright law
International Bill of Human Rights, 133–135, 223–224n18
International Convention on Economic, Social and Cultural Rights (ICESCR, 1966): core obligations, 225n31; history, 137; on moral rights, 225n30; overview, 134; on public access, 144–145
International Covenant on Civil and Political Rights (ICCPR, 1966), 134–135, 223–224n18, 224n19
intertext, 214–215n118
intrinsic creativity, 11–22; as gifted, 14–16; as inspired, 13–14; overview, xiii, 5–6; as self-transcendence, 15–17; as stewardship, 18–19, 173n64, 173n67. *See also* creativity
intrinsic motivation, 11
Intrinsic Motivation Principle, 11
invasion of privacy. *See under* privacy
inviolate personality, 4

Jewish copyright law, 138–140
Jews for Jesus, 126, 164
joint works, 103
Joyce, Craig, 195–196n77
Jung, Carl, 11, 16

Kakutani, Michiko, 125
Kant, Immanuel, 40
Koons, Jeff, 84
Kozinski, Alex, 118
Kübler-Ross, Elisabeth, 20

Laemmle, Carl, 116
LaFrance, Mary, 215n129
Lamartine, Alphonse de, 39
Lange, David, 63–64, 80
Lanham Act, 30–32, 177n63, 178n65. *See also* attribution, right of
Larson, Jonathan, 102–104
Lastowka, Greg: on attribution, 144, 153; on an author trademark, 88; on ghostwriting, 91

Lawrence, Florence, 116
Lee, Edward, 64
L'Engle, Madeleine, 14, 17
Lennon, Kathleen, 15
LeRoy, JT, 88
Les Miserables (Hugo), 43–44
Lessig, Lawrence, 65–66
Levine, Sherrie, 84
liability rule, 65–66
liberty model of First Amendment
    protection, 62–63
licensing under work for hire doctrine,
    210n45
Liemer, Susan, 6, 140
Lilley v. Stout, 75–76
Line of Control (Clancy, Rovin), 92
The Little Rascals, 117
Locke, John, 25
Loft v. Fuller, 124
look-alike/sound-alike, 123
Lowell, Amy, 12
Lutzker, Arnold, 181–182n42

Madison, James, 24
*Martha Graham School v. Martha Graham
    Center*, 99, 101, 210–211n55
Mason, Jackie, 126–127, 164
Masur, Richard, 170n37
McFarland, George ("Spanky"), 117
McIntyre v. Ohio Elections Commission, 90
McKenna, Mark, 119, 220n62
meaning: authorship dignity and, 4–5;
    defined, 2–3; in moral rights reform,
    150, 157; through the intrinsic
    creative process, 6
Meir, Asher, 228n79
Mengele, Josef, 100–101
Merges, Robert, 66
Merryman, John, 142
message: authorship dignity and, 4–5;
    defined, 2–3; in moral rights reform,
    150, 157; through the intrinsic
    creative process, 6
MGM v. Grokster, 141–142, 228n79
Midnight Flight (Andrews), 91
Miller, Henry, 12
Mitchell, Bonnie, 107

modification of work. *See* commodification
    of art; waivers
monist theory, 40
Monty Python. *See Gilliam v. ABC*
moral, 227n66
moral rights distinguished from copyright,
    55–56
moral rights doctrine: in civil law systems,
    38–47; in common law systems,
    47–51; degree of originality and, 72;
    duration, 46–47; First Amendment
    objections, 59–63; in foreign
    copyright law, xiii; Francis's claim,
    169n35; freedom of expression and,
    224n19; as human rights, 133–145
    passim; in the ICESCR, 225n30;
    intrinsic creativity and, 6; opposition
    to, 30; state vs. federal, 29–30; type of
    work and, 69; in U.S. copyright law,
    25–35 *passim*
moral rights protection: ghostwriting and,
    90–92; for meaning and message, 3; in
    trademark law, 88–89
moral rights reform, 147–165; anonymity
    and pseudonymity, 149–150;
    attribution rights, 149–154, 157;
    authorship, 157–158, 158–159;
    damages, 231n20; destruction of
    works, 156; dignity in, 156–157;
    disclaimer remedy, 151–155, 159;
    duration of protection, 159–161; fair
    use doctrine, 159; integrity rights,
    148–154, 155–156; overview,
    147–148; personas, 162–164;
    preemption of current statutes,
    161–162; summary, 164–165; work
    for hire doctrine, 157–158
morality, authorship, 4
motivation, 11, 18–19
music: artistry and creativity in, 203n89;
    originality and creativity in, 79; right
    of integrity and, 43, 236n90; in U.S.
    copyright law, 26. *See also* sound
music videos, 203n89
mutilation violations, xv
mutual intent standard of joint authorship,
    104

National Film Preservation Act (1988, 2005), 232n30
natural law, 25
nature photography, 77, 202n76
Nazi inmate's creativity, 20
neighboring rights under the WPPT, 180n14
Neruda, Pablo, 18
neutrality of copyright law, 61, 194–195n70, 194n68, 195n71
Nevins, Allan, 98
Nike, Inc., 105–106
Nimmer, David, 89, 182n48
novelty distinguished from originality, 71
Nozick, Robert, 1
Nussenzweig v. DiCorcia, 126–127

Oliar, Dotan, 56
Onassis, Jacqueline Kennedy, 123
Op-Center (Clancy), 92
open-source software, 108–109
origin, 31–32
originality: degree of, and copyright protection, 70–72; degree of, and integrity rights, 42–43; distinguished from creativity, novelty, 71; evidence of, 76; as legal fiction, 199n18; levels of, 80–81; in moral rights reform, 156; proving, 80; standard for, 199n23
Orphan Works Reform Bill, 229–230n97
Our Gang, 117
owner, ownership. See copyright owner, ownership; public domain

Pacino, Al, 7
parental metaphor of creation, 13–14, 107–108
parodies: attribution and integrity in, 234n63; of celebrity, 235n85; in moral rights reform, 163
participation and compliance, 5
Patry, William, 71
Patterson, L. Ray, 195–196n77
The Perfect Storm (film), 125, 162–163
performance under the WPPT, 38. See also dance
Perkins, Carl, 8–9, 126, 154, 164

persona violations, 9, 111, 123, 126–127, 164, 170n37
personal responsibility and authorship, 1
personality. See inviolate personality
personas, 111–131; celebrity packaging, 115–117; copyright protection of, 117–119; copyrightability, 111–113, 217n14; creation of, 117–118; of deceased people, 129–130, 222n105; factual use, 125–128; fame, 113–114; fictional use, 124–128; identification with celebrity, 114–115; informational use, 123–124; in moral rights reform, 162–164; publicity violations, 119–122; unauthorized use of, 122–128, 219n49; under work for hire doctrine, 217n11; as works of authorship, 112–113
persona-text, 112, 117–119, 127–128
photography, 75–76, 76–78, 78–79
physical separability test of copyrightability, 81
plagiarism: authorship norms and, 143–144; defined, 229n86; derivation, 14; distinguished from attribution violations, 143; in Jewis copyright law, 139–140
play and creativity, 11
Poincaré, Henri, 12, 21
Pollack, Malla, 64
Posner, Richard, 215n129
postmortem copyright duration, 160–161
postmortem personas, 129–130, 222n105
Pound, Ezra, 18
Prince of Tides (film), 8
prisoner status under work for hire doctrine, 100–101
privacy, invasion of, 33–34
privacy distinguished from publicity rights, 34
privacy violations applied to persona, 120–122
property law and authorship norms, 141–142

pseudonymity: in international copyright law, 207n10; in moral rights reform, 149–150; overview, 87–90; under VARA, 28; waivers and, 46

public authorship and copyright, 170n8

public domain and ownership, 53–67; in civil law systems, 65; Copyright Clause, 57–58; Lanham Act and, 32; overview, 53–55; speech entitlements and, 55; theories of, 63–66

public morality and compliance, 5

publicity, right of: commercial distinguished from noncommercial use, 130–131; of deceased people, 129–130, 222n105; distinguished from right of privacy, 34; persona protection, 111; in U.S. copyright law, 34–35; violations, 119–122

publishing, signature requirement in, 207n9

Qimron, Elisha, 41–42

quilts, copyright protection of, 205–206n112

random acts of creativity, 82–83

Rashi, 15

reasonableness criterion, 45, 49–50, 188n125

recognized stature, 74, 201n43

Red Room at Five (Stout), 75–76

Redish, Martin, 62–63

Reed, Matthew, 105–106

Reese, Anthony, 64–65

Reid, James Earl, 95–98

Rent (play), 102–104

reproduced art, 74–75, 156, 201n52

responsibility. See personal responsibility

Restatement of Agency, 96

restored works, copyright of, 194n56

reverse passing off, 31–32, 149–150, 177n58

Rigamonti, Cyrill: on civil vs. common law, 179n2; on modification of work, 46; on moral rights in copyright law, 181n35; on waivers, 51

right distinguished from duty, 139

rights. See under anonymity; attribution; disclosure; integrity; privacy; publicity; withdrawal

Rilke, Rainer, 18

Rose, Mark, 22, 38–39, 57

Roseanne, 118

Rothman, Jennifer, 143–144

Rovin, Jeff, 92

rugs, copyright protection of, 205–206n112

Russell, Bertrand, 12

Samuelson, Pamela, 53–54

Santilli, Marina: on anonymity, 89; on duration of rights, 47; on ghostwriting, 90; on pseudonymity, 88–89; on work for hire, 40–41, 100

Sarah (LeRoy/Albert), 88

Scafidi, Susan, 11–12, 117, 170n6

Schemers, H. G., 137

Section 43(a). See Lanham Act

self-definition, 220n62

self-executing adherence, 176n33

self-realization model of First Amendment protection, 62–63

self-transcendence in creativity, 15–17

Sessions, Roger, 14

The Seventh Cross (film), 41

Shanks, Hershel, 42

Sigall, Julie, 228n79

signature requirement in book publishing, 207n9

silence and dignity, 4

Silverstein, Elliot, 14, 200n29

Simpson, O. J., 121

site-specific art and joint authorship, 105–106

Smith, Tim, 79, 203n89

Snyder, Gary, 14–15

Soloveitchik, Joseph, 4, 13

sound, 174n1. See also music

"Spanky," 117

speech entitlements, 55, 62, 195n76. See also First Amendment

speechwriting, 91

spiritual, spirituality, xiii–xiv, 167n1 (Intro.)

Stamatoudi, Irini, 187n117
stature, recognized, 74, 201n43
Statute of Anne, 174n3
statute of limitations, 230n3
Stern, Sacha, 139
stewardship doctrine: copyright duration and, 58; of creativity, 18–19, 173n64, 173n67
Strugnell, John, 41–42
substantial similarity test, 83–84
Sunder, Madhavi, 141, 142
synthespians, 127–128

tattoos, 105–106
The Temptations (film), 125
Ten Utterances, 172n54
term extension. See copyright protection: duration
textual integrity, xv, 1–9. See also integrity
Thomson, Lynn, 102–104
Thomson v. Larson, 102–104
Tin Pan Apple v. Miller Brewing Co., 123
Torremans, Paul, 134, 136, 222n5
trademark law, 88–89, 118–119
Trade-Related Aspects of Intellectual Property Rights (TRIPs), 37–38
translations. See deciphered text
Travers, Pamela, 16
treaty power and moral rights protection, 191n27
TRIPs (Trade-Related Aspects of Intellectual Property Rights), 37–38
Turner Entertainment, 41
Tushnet, Rebecca, 143, 231n22
Tyler, Tom, 5

UDHR. See Universal Declaration of Human Rights (1948)
"unconscious machine," 12
unintended creativity, 21
Universal Declaration of Human Rights (UDHR, 1948): balancing provision, 223n7; history, 137, 223n11; overview, 133–135; on public access, 144–145
Uruguay Round Agreements Act (URAA), 194n56

utilitarian function: copyright infringement and, 141–142; right of attribution in, 85; separate from artistic features, 81–84
utilitarian model of copyright law, 24–25

Valentine v. C.B.S., Inc., 124
VARA. See Visual Artists Rights Act (1990)
virtual actors, 127–128
visual art, 94, 99
Visual Artists Rights Act (VARA, 1990): on anonymity and pseudonymity, 89; damages, 176n47; on destruction of works, 156, 212n65, 233n49; on duration of rights, 160–161; excluding work for hire, 94, 99, 101, 158; on joint authorship, 109, 215n138; lack of challenges, 193n47; limited integrity protection, 155–156; moral rights protection and, 55; overview, 27–30; on preemption of current statutes, 161–162; on reproduced art, 201n52; on visual art, 74–76. See also moral rights reform
von Gierke, Otto, 40

Waiting for Godot (Beckett), 45
Waits, Tom, 34
Waits v. Frito-Lay, 34, 123
waivers: in civil law systems, 45–46; in common law systems, 50–51; in moral rights reform, 156–157; under VARA, 28–29
Wallace, Rasheed, 105–106
Walterscheid, Edward, 24, 69, 198n6
Warner Brothers, 7–8
Washington National Cathedral, 7
Weinstein v. University of Illinois, 110
Wheaton v. Peters, 59
Wheel of Fortune (TV show), 128
White, Vanna, 128
Williams, Otis, 125
WIPO (World Intellectual Property Organization), 37, 38, 89, 160
WIPO Performance and Phonograms Treaty (WPPT), 38

withdrawal, right of, 44–45
Wolfe, Thomas, 15, 19
Woodmansee, Martha, 1
work for hire doctrine, 92–103; case law, 94–99; colloquial authorship, 230–231n10; contractor status, 94–99, 210n50, 211n62; copyright and, 40–41; copyright infringement and, 177n60; in copyright law, 87; defined, 94; determination of status, 212n74; duration of copyright and, 210n45; employee status, 99–102, 211n57, 213n83; internationally, 208n28; joint authorship in, 102–104; licensing and, 210n45; in

moral rights reform, 157–158; personas, 217n11
World Intellectual Property Organization (WIPO), 37, 38, 89, 160
A World Made New (Glendon), 133
WPPT (WIPO Performance and Phonograms Treaty), 38
writings, 69–70, 111–112

Yen, Fred, 2
Yu, Peter, 136, 141, 223n11

Zimmerman, Diane, 53, 71
Zinnemann, Fred, 41
Zornberg, Avivah, 172n52